Birth of a Global Community:

Appreciative Inquiry in Action

Charles Gibbs and Sally Mahé
United Religions Initiative
San Francisco, CA

Lakeshore Communications, Inc.

24381 Aurora Road, Suite B8
Bedford Heights, OH 44146
(440) 374-2500   (800) 537-7054

Published by:

Lakeshore Publishers, Div.
Lakeshore Communications
24381 Aurora Road, Suite B8
Bedford Heights, Ohio 44146
(800) 537-7054 (440) 374-2500

Address inquiries to:
College Permissions, Lakeshore Communications, Inc. 24381 Aurora Road, Suite B8, Bedford Heights, OH. 44146

Printed in the United States of America
B C D E F G E
ISBN   1-893435-423

This publication is designed to provide accurate and authoritative information with regard to the subject matter involved. It is sold with the understanding that the publisher is not engaged in rendering legal, accounting or other professional advice. If legal advice or other expert assistance is required, the services of a qualified professional person should be sought.

From: **A Declaration of Principles**, jointly adopted by a Committee of the American Bar Association and a Committee of Publishers and Associations.

Visit our home page at: http://www.lakeshorepublishers.com

Publisher: Roger L. Williams
Production Coordinator: Nicholas Connavino
Copyediting: Marianne Miller
Proofreading: Sue Henderson
Cover and interior design: James Fedor
Graphic arts production: Tia Andrako

Birth of a Global Community:

Appreciative Inquiry in Action

CONTENTS

FOREWORD

In 1937, about ten years before his assassination, Mohandas K. Gandhi made a plea for a new mode of relationship between people of diverse faiths. It was a radical plea. Sitting in the turbulent vortex of ethnic and religious conflict, which was often perpetuated in the name of God, Gandhi called not just for nonviolence or tolerance, but also for a more radical kind of appreciative interchange. He called for a stance of openness and learning whereby people would actively seek to know the deepest and best in each other's religious wisdom, knowledge, and spiritual practice. He called it a "reverence for other faiths" – something that, with simple humility, recognizes how all faiths are imperfect ("as they pass through the human medium") and how all have something to teach and share. He went even further, however. He proposed that people might, in their active appreciation of others, discover surprising things that are so good in others' traditions that they would not only not hesitate, but also think it their duty to bring into their faith every acceptable feature of the other faiths.

Radical for Gandhi's times? The answer is obviously yes, as, tragically, Gandhi himself was killed for such views. But the real question is this: What about these times? Still radical? How about Catholics and Protestants sitting down together in this Gandhian-like way in Ireland or Palestinian Muslims and Israeli Jews in Jerusalem searching for the deepest and best in each other and each other's religious and spiritual traditions? Impossible? Read on.

This book is about the most important agenda of the twenty-first century and about a new kind of global organization being created to carry out that agenda. This book is about the dramatic story of the birthing of a United Religions Initiative, something that in spiritually appropriate terms could be to the world of religions what the

United Nations is to nation-states. And it is about Appreciative Inquiry (AI) — a leading approach to organizational development and change — and how it has simultaneously been challenged, humbled, and inspired in this new domain of unimaginable complexity.

My own life changed dramatically when I first heard about a bishop's vision. It was a Saturday morning in 1995, during the fiftieth anniversary celebration of the United Nations. I was at home in Cleveland reading the morning paper, *The Plain Dealer*. In it was a picture of Bishop William Swing making a speech at the United Nations fiftieth anniversary celebration. It was a tiny picture of the Episcopal bishop of California with a one-paragraph news report. (I later learned that the press release leading to this article was picked up nationally and internationally by only one paper — *The Plain Dealer*.) When I read the piece about a vision for a United Religions to compliment the work of the UN, I remember being slightly impressed, but I tossed the paper in the recycling bin, not giving it another thought. However, later in the afternoon, I shared what I had read with Nancy, my wife. She said she wanted to read it too. So I recovered the article from the trash barrel in the garage, and we read it together. This time my heart started pounding because my research interests at the Weatherhead School of Management at Case Western Reserve University had recently turned to studies of "new forms of human cooperation and global action."

While most of my work was in the business world, I started to think about the implications of a United Religions Initiative. Its purpose would not be to create one unified world religion (just like the UN is not to take away from the sovereignty of nations), but to provide a place to work out global interdependencies. The logic was compelling. Indeed, reports show that over half of the world's armed conflicts are not between nation states at all, but between groups of differing ethnic and religious identities. What are the world's religious leaders doing, not alone but together, about these conflicts?

I also asked myself, after seeing pictures on CNN of blacks and whites coming together (such as Mandela and DeKlerk spontaneously holding up each other's hands in the soccer stadium),why there were no similar pictures of religious leaders (for example, the Pope and Dalai Lama) doing the same? Do many believe – did I believe – that religions together could be more of a worldwide force for peace and cooperation than bitterness and separation? I turned to Nancy and said, "If something like a UN among people of the world's religions could be created, it might well help change human relationships more than any other kind of organization I know."

As a scholar and researcher, I wanted to study Bishop Swing's vision. I wanted to see the whole thing evolve from the beginning moments of creation. I wrote a long letter to the bishop that night. I sent him a chapter from a new book I was writing with Jane Dutton at the University of Michigan, *The Organization Dimensions of Global Change: No Limits to Cooperation*. But I was open about our work: "We are infants in our understanding about how to create organizations of the kind you are speaking about. So it would be an amazing privilege to be able to observe, to document, and to learn."Three days later I received a call from the bishop's key colleague in the initiative, the Reverend Charles Gibbs. He came to Case Western Reserve University right away. Shortly after that an advanced doctoral student in Organizational Behavior, Gurudev Khalsa, and I visited the initiative's entire team in San Francisco. Bishop Swing had just returned from a trip around the world. His report showed that about half of the world's religious leaders thought his idea was totally utopian and the other half thought it was definitely needed. Almost all said they would pray for it.

Within 30 minutes, the bishop challenged us when he said, "We do not need you to stay in the ivory tower and study the effort at arm's length. We invite you right here to join us, to bring your organizational development backgrounds and the spirit of the appreciative inquiry to our first summit." Gurudev and I signed on. Without any discussion, we agreed to partner. And we said yes about bringing the AI Summit approach – a whole systems, strength-based, large-group planning methodology – to help launch a five- year process for creating a vision, a charter, and a plan for a United Religions Initiative.

Two minutes after that meeting, we jumped into another with Sally Mahé and Charles Gibbs, the authors of this amazing book. They introduced us to the host committee of the first global summit for creating a charter for a United Religions Initiative. The summit dates were already set. And the summit, which was to be held where the UN Charter was drafted at the Fairmount Hotel in San Francisco, was less than two months away. We started designing and preparing for it that day. It was thrilling.

This book tells the organizational development story of the next five years: the global AI Summits held at Stanford University, at the Fairmount Hotel in San Francisco, and at Carnegie Mellon University in Pittsburgh; the charter-writing meetings taking place all over the world in Caracas, Oxford, Buenos Aires, Nairobi, New York City, and others; the dozens of organizational design meetings with business leaders such as Visa's Dee Hock; and, of course, the exciting moments of birthing the URI at the charter- signing celebration at Carnegie Music Hall in Pittsburgh in June of 2000. Right now, as I write these words, more than 200 United Religions Initiative centers, or Cooperation Circles, on every continent are bringing together Hindus, Muslims, Christians, Buddhists, Jews, Zoroastrians, Jains, indigenous spiritual traditions, Bahai, and many more. The mission is strong: *The purpose of the United Religions Initiative (URI) is to promote enduring daily interfaith cooperation, to end religiously motivated violence, and to and create cultures of peace, justice, and healing for the Earth and all living beings.*

I believe the URI, like the International Physicians for Nuclear War, can be one of the few organizations that is nominated for and receives a Nobel Peace Prize. The work of the URI is that important. It could happen in our lifetime.

Remarkable in its in-depth view of the promises and potentials of appreciative inquiry, organizational design, large-group summit methods, and spiritual practices for bringing people together across boundaries of all kinds, this book is a unique resource for people involved in organizational development and change leadership. To be sure, this volume is a practical guide with tools and insights. But it is not your typical guide. It is not superficial. It is not just about forms and worksheets. It is a narrative guide, teaching while telling a story. It shows the reader a "way" without prescribing a narrow or misleading "six surefire steps." Work in the real world is emergent and dazzling. And this book is about the real thing. Through storytelling like Margaret Mead might do, one learns at levels that are tremendously beneficial. This book should be in the library of every person interested in organizational design, interfaith and international relations, social movement organizing, and appreciative inquiry.

My many feelings of gratitude are offered to Charles Gibbs, Sally Mahé, and all the people of the URI that have helped bring a new hope to the world. In this seminal work, Charles and Sally have provided each one of us with a gift. It is a gift of passion and compassion, of courage and humility, and of literary inspiration. Most of all, it is a precious example, much like the Dalai Lama's *The Good Heart*, of the power of appreciative ways of knowing, valuing, and learning from the Other.

David L. Cooperrider
Weatherhead School of Management
Case Western Reserve University

November 2003

PREFACE

Birth is an abiding mystery and miracle. The birth of an organization no less than the birth of an individual. This is the story of a birth of a transformative global community, the United Religions Initiative (URI). And the story of the extraordinary midwife, Appreciative Inquiry (AI), serving that birth.

A skilled midwife creates the safety and comfort that nurture a mother and family during the birthing process. She believes in the birthing abilities of mother and the baby. She suggests actions to prepare for a healthy birth, and to relieve pain and stress. She trusts that natural forces will follow their own momentum to give birth to a new life and the nurturance of that life. She knows that the birthing process is unpredictable and that the unexpected occurs even in the most well prepared households. A good midwife guides the expectant family on a trust walk through the exhilarating, frightening, disorienting unknown of the birthing process into the promise of new life.

As midwife, AI led a growing global community on its trust walk of cocreation. It opened the door for hundreds and eventually thousands of people to join in an unprecedented act of global cooperation in giving birth to the URI.

An organizational development methodology that is changing human history facilitated the birth of a global interfaith organization with the potential to change human history.

AI is rooted in the simple and profound act of appreciation, a life-giving human action that evokes and recognizes the good in people, all kinds of people. By harnessing appreciation as an active ingredient in supporting change, AI processes become a portal through which one of the most extraordinary resources on Earth, the ingenuity and resourcefulness of the human spirit, is tapped.

AI is a dynamic phenomenon that calls forth the best in people and asks them to focus on the best of all possibilities. It creates a climate where people believe that their organization really means something and so do they. It is founded on a practice that can be described as sacred listening and on a belief that every voice matters. AI invites the "whole system" of affected parties to cocreate the vision of a new future. It carries a belief that a gathered community contains sufficient wisdom, without the necessity of privileged 'expert' voices, to create the plan and commitments necessary to realize that vision.

In URI's case, the whole system is the diverse religions, spiritual expressions and indigenous traditions throughout the world. The vision is of a global organization whose purpose is to promote enduring, daily interfaith cooperation, to end religiously motivated violence and to create cultures of peace, justice and healing for the Earth and all living beings. The plan and commitments? You'll have to read this story to find out.

In this story of how AI served as midwife at the birth of the URI, the authors want the reader to understand the practical ways that AI elicits the best in people and how it offers a safe space for all voices to be heard. The authors want the reader to understand how AI is rooted in a fundamental trust in the human spirit to serve a collective good, and how AI preserves a reverent approach to work that allows the glory of the sacred to enter.

And the authors hope the reader will be inspired by the story of how, in a world too often characterized by mistrust and deadly violence, people of diverse faiths dared to dream of a different way and committed their lives to making that dream a reality through the United Religions Initiative [www.uri.org].

Charles Gibbs and Sally Mahé
United Religions Initiative
August 2003

DEDICATION

There are as many stories of the birth of the URI and the role AI played as there are people who lived through the years of this birth. We hope this book gives at least a whisper of the thousands of voices who are a part of this story. We hope this story is one where people who shared in URI's creation can find their place, whether they're mentioned by name or not. And, we hope that those who read this book will find that they are inspired to join the journey of transformation.

Especially, we dedicate this book:

To those URI pioneers who helped blaze the trail
in this life and have now crossed over to blaze the trail
in the next.

Luis Dolan, Mary Ellen Gaylord, Gary Smith,
Juliet Hollister, Gedong Bagoes Oka,
and Joel Beversluius.

ACKNOWLEDGEMENTS

To the thousands of people who each day, make URI a living force for a better world.

To Bishop William Swing, whose tenacious and gracious vision, fundraising prowess and tireless dedication gave URI wings to fly.

To those visionary souls who have served URI on its Board, Interim Global Council and Global Council for their passion and commitment.

To William Bowes, Richard Goldman, and Arch and Anne McClure for their visionary philanthropy and enduring commitment to the URI vision; and to all whose financial generosity makes URI possible.

To the AI community, especially to Dr. David Cooperrider for his incomparable vision, humility and heart; to Dr. Diana Whitney for her guiding light, penetrating questions and deep spirituality; and to Gurudev Khalsa for his commitment to team facilitation that helped us be the global community we sought to create.

To Dee Hock, Geoff Strawbridge and Robin Myren for their chaordic vision and practice.

To the URI staff, past and present, global and regional for their loving friendship and utter dedication.

Charles: My deepest thanks and love to my wife, Debbie, and to my children, Ben and Naomi. My work for URI could not have been done without their loving and sacrificial support. Thanks to my mother, Ruth for grounding me in the values that guide me; to my brother, Eric, for teaching me that every individual is a precious sister or brother; to my sister, Ruthie, and my brother, Peter, for their love and support; and to my coauthor, Sally Mahé, an inspiring midwife in her own right.

Sally: I am grateful to Susan Switzer, Sheri Ritchlin and Deborah Schweng for their encouraging spirit; to my coauthor, Charles Gibbs for his unflagging faith and light; to my daughters Elizabeth and Katherine for their love; to my mother and father, Nadine and George Mahe and to Sanford Garner, my first AI partner at the Global Summit in 1996, who told me "I was perfect to do this work."

CHAPTER 1

The Bishop wanted to know what others in the field thought about the vision of a spiritual analog to the United Nations. Was there any existing organization already working on such a project? If so, how could we help? If not, was there any advice about how we might proceed?

At this point the "we" was a small circle — the Bishop and a few other people — but a circle seized by a powerful vision that they could not put aside.

The Birth of a Vision

In May 1999, the United Religions Initiative (URI) cosponsored a historic interfaith conference in Brazil. A total of 125 people from 35 different religious, spiritual, and indigenous traditions attended. The gathering provided an essential opportunity to make known and to celebrate existing interfaith work in Brazil, to explore how connecting Brazilian interfaith work to the URI's global effort might be mutually beneficial, and to begin to forge strategic alliances for future work. An image of the future URI wished to create materialized during the second night of the conference, an extraordinary experience.

Participants gathered at night in a large circle on a mountain, in the middle of the Brazilian rain forest. The only light came from a bonfire in the center of the circle and from a full moon occasionally concealed by the clouds drifting across the night sky. The participants were led by representatives from four indigenous nations that had been pushed to the brink of extinction by ancestors of many of the people standing in the circle. Dressed in their ceremonial regalia, the indigenous representatives shared a ritual of sacred dance and chant. One *after another each nation danced, the chants rising past the clouds, past the moon, to the great spirit of life. Then all four shared a common dance.*

It was a historic moment. Ancient divisions among the groups were so strong that they had never before danced together. The previous night they had struggled into the early hours of the morning over how to lead the whole group in sacred ritual for healing and peace. Someone had then said that if they were to lead a ritual for healing and peace for the whole group, they must first heal ancient enmities and make peace among themselves. The manifestation of that peace was their shared dance.

At the end of the shared dance, the whole group was invited to dance. All joined hands and danced until they were exhausted. Around the circle were indigenous people in their native dress, a Zen Buddhist monk, a Tibetan Buddhist monk, two Dominican monks, a Hindu swami, and a Muslim sheikh — all sizes, shapes, ages, and colors of men and women in regular clothes and in ritual clothes, hands joined, dancing together as one community, extraordinarily diverse and yet united. In that moment, it felt as though the participants were living their vision of a better world. They were what they sought to become.

A VISION

A vision of interfaith cooperation for global good has been central to the United Religions Initiative since the seed that has grown into the URI was first planted. From one perspective, that seed was planted and the URI story began in the winter of 1993. The United Nations invited the Episcopal Bishop of the Diocese of California, William Swing, to host a one-hour interfaith service at Grace Cathedral on June 25, 1995. The service was to be part of a week of activities commemorating the 50th anniversary of the signing of the United Nations Charter in San Francisco. When the Bishop expressed his delight at hosting this service, the UN representative said, "We'll bring 185 nations to this celebration. You please bring the world's religions." The Bishop said, "Fine," went home, and found it difficult to fall asleep that night.

From a longer-range perspective, the story began in 1893 at the Parliament of the World's Religions in Chicago. This event marked the first time a major Hindu leader, Swami Vivekananda, shared a platform in this country with major Christian leaders. His opening remarks, which follow, remain an inspiration for all who yearn to see religion as a source of good and interreligious cooperation as a vehicle for a new day of peace, justice, and healing.

Swami Vivekananda's Remarks to the Parliament of the World's Religions in Chicago, September 11, 1893

Sisters and Brothers of America,

It fills my heart with joy unspeakable to rise in response to the warm and cordial welcome which you have given us. I thank you in the name of the most ancient order of monks in the world; I thank you in the name of the mother of religions; and I thank you in the name of the millions and millions of Hindu people of all classes and sects.

My thanks, also, to some of the speakers on this platform who, referring to the delegates from the Orient, have told you that these men from far-off nations may well claim the honour of bearing to different lands the idea of toleration. I am proud to belong to a religion which has taught the world both tolerance and universal acceptance. We believe not only in universal toleration, but we accept all religions as true. I am proud to belong to a nation which has sheltered the persecuted and refugees of all religions and all nations of the earth. I am proud to tell you that we have gathered in our bosom the purest remnant of the Israelites, who came to southern India and took refuge with us in the very year in which their holy temple was shattered to pieces by Roman tyranny. I am proud to belong to the religion which has sheltered and is still fostering the remnant of the grand Zoroastrian nation. I will quote to you, brethren, a few lines from a hymn which I remember to have repeated from my earliest boyhood, which is every day repeated by millions of human beings: *"As the different streams having their sources in different places all mingle their water in the sea, so, O Lord, the different paths which men take through different tendencies, various though they appear, crooked or straight, all lead to Thee."*

The present convention, which is one of the most august assemblies ever held, is in itself a vindication, a declaration to the world, of the wonderful doctrine preached in the Gita: *"Whosoever come to Me, through whatsoever form, I reach him; all men are struggling through paths which in the end lead to Me."* Sectarianism, bigotry, and its horrible descendant, fanaticism, have long possessed this beautiful earth. They have filled the earth with violence, drenched it often and often with human blood, destroyed civilization, and sent whole nations to despair. Had it not been for these horrible demons, human society would be far more advanced than it is now. But their time is come; and I fervently hope that the bell that tolled this morning in honour of this convention may be the death-knell of all fanaticism, of all persecutions with the sword or with the pen, and of all uncharitable feelings between persons wending their way to the same goal." (Swami Vivekananda, Chicago Addresses. (Nabajiban Press, Calcutta, 1992, pp. 1-4.)

4

The Parliament also marks the birth of the modern interfaith movement, which is based in the belief that enhanced understanding and cooperation among people of different faiths is central to the future of humanity. This movement also has given birth to many international interfaith organizations. Among these are the International Association of Religious Freedom, the World Congress of Faiths, the Temple of Understanding, the World Conference on Religion and Peace, the Council for the Parliament of the World's Religion, and the International Interfaith Centre.

From yet another perspective, the story began before the dawn of recorded history, when the first religious impulses stirred in the souls of ancient peoples. It began before formal religions, when early humans first found themselves drawn into a conscious relationship with a mysterious Other. Out of these first relationships has evolved the rich and varied wisdom of the world's religions, spiritual expressions, and indigenous traditions. The URI story begins in the use, abuse, and potential for transformative good of this wisdom and these traditions.

The Reverend Marcus Braybrooke has told the story of the modern interfaith movement in his book, *A Pilgrimage of Hope*. Many writers, perhaps most notably Dr. Huston Smith, have told the story of the birth and growth of the world's wisdom traditions. While building on these stories, this book will tell its own story, beginning in the winter of 1993.

So, returning to that night in 1993, Bishop Swing, unable to sleep, began reflecting on the invitation from the United Nations – an invitation to celebrate 50 years of unprecedented peacemaking dating back to 1945. During that time, the nations of the world, even when they were at war with each other, had had the moral courage to meet on a daily basis at a permanent center to work for peace. The bishop realized that during that same 50 years, even though they were often implicated in the violence that helped make the twentieth century one of the bloodiest in human history, the religions of the world had barely talked with each other.

From this insight was born the vision that has animated the URI since its inception: the creation of a global forum where the religions and spiritual communities of the world would meet on a daily basis in mutual respect, prayerful dialogue, and cooperative action to make peace among religions so they might become a compelling force for global good. As the bishop shared this vision with people in his diocese, he found many responding with enthusiasm and a desire to help make the vision a reality.

As Bishop Swing readily admits, this vision was born in an "invincible ignorance" of 100 years of growing interfaith work and of the existing global interfaith efforts. This led him to the United Nations in June 21, 1993, to a meeting he organized, with the help of Gillian Sorensen, UN Deputy Secretary, for leaders from other major international interfaith groups, including the Temple of Understanding, the World Conference on Religion and Peace, the World Congress of Faiths, and the International Association of Religious Freedom.

The bishop wanted to know what others in the field thought about the vision of a spiritual analog to the United Nations. Was any existing organization already working on such a project? If so, how could we help? If not, was there any advice about how we might proceed? At this point, the "we" was a small circle, (the bishop and few other people), but a circle seized by a powerful vision they could not put aside.

Out of that meeting emerged a clear sense that while a wide array of interfaith work was going on, no one was endeavoring to create the kind of forum the bishop was imagining. Indeed, some of those attending were opposed to the idea. Among the reasons for this opposition were the belief that it was too idealistic, that others had tried and failed, and that the differences were too great between the world of religion and the world of nation states. While one can go to the leader of Germany and ask for an official representative, he or she cannot similarly go to "the leader" of Christianity and ask for a formal representative of all Christians. There are different branches of

Christianity, and within each branch, different practices and structures of leadership are commonplace. The vision founders, some believed, on this crucial issue.

At the same time this well-founded skepticism was voiced, others heard in the bishop's vision a calling of the Spirit and were more encouraging. One suggestion was that a way to take a significant next step might be to convene an interfaith conference of young people that would be part of the lead-up to the 50th anniversary interfaith service. Let the young people engage with this vision and see what they make of it. Coming out of that meeting, the bishop recognized that no one was seeking to create what he had envisioned as a spiritual analog to the United Nations. While many interfaith leaders were skeptical of the idea and others believed it would be extremely difficult but was worth trying, there was a clear message from a few that working toward a youth conference would be a good way to ground the URI effort in more than one person's vision.

Over the next two years, two parallel *ad hoc* interfaith groups worked in San Francisco. One worked to plan the one-hour interfaith service at Grace Cathedral, and the other worked to plan a conference for 200 young people to be hosted by the University of San Francisco, a Jesuit university. Though these groups worked largely independently of each other and were staffed by different people, they contained among them many who would go on to be part of the URI's founding board of directors, or key supporters. Among these were Rita Semel, a San Francisco civic leader as well as a leader in the Jewish community and a pioneer of interfaith work in San Francisco, and Father Gerry O'Rourke, Ecumenical and Interfaith Officer of the Roman Catholic Archdiocese of San Francisco and an interfaith pioneer in the city. Sister Chandru Desai, the head of the San Francisco Brahma Kumari Center, was a key participant, as were Dr. Waheed Siddiqi, a member of United Muslims of America; the Reverend Paul Chaffee, director of the Interfaith Center at the Presidio; and the Reverend Charles Gibbs, a local Episcopal priest who would become the URI's founding executive director.

"REDISCOVERING JUSTICE"

The conference was called "Rediscovering Justice," a title that came more from the University of San Francisco side of the partnership than from Bishop Swing. The bishop, who is an extraordinarily gifted fund-raiser, was responsible for most of the money raised to fund the conference. In fact, as the planning for the conference evolved, the bishop found himself struggling to maintain a focus on the vision of a United Religions Organization. Whether that struggle was ultimately won or lost, the conference provided great teachings about the challenges of organizational partnerships and created a living model of interfaith cooperation that held within it the seeds of what the URI has become.

"Rediscovering Justice" gathered an international group of 200 young people from 35 spiritual traditions to hear eminent religious leaders, including two Nobel Peace laureates, Betty Williams and Desmond Tutu, speak about the role faith had played in their actions for a better world. In addition, the participants had the opportunity to learn from each other in small groups, to reflect on what they had been hearing, to engage the vision of a United Nations-type organization for religions, and to reflect on what they believed their religions had to offer for the good of all people, not just the members of their faith. What emerged was an early and vibrant image of what the URI might be like.

"Rediscovering Justice" was the first significant interfaith engagement for many of the participants. For instance, many of the young Christian participants had never met a Sikh and had not even known that Sikhism was a religion. Predictably, as inspiring as the talks were, the participants were most animated by the time they spent in small groups, where they had the opportunity to explore their own faith in new, deeper, and often more challenging ways and to learn about the faiths of others. This grounding in the sacred and in the conversations that flowed from it created a powerful sense of community among 200 strangers and led them to claim the conference as their own, rather than as something being done to or for them. The organizers did not know it at the time, but this dynamic would come to characterize the URI. Over time, URI organizers would become quite skilled at bringing people together and creating a community grounded in richly diverse expressions and practices of the sacred, ready to claim this initiative as its own.

On the last day of the conference, the two Nobel laureates electrified the group with their messages of faith leading to sacrificial action for good in the face of extreme violence and hatred. As the session was about to adjourn, one of the young people stood up and said, "Anyone who would like to join in a brief time of prayer together, please meet outside on the way to the reception."

Within minutes, 200 people had formed four concentric circles on a grassy lawn under the midmorning sun. For the next 45 minutes, one after another, people stepped into the center of the circle and offered a prayer, a passage from a sacred text, or a thought of inspiration as the others listened with open hearts and minds. For 45 minutes, unabashedly and freely, people of diverse faiths shared what was most important to them and appreciated what was most important to their newfound sisters and brothers. In this moment of movement of the spirit, theological differences took a back seat to a yearning to share the riches of various traditions for the uplifting and inspiration of all.

The interfaith service took place the following day at the cathedral and was televised around the world. Though UN ambassadors from all over the world and several heads of state attended, only two people were given the opportunity to address the gathering – the UN Secretary-General, Boutros Boutros Ghali, and Farid Senzai, a young Afghani Muslim. Security was extremely tight, involving the Secret Service, the San Francisco police, and Grace Cathedral's security. Streets were cordoned off for blocks around the cathedral. Everyone entering the cathedral had to pass through a metal detector.

In an action expressing the potential for interfaith engagement to lead to compassionate action, the young people expressed their solidarity with the poor by electing to walk, rather than ride, from the University of San Francisco to Grace Cathedral. "We'll march," they announced. "Please use the money you save on the buses to help feed people who are hungry." As people filed through the metal detector at the cathedral, a young Sikh woman, who was wearing her ceremonial dagger, triggered the alarm. She was told to remove her dagger or she would be denied admission. Though the rest of the group was inside, word quickly spread that one of their sisters was being held outside. Three days before, these 200 people had been strangers. Many had never met a Sikh and knew nothing about Sikhism. Still, in that moment, they stood as one. All 200, including Farid Senzai, who was to share the pulpit with the Secretary-General of the United Nations, declared their intention to leave if their sister was not allowed in. After some hasty interfaith education, the Secret Service agreed that as long as the young woman was not near enough to stab anyone they were guarding she could come in. The San Francisco police agreed as well. The cathedral's security agreed to have someone sitting nearby in the unexpected event that his or her intervention was needed. Almost lost in the service that followed was a challenge to the world issued by Bishop Swing to create a United Religions organization.

Also attending the Rediscovering Justice conference were representatives from many of the interfaith groups who came to facilitate small groups, to serve as interfaith resources, and to meet in parallel sessions to discuss the evolving vision of a United Religions Organization. Offered as a conversation-starter was a white paper prepared by a Bay Area visionary and activist, Peter Hart. The document imagined the creation of a UN-style organization that would be centered in San Francisco's Presidio, the oldest military base in the country that was in the process of being converted into an urban national park dedicated to peace and the environment.

The people participating included Dr. Robert Traer, General Secretary of the International Association of Religious Freedom; respected interfaith scholars and activists the Reverend Marcus Braybrooke and Mary Braybrooke; Venerable Chung Ok Lee, Won Buddhist priest and chair of the Religious NGO Association at the United Nations; Peter Stewart and Elizabeth Espersen of Thanksgiving Square in Dallas; and Dr. Diana Eck from the Center for World Religions at Harvard University.

As veterans and pioneers in the interfaith movement, these people brought an extraordinary experience, belief in the power and potential of the interfaith movement, hope, and skepticism. The conversations were wide-ranging and frank. Though the white paper had been intended as a conversation-starter, many people believed they were being asked to put their personal and/or organizational stamp of approval on a project they had had no part in developing. Who would own this effort, they wanted to know? How would decisions about its development be made, and who would make them? Would the project's development be truly global? How would this effort connect with and be respectful of existing global interfaith work? How was this effort connected with growing grassroots interfaith work around the world? Was the organizational model appropriate? Did the world need another superbureaucracy? Who was going to lead it? How was it going to be funded?

Some expressed the conviction that the movement needed a charismatic leader who would dedicate his or her life to this work, if it ever happened. Others stressed the importance of the organization being widely owned and cocreated. Bishop Swing stressed the need he sensed for the world's religions to find a common vocation for peace — and his intention to help create an organization with that as its primary purpose. He invited any of those interested to share in the effort. By the end of the conference, many questions were on the table, but few, if any, had been answered. The questions would be expanded and sharpened by many people in the years ahead. For this group, the emerging relationships were characterized by varying degrees of interest, trust, skepticism, and commitment to remain in the conversation if it moved forward. The group dispersed with no formal resolutions, but with a verbal commitment to remain in communication and with an invitation from Venerable Chung Ok Lee to Bishop Swing to address a major gathering of religious nongovernmental organizations (NGO's) at the United Nations the coming October.

EARLY ORGANIZATIONAL CHALLENGES

In the exhausted aftermath of the youth conference and the service, a small group, including Bishop Swing, Peter Hart, and Charles Gibbs, met in Bishop Swing's living room to ask whether and how to move forward. The consensus was to move forward. The plan of action included incorporating and filing for nonprofit status; making a trip to the United Nations in October; using a three-month sabbatical journey by Bishop Swing beginning the following February to seek endorsements from religious and interfaith leaders around the world; and planning a small global interfaith summit to take place the following June. This summit would fall during the week which included the anniversary of the UN charter signing and would convene to write a charter for the United Religions organization.

Reality quickly set in. Having paid the bills for the youth conference, little money was on hand; the group knew only a few interfaith leaders, and some of them, as the group had rediscovered at the recent conference, were not too enthused about the effort to create a United Religions organization. Into this sobering reality came some sound advice: "Without losing the sense of urgency, move slowly enough to build participation and create broad-based, shared ownership of the project." Thus, the primary objective changed. Rather than seek to write a charter with a small group in a week in June 1996, the new goal was to gather a credible group of religious and interfaith leaders to plan the *process* that would produce a charter that had global input and ownership and would eventually be signed in June 2000.

Water finds its own way around obstacles; so does the creative spirit of the universe, called by whatever name. The movement of the Spirit has a way of transforming obstacles into openings, of putting doors into brick walls so one can pass through them. A key element of leadership is to discern the movement of the Spirit. Often the obstacles that present themselves are invitations to see the path before oneself in a new way. The challenge is to hold fast to a central guiding vision while being supple enough to allow one's understanding of how to realize that vision to evolve. This openness to the Spirit has been an essential element of the birth of the United Religions Initiative (URI). The vision of finding an enduring way to help religions recognize and realize their common vocation for peace and cooperative action for global good animated the quest to create a United Religions organization. That vision remains at the heart of the URI. But much has changed along the way.

The June 1993 meeting at the UN and the Rediscovering Justice conference were two key moments in the early history of the URI, when a vision held essentially by one person began engaging a broader community with an array of diverse religious and spiritual, cultural, ethnic, generational, and vocational backgrounds. Through this engagement, it became clear that no one had a monopoly on vision or wisdom and that different and sometimes seemingly divergent visions often pointed toward a common destination – a world that reflected a larger measure of peace and justice for all. One cannot be in serious dialogue with another without having his or her vision and insights reinforced and challenged; one cannot honor that dialogue without being prepared for his or her vision and insights to evolve. The history of the URI has been one of a movement, learning more and more effectively how to create the conditions for meaningful dialogue around a central vision so all voices are heard and all have an opportunity to shape the development and realization of the vision, yet the central vision remains vivid and compelling. This pattern of growth accelerated in the year between "Rediscovering Justice" and the URI's first Global Summit in June 1996.

In the extraordinary effort to produce "Rediscovering Justice" and the interfaith service for the UN 50th Commemoration, little attention had been paid to what might happen after these grand events. Conference organizers had hoped to create a communications network that would keep the community of young people connected with one another. Communication for this effort was problematic. email was still so new that a critical mass of participants did not have access to reliable email. Further, many of the students moved over the summer and then again in the fall. The staff at USF moved on to other projects, and this potentially powerful tool for change dissolved. The same was initially true of the planning committees of these two events. There had been such a focus on producing the events, and such exhaustion in the aftermath, that the working interfaith coalitions that enabled these events dispersed. Fortunately, through the fall of 1995 into early winter 1996, key members of these groups came back together and new members joined to form the host committee that would give birth to the URI's first official board of directors and provide the planning muscle for the first Global Summit. During this time, Sally Mahé and Paul Andrews, who would become part of the founding staff of the URI, became directly involved.

Over some months, a consistent core developed. In addition, there were always new invitees. Some joined for the long haul; others drifted away. Though never seeming diverse enough (a point regularly made by someone whenever the host committee met), the diversity grew — women and men, clerics and lay people, younger and older, many flavors of Christians and often only one Jew or Muslim or Hindu or Buddhist or Brahma Kumari, many Caucasions and few (but a growing number of) people of color.

Beginning each meeting with an invocation of the sacred from one of the traditions represented, the host committee focused on a wide range of issues — from the most global and visionary to the most local and practical. In discussing their incorporation, the founders had to imagine more fully what a United Religions organization might look like, how they would actually give birth to it, and what the host committee's relationship would be to what it was seeking to create. One reflection of this issue was the deliberation about what to call the new organization. Was the name to be the United Religions Organization, the United Religions Initiative, or simply United Religions? After lengthy debates, the host committee decided to incorporate as United Religions and to lay claim to the name but to operate as United Religions Initiative until the charter was written and signed.

With this decision came an essential distinction that would shape the URI's work over the next four years. The host committee represented not the baby to be born, but the midwife to assist in the birth. The committee was not the building to be built, but the scaffolding that would enable the building to be built. Both of these images exemplified that the host committee was not seeking to create something for its own aggrandizement, but was performing an act of service to the world. As the midwife steps out of the way after a successful birth and as the scaffolding is dismantled after a building is ready for occupancy, so the host committee would not attempt to control the forum it was seeking to create; it would step out of the way and leave it to the "religions" to inhabit and use. This ethic of spiritual service to a higher good was implanted in the URI's genetic code almost from the moment of inception.

Every decision was made more complex by the vision of the diversity of the world's religions and peoples to be served. Questions such as deciding on letterhead — would there be just words? Should there be a logo? If so, what should the logo look like? — led to near paralysis. Many favored using symbols from different faiths to represent the interfaith nature of the organization. Others were firmly opposed to a logo, believing it was inappropriate to omit religion from a logo but impossible to include them all. Some brought deep experience in interfaith work; some, deep experiences of exclusion; some, fervor for the cause but no real interfaith experience or sensitivity; some, a passion to have a good graphic design. The committee had no formally articulated decision-making process. Typically, such deliberations plunged the group into a swirling chaos of seemingly competing visions and values. Sometimes the chaos inexplicably resolved itself into something approaching consensus, but time and again the group was kept from drowning in chaos as a decision made by a few enabled the members to move forward.

In early October, Bishop Swing and Charles Gibbs journeyed to New York City, where the bishop was to address the annual gathering of religious NGOs at the United Nations, organized by Venerable Chung Ok Lee. Dr. Robert Traer was to be a primary respondent to the bishop's remarks. This presentation laid the groundwork for what would become a fruitful relationship between the evolving URI vision and NGOs, who had been part of the UN system for years. From members of these groups came a clear and nearly unanimous response to the Bishop's presentation:

> *We love the vision of religions working together for peace; we think the organizational model of the UN is all wrong. The world doesn't need another super-bureaucracy that tells the rest of the world what to do. The peaceful revolution in the Philippines and the fall of the Berlin wall make it clear that this is the era of people power. The power needs to be in the grassroots, not in the religious hierarchies.*

This pattern of response would grow over time and would reach a crescendo at the Global Summit in June 1996, which would fundamentally alter the development of the URI.

In a continuing practice of working cooperatively in this effort, conversations in November eventually led to three additional cosponsors of the June summit: Jim Garrison, head of the Gorbachov Foundation and later the State of the World Forum; Richard Blum, who held a vision of an organization to be called the Foundation for Religious Understanding and was a longtime supporter of His Holiness the Dalai Lama; and William Vendley, General Secretary of the World Conference on Religion and Peace. Though the early hope for these partnerships was never realized (the WCRP withdrew its cosponsorship, and the other two individuals and their organizations never participated actively), they did stimulate the thinking at an early stage about who should (and who should not) attend and what the summit might accomplish.

In early February 1996, Bishop Swing and his wife, Mary, left San Francisco for a three- month trip that would take them through India, Pakistan, Egypt, Jordan, Israel, and different countries in Europe. Along the way, they would meet with a wide array of religious leaders, scholars, diplomats, and interfaith leaders. Among others, they met with Mother Teresa; the Dalai Lama; the Shankaracharia of Kanchypuram; the Grand Mufti of Cairo; Cardinal Arinze in the Vatican; the Coptic Pope Shenouda; Chief Rabbi Mordecai Peron; and the renowned Roman Catholic theologian and proponent of interfaith work and a global ethic, Dr. Hans Kung, whose famous formulation — there will be no peace among nations until there is peace among religions, and there will be no peace among religions until there is dialogue among religion — is a resounding call to many in the interfaith world. Dr. Kung suggested that the United Religions faced a crucial choice: it must focus either on the grassroots of religions or on the high-level religious leaders. His suggestion helped open the door to the URI's future uniqueness, as it chose to emphasize the grassroots.

In these meetings, the bishop shared his vision of a United Religions organization and sought counsel, endorsement, and commitments to attend the charter signing. Most people listened attentively and gave counsel freely. A few, such as Mother Teresa and the Dalai Lama, expressed great enthusiasm for the idea; but most were either cautiously skeptical and expressed a wait-and-see attitude or overtly hostile to the idea. Other positive support came from diplomats, who were keenly aware that religion was an essential and essentially missing player in efforts for peace around the world. The bishop returned from the trip with enough memories for a lifetime, a deepened sense of the complexity of the world of religions and religious leaders, and the challenge of creating a United Religions. He also returned believing more firmly than ever that a United Religions was essential to the positive future of humanity and that this was the time to make it happen.

During these three months, the host committee, absent the bishop, who had served as its chair, chief visionary, and fund-raiser, was hard at work planning the Global Summit. Charles Gibbs devoted a sabbatical from his parish to work on the summit, and members of the bishop's staff provided invaluable support. The key questions: Who should be invited? Where will it be held? What will it cost? What will happen? Initially, each of these questions seemed nearly insurmountable, with wrong answers far easier to find than right answers. The committee had too little time and too little experience, and there were too many pitfalls. And yet the group continued to meet, continued to invoke sacred guidance, and continued to move forward.

Slowly, with many consultations, an invitation list was compiled that reflected religious, geographic, and gender diversity. An invitation letter was crafted and sent out. Responses, more affirmative than negative, came in. After initial hopes of holding the summit in the Presidio proved impractical, the Fairmont Hotel, which figured prominently in the signing of the UN Charter, was chosen as the site. Knowing all this, the host committee was able to put together a budget. Finally, the fledgling URI had a budget, a place to meet, and people to attend. Out of a sea of unknowns, an island of the known had emerged.

From that point, the host committee faced the remaining daunting question: What do we do with these people for five days? The committee members knew they wanted this group to imagine more fully what a United Religions organization might be and do. The committee members wanted the group to imagine how to ground this effort around the world and in a great diversity of religions. The committee members wanted the group to help plan how to attract the right people and to write a charter. But the staff did not know how to make that happen.

ENTER APPRECIATIVE INQUIRY

As this question hung in the air, a miracle arrived in a FedEx envelop from Cleveland, Ohio. It contained a cover letter from Dr. David Cooperrider, an article about something called Appreciative Inquiry (AI), and material about programs called Global Excellence in Management (GEM) and Social Innovations in Global Management (SIGMA). Dr. Cooperrider explained that through an organizational development methodology called Appreciative Inquiry, these programs helped with the development of organizations all over the globe dedicated to transboundary work for a better world. He explained that he had read an article in Cleveland's newspaper, *The Plain Dealer*, about Bishop Swing's vision and believed it was the most exciting global initiative he had ever heard of. He, using GEM and SIGMA, would be honored to participate if he could be of help. Would the bishop be willing to meet with him to explore this option?

Since the bishop was on the other side of the world, it fell to Charles Gibbs to respond. Within a few weeks, he was flying to Cleveland for a consultation, during which it became clear that what the host committee was seeking to do intuitively, the practitioners of AI did from a theoretical basis refined through years of practice. Within a week, the host committee had agreed to use SIGMA to produce the URI's first Global Summit.

During his first planning trip to California in mid-April, David Cooperrider challenged the host committee to think more broadly: You are planning to bring together 30 religious and interfaith leaders. But what about businesspeople? teachers? doctors? members of the media? Every area of human endeavor will be affected by a United Religions. You need to have participants from many different vocations. You need to have the whole system in the room.

Two months before the Global Summit, its size doubled and the second phase of the invitation process began, as did the program planning. There was no more talk of the organizers not having enough time or not knowing what they were doing. They were about to embark on a journey of faith.

CHAPTER 2

Join a world waiting...
for the birth of new light...
The United Religions Initiative

Moving Toward the Vision

URI MEETS AI

A postcard was created for Bishop Swing to give away on his three-month sabbatical journey to seek endorsements from religious and interfaith leaders around the world. On one side was the photo of the birth of a star taken from the Hubble telescope. It was a blazing, glorious explosion of fresh light. The postcard read, "The world is waiting for the birth of new light – the United Religions Initiative." On the back of the card was an invitation to enter into a sacred trust, to join in prayer and meditation to prepare for the coming of a United Religions that would change the world.

This card reflected the starting point for the URI host team in San Francisco when they first met Cooperrider and his colleagues from the SIGMA program. The vision of the URI was held as a sacred trust, a vision to be shared with humility and prayer, a plan to be developed with the help of people everywhere who felt drawn to its promise and light. The vision of the URI included a challenge to solve big problems in the world, beginning with work "to stop killing in the name of God and to start learning to live together." The vision also carried an invitation to people of their own goodwill everywhere to share the responsibility for the URI's success by acting in accord with their deepest values and best understanding of Divine will. The host committee was motivated instinctively to ground the URI in service through people everywhere acting in accord with a greater good and an adherence to Divine purpose. In a moment of extraordinary synergy, David Cooperrider and AI matched that instinctive motivation with a globally tested process for URI's development that gave these inclinations direction, structure, and form.

In mid-April 1996, shortly after Bishop Swing had returned from his three-month pilgrimage and a scant six weeks before the URI's first Global Summit, Cooperrider and a graduate student colleague, Gurudev Khalsa, journeyed to San Francisco for the first substantial meeting between the URI and AI. They met with a small group of committed regulars from the loosely-organized host committee, (Paul Andrews, Sally Mahé, Jennifer Peace, Lois Gundlack, and Iftekhar Hai) who had volunteered to work with Charles Gibbs and Bishop Swing to help make the first URI summit happen. The representatives of the host committee were clear about the purpose of the summit: to plan a year of engagement that would share the URI vision around the world and to gather a truly global and religiously diverse group in San Francisco in June 1997 to begin drafting a charter for the United Religions. They were also clear about who would attend the summit: 30 religious and interfaith leaders with as much geographic and religious diversity as possible. In addition, the host group was discussing issues such as these: How might the city of San Francisco provide a hospitable welcome for the guests? Should a prayer vigil be held in Grace Cathedral, only a block from the meeting, to support the activities at the summit? In what capacity, if at all, would volunteer staff be able to share in this invitation-only summit?

After the San Francisco group shared this background, David gave an overview of his work. He explained that in the field of organizational development, the dominant paradigm had been "problem solving," which called on people to identify what was wrong and to try to fix it. AI arose out of David's concern that problem solving was inevitably tied to and limited by what wasn't working in the past and present. Rather than focusing on what was wrong in a system, AI asked people to focus their work on a positive outcome for the future. Building on this focus, the group is asked to discover the best practices and resources of the past and present, to cocreate a positive vision of the future they wished to inhabit, to plan how to use the best practices and resources as tools to create that future, and to commit to "living into" the plan to make their shared vision a reality. In such a process, David believed, problems would be taken care of indirectly as people worked together for a positive future.[1]

AI is founded on a practice that might be called sacred listening and on the core democratic value that every voice matters. The "whole system," everyone who might have a stake in the outcome, must be in the room when an organization goes through the four fundamental steps of AI: Discovery, Dream, Design, and Destiny (the 4-D process; see below). This approach carries a belief that the gathered community contains sufficient wisdom, without the need of privileged "expert" voices, to create the vision, plan, and make the commitments necessary to create a desired future. An AI conference is not a passive gathering where a few people talk and most of the people sit and listen. In general, there are no speeches. The conference is fully participatory, with participants working in groups of eight, organized for maximum diversity, sitting at round tables.

With this background, David first challenged the local group to come up with a crisp thematic statement that would focus the work of the summit. A summit, as the name implies, is a key meeting of diverse stakeholders. After a time of energizing exploration, the group settled on *A Time for Action: Discovering the Steps for a United Religions Charter*, which became the title of the summit. Building from there, David gently but firmly insisted that the group adopt the concept of having the "whole system" in the room, all the stakeholders. It was a mistake,

---

1 See David Cooperrider, et. al., *Appreciative Inquiry Handbook* (Euclid, Ohio: Lakeshore Communications, 2003).

he believed, to limit the summit to religious and interfaith leaders when all of humanity had a stake in the creation of a United Religions. In addition to a balance of men and women and age, ethnic, religious, and geographic diversity, the planners needed to include people in business, education, the arts, politics, the media, NGO's, and so on. They accepted David's insights and challenges. With his help, the team would set out to bring a microcosm of the whole system, people from many different sectors of society, into the room, doubling the size of the conference from 30 to 60 people. This broader sense of inclusion struck a resonant chord and became a guiding value for the URI's work for the summit and beyond.

THE DISCOVERY PROCESS

David and Gurudev engaged the San Francisco planners as partners in designing the program for the summit. It was evident in these initial planning sessions that the more conventional management style (where a few people "in charge" decided the purpose, participants, agenda, speakers, and activities) was being replaced by a different set of values and behaviors. The planning meetings involved people who were less interested in having the answers to all of the questions than in engaging in an inquiry that might help discover, if not the answers, then at least the best questions to ask. It was all right, in fact appropriate, not to know the answers so others could be invited to share in the challenging journey of discovery.

In those first planning meetings, the URI planners and the SIGMA team had conversations about the desired atmosphere and intentions for the gathering. When David asked members of the team to think about their best intentions for the Global Summit, people around the table offered their ideas spontaneously. Some highlights of these intentions were:

✚ To create a spirit of hospitality and openness.
✚ To share at a personal level from the beginning of and throughout the summit.

✜ To honor each person for who they are and what
  they bring.

✜ To avoid the making of speeches as a conference
  norm.

✜ To reserve time for silence, pausing to reconnect.

✜ To incorporate sacred practices explicitly, with
  sensitivity and optional participation.

✜ To have this be a time for retreat and renewal as
  well as productivity.

✜ To make space for storytelling, both one-to-one
  and in the community.

Building on these considerations, the planning team wanted a
gathering that would engage a core community to design and initiate
the global development of a charter. David and Gurudev proposed a
process called an "Appreciative Future Search." The key concepts of
this process were included in an advance letter to the invited guests:

This conference will be a space for us all to discover
our calling to this initiative and the resources we bring
to find our common ground together, and to mobilize
ourselves toward actions that can bring our dreams
into reality. It is appreciative in that we will conscious-
ly value the personal experiences and trends in interfaith work supporting this initiative now, and it is a
future search in the sense that none of us knows now
what the United Religions Initiative will be or how it
might come into being until we engage in the process
of creating it.

The members of the planning team went on to discuss the values
and directions they thought were important. This list became the
starting point for planning the agenda. Among the values discussed
were evoking and honoring each person's unique call to the URI

vision and his or her unique gifts; engaging people's imaginations and capacity to dream; recognizing those who had come before and drawing upon the research, success, and collective wisdom of the world; creating and sharing a collective understanding of the historical trends that had shaped them; and trusting that even if they did not initially know how they were going to reach their goal, they could "build the plane as they flew it."

Building on these values and using the fundamental concepts of AI to plan the agenda for the five-day conference, the planning team embarked on its journey to establish a new United Religions organization. This organization would embody the spirit expressed in the Preamble to the United Nations Charter:

> We the peoples of the United Nations determined to
> save succeeding generations from the scourge of war,
> which twice in our lifetime has brought untold sorrow
> to mankind, and to reaffirm faith in fundamental
> human rights, in the dignity and worth of the human
> person, in the equal rights of men and women...

But this United Religions organization would not replicate the centralized and representational structure of the United Nations. Instead, the organization would be built on relationships and participatory processes that supported a shared vision and mission. The organization would give increasing numbers of people an opportunity to create a global community that reflected and enacted the positive values they cared about so deeply.

These values and intentions were reflected in the planning process. The atmosphere was one of invitation, respect, passion, appreciation, cooperation, and commitment. Each person present was invited to offer ideas, to ask questions, and to discover his or her place in designing the summit. These ideas and contributions were woven into the fabric of the planning. The planners celebrated insights and breakthroughs. Moments of confusion and low energy became an invitation to become silent and to invoke divine wisdom. The organizers felt tremors of fear and exhilaration before the magnitude of this endeavor and a conviction that what was beginning here could not be stopped. With the UR vision as a polestar and planning processes consistent with the organization's deepest values, the team moved forward as friends, colleagues, and cocreators into an unknown future of extraordinary promise.

Primarily through David's connections, the team constructed an impressive invitation list of people who, while motivated by religious or spiritual values, worked in secular organizations.

Preparation

The team grew to include Kathryn Kaczmarski, another of David's graduate student colleagues. It developed a plan for the week using a methodology called Appreciative Future Search. The participants would systematically proceed through the phases of Discovery, Dream, Design, and Destiny, explained below. The 4-D process introduced a range of activities during the five-day summit that called upon participants to cocreate the next steps toward developing a charter that would establish the United Religions.

The 4-D Process of Appreciative Inquiry

Discovery calls people to share with each other what is most deeply meaningful for them, to appreciate the gifts they and others bring, and to cocreate a shared sense of historical trends.

Dream invites people to envision a positive future built on the best experiences of the past, a future where the world's religions are working for global good.

Design challenges people to engage wisdom from related fields; to develop consensus around common themes such as the organization's mission, vision, values, structure, and actions; and to create plans for future work.

DESTINY invites people individually and collectively to make specific commitments to work toward the realization of their dreams and plans.

In addition to the core 4-D process, the week was designed to create space for deep listening and sacred wisdom, for community building, and for an appreciation of the Earth. Each morning before breakfast, a different participant led an optional meditation/prayer practice in a meditation room set up especially for this purpose. The practices included reflection based on the prayer of St. Francis, the patron saint of San Francisco; Jain chanting; and Raja Yoga meditation. Morning and afternoon sessions were to begin with a time of silence and prayer. These were to be offered by the participants, ensuring as broad a diversity of religious expressions as possible. Planned for midweek renewal were a picnic and hike through the natural environment of the Presidio, followed by an interfaith service at the Presidio's newly rededicated interfaith chapel and a special evening of hospitality offered by Charlotte Swig at her home overlooking San Francisco Bay.

As its work unfolded, the planning team was assigned different leadership roles, with attention paid to gender balance. Props to support the different activities were gathered: flip charts, several 4' x 8' sheets of foam core, colored dots, colored markers, binders full of worksheets, name tags, and more. The day before the summit opened, the ornate circular meeting room at the Fairmont Hotel was transformed from an ideal space for an elegant wedding reception into a working space for 55 people. The large sheets of foam core were taped together and attached to the walls to create a vast, inviting blank slate that encircled most of the room. Flip charts stood at attention next to each table, and tables were adorned with colored markers, scissors, glue sticks, and colored dots. Upstairs, the furniture was removed, and a hotel bedroom was transformed into a serene and beautiful place for participants to find refuge and silence at any time during the day or evening. In addition, the week's agenda was being fine-tuned, worksheets were being finalized and copied, and binders for the participants were being assembled.

At noon that day, Iftekhar Hai, a Muslim and member of the host committee, was helping to carry assorted supplies from the basement of Bishop Swing's diocesan office across the street to the hotel meeting room. As the Cathedral bells chimed 12 noon, Iftekhar said he needed to stop to pray. With no prayer rug handy, Iftekhar improvised. He deftly placed a flip chart on the floor and, facing east, knelt on it and quietly chanted his prayers. The rest of the team paused in awe and appreciation – the feverish pace stilled by a devout Muslim in prayer. In the lighthearted aftermath, all applauded Iftekhar's innovative use of a flip chart. Through all of this, members of the host committee worked as calmly as possible while nonetheless at a feverish pace. Some, such as Iftekhar Hai, knew they would be participants in the summit. Others, such as Sally Mahé and Paul Andrews, who (though no one knew this at the time) would become the core of the URI's founding staff, had no idea whether they would be serving water or helping to cofacilitate one of the sessions. Regardless, all worked with a single-minded focus on serving the success of the summit.

1996, THE FIRST URI GLOBAL SUMMIT: A TIME FOR ACTION

DISCOVERING THE STEPS FOR A UNITED RELIGIONS CHARTER

On Monday morning, June 24, 1996, anxiety about how all of the carefully crafted plans would actually work was masked by the planning team's gracious hospitality, welcoming an eclectic mix of 55 people assembled in a transformed banquet room in the Fairmont Hotel in San Francisco. In addition to local interfaith leaders from the host committee – Rita Semel, Father Gerry O'Rourke, Sister

Chandru Desai, and Reverend Paul Chaffee — participants included Dr. Robert Muller, former Under-Secretary at the UN and current president of the UN University of Peace in San Jose, Costa Rica; Sister Jayanti Kirpilani of the Brahma Kumaris, a spiritual movement based in Hinduism and founded in India; Dr. Jane Pratt, CEO of The Mountain Institute, a global NGO of and for people who inhabit the highest places on earth; Venerable Chung Ok Lee; John Caron, a Connecticut businessperson; Sister Joan Chatfield, a Maryknoll sister and veteran of interfaith work; David Storey, a British veteran of interfaith efforts; Jim Lord, an international philanthropic consultant; Father Luis Dolan; Juliet Hollister, founder of the Temple of Understanding in New York City; Dr. Nahid Angha, a Sufi scholar; Bawa Jain, a Jain interfaith leader; and Bettina Gray, a video journalist.

DISCOVERING THE STEPS FOR A UNITED RELIGIONS CHARTER

The participants had been invited to engage with the URI vision and to discover together what steps might be taken to develop a charter and to create a United Religions. The premise was that no one person knew how to bring the UR into being, but that a group of concerned stakeholders could collectively discover what these steps might be. Participants were invited as guests of the URI, with the summit being funded largely with money left over from the Rediscovering Justice Conference. As the summit began, participants found their places at round tables of eight, designed to have a balanced distribution of women and men and a maximum diversity of geography, religion, vocation, and age. Almost everybody knew somebody; nobody knew everybody. Some came energized by the URI vision and anxious about the success of the summit. Others came deeply committed to interfaith work but skeptical about the URI. Still others came having trusted David Cooperrider's belief that this was a remarkable moment in a movement with the potential to transform world history. A few had experience with AI; most had no idea it even existed. No one knew quite what to expect. Even David looked nervous that first morning and later admitted that he had been shaking with a sense of the magnitude of the moment as he prepared his introductory remarks.

Charles Gibbs offered a warm welcome and gracefully recited a poem he had written one year earlier, "Hymn for a Hatching Heart," calling the participants "to come journey on" into the unknown of this week together.

HYMN FOR A HATCHING HEART
by Charles P. Gibbs (July 1993)

The voice of Sophia, the voice of God's Wisdom,
Insistently calls us to come journey on,
To pack few belongings, to trust in her guidance,
To set out in darkness, to come journey on.

The voice of Sophia calls us out of bondage,
Held captive by Pharaoh and fearful of dawn.
She leads us in darkness, through death to deliverance,
Then into the wilderness, come journey on.

The voice of Sophia, in cloud and in fire,
Inspires our courage and guides us toward dawn,
Obscured by resistance. Then God's transformation:
Light shines in the wilderness, come journey on.

O voice of Sophia be spoken within us.
Enlighten our struggle from darkness to dawn.
Enliven the joy that is trembling within us,
Deep joy at our calling to come journey on.

Bishop Swing, wearing a golf sweater and slacks rather than his formal clerical attire, intuitively recognized the need to use this conference to give his vision away to others to see what could happen. His welcome and introductory remarks to the participants spoke humbly but passionately of his vision, his conviction, and his determination that one day there would be a United Religions. He likened this effort to the first notions that people might be able to fly, as reflected in his comments below.

> At the first of this century, there was a time when human beings knew in their bones that we should fly, so all kinds of people glued feathers to their arms, climbed to the top of the barn, began flapping and jumped off. And sure enough, right around that time, we learned to fly. I don't mind standing in front of you today smelling of feathers and sticking with glue. I'll tell you right now, I'm jumping. This Summit comes down to one invitation to you around the creation of the United Religions, "Come, let's fly!"

> — an excerpt from Bishop Swing's welcome
>   at the first Global Summit

DISCOVERY

BRINGING WHO WE ARE TO THE TABLE

After the bishop's remarks, David and his colleagues from SIGMA gave a brief overview of the week and the 4-D process. They talked about conditions for success. Since the participants' work would steadily build, everyone needed to participate fully for the entire week. Coming and going, typical conference behavior, would not work with this process. People needed to commit to careful listening. Every voice mattered and no voice was privileged. The facilitators were more guides than directors. Self-organizing was an essential value. The conference participants had to take responsibility for their own work, including monitoring time and recording deliberations on flip charts. David and his group also described the different metaphoric rooms the participants would journey through during the week – exhilaration, insight, frustration, and so on. David and his colleagues assured the participants that it was natural to find themselves in any of these rooms. The participants needed to trust these contradictory feelings as part of the process that would ultimately lead them to a shared sense of clarity.

With this background, AI facilitators guided the group in the first activity – appreciative interviews. People were asked to pair with another person at their table, preferably someone they did not know, find a comfortable place to sit, and engage in a mutual interview process guided by a worksheet in their conference binder.

The worksheet "An Appreciative Inquiry – Discovering Steps to a United Religions" framed the essential question: Should there be a United Religions that would, in appropriate ways, parallel the United Nations? The introductory paragraphs explained that the United Religions was not yet a reality but that there was an urge to "establish a United Religions that would be a permanent gathering center where all religions of the world are united on a daily basis in bringing their spiritual gifts to a common table, to enrich, whenever possible, all life on earth." The worksheet included directions for conducting the interviews, as well as the invitation to embark on a journey of discovery – to ask themselves and others how to act collectively on this urge and join with a world waiting for the birth of this new light.

The heart of the worksheet was the interview questions themselves. They had been carefully crafted to elicit stories of powerful personal experience and competence that would help the interview partners connect on a deep level and identify resources they might draw on over the coming five days.

THREE QUESTIONS FROM THE
APPRECIATIVE INQUIRY WORKSHEET:
(for complete set of worksheets from the 1996 Global Summit, see Appendix 1)

1. TO START I'D LIKE TO LEARN A LITTLE BIT ABOUT WHO YOU ARE, what interests you, excites or draws you to participate in this conference? What was it that compelled or called you to this work?

2. A "HIGH POINT" IN YOUR LIFE. To get to know you better as it relates to experiences that you have had that might make a difference here during the course of this conference, I would like you to reflect upon your life and life's work. Obviously you have experienced ups and downs, peaks and valleys, etc. For the moment I would like you to reflect on a high point — a time when you were involved with something significant or meaningful and felt most alive, proud, creative, effective, engaged, etc. Share the story of this high point experience. What made it a peak experience? What felt truly special? Are there lessons that might be brought to this work?

3. VALUING: We can draw upon many different qualities and skills, resources, positive global changes and trends, and historical experiences as a United Religions vision is given birth and grows. We would like to engage in a process of valuing those many resources at several different levels — yourself, your religion or faith community, and global trends.

   A. Without being too humble, what is it you value most about yourself as it relates to things you

bring to this conference and the work of interfaith cooperation? What are your best qualities,
skills, approaches, and experiences?

B. Each of our communities of faith have special
gifts – traditions, beliefs, practices, values – to
bring to the arena of interfaith cooperation and
action. As you think about your community of
faith, what are some of the most positive qualities or gifts that make it capable of entering
into cooperation with others to build something like a United Religions? Do special texts
or passages that stand out for you? a story or
parable? historical experiences? capabilities or
commitments? values?

When the participants rejoined their table groups an hour and a
half later, people's relationships and the energy in the room had been
transformed. The atmosphere was alive with a joyful energy that came
from connecting with another person on a deep level; from feeling
honored by another; and being amazed at the experience, passion, and
vision shared. No longer a collection of randomly connected individuals, the participants were a community inspired to work together.
This energy and sense of community grew as people introduced their
interview partners to the rest of their table mates by offering the
moments of recognition and inspiration that had been the high
points of their conversations.

The challenge with this exercise was not to provide lively introductions, but to have the whole group introduced in the assigned
amount of time. An exercise that, with all the enthusiasm, could easily have taken several hours had to be accomplished in 45 minutes. To
accomplish this, each table was asked to self-organize using four key

roles: a discussion leader, who was to ensure that everyone had an opportunity speak and that no one dominated the conversation; a timekeeper, who was responsible for making sure the participants moved through their work at a pace that would allow them to finish on time; a recorder, who would be taking notes of the conversations; and a reporter, who would be responsible for sharing the work of the group with the whole. The people in these roles made it clear that the participants were responsible for their own work and that they had to work cooperatively if they were to get their work done. These roles would become very familiar to the participants as the week unfolded.

Following an animated 45 minutes of introductions, the sense of connectedness and amazement in the room was expanded still further as the reporter from each table introduced with highlights his or her members to the whole group: "No one has to die for God anymore." "Dag Hammarskold and U Thant were his spiritual teachers at the UN. They influenced him to bring spirituality into the dialogue at the UN." "She believes that 'if you want to live in a good world, it must be good for all.' " "She sees miracles happening all around her. 'Even Muslim groups as diverse as Farrakan's Nation of Islam and Sufi dervishes are sitting down together.' " "The most precious gift is the awareness of being a soul, a sparkling child of God, and of recognizing the soul, the essence of life, in each one of us."

By lunchtime, the participants viewed one another and themselves in a transformed way. The deep humanity, aspirations, experience, talents, core values, diverse perspectives, vocations, and personal callings present in the participants were suddenly visible and charged the atmosphere with enormous possibility. This energy lit up the room, revealing 55 people "smelling of feathers and sticking with glue, holding hands at the edge of a precipice saying in one voice, "Let's fly.""

Creating a Timeline

After lunch and a sacred opening to begin the afternoon session, the participants developed three timelines that created a shared historical context for their work and surrounded them with a visual representation of noteworthy global, religious, and interfaith events in the hundred years since the first Parliament of the World's Religions. First, using a worksheet in the binder, the participants worked individually to recall historic milestones or turning points from the perspectives of world history, the history of their particular faith tradition, and the history of the interfaith movement. This generally orderly work at tables turned into a river of chaos when 55 people armed with worksheets, colored markers, and their best artistic skills flooded to the blank 20-foot long timeline that encircled the room. As people joined their individual timelines together, they regularly exclaimed, "Oh, I had that too." and "I didn't know that." In short order, they deepened their sense of connectedness, learned some new history (for instance, in 1976 Sushil Kumar created a great uproar in his homeland when he became the first Jain monk to leave India), and transformed the blank walls into a group mural. This mural alive with words and symbols that painted an eclectic picture of 100 years of history, created an embracing, if incomplete and idiosyncratic, historical context for their work.

No sooner had the participants finished this marvelous creation than they were directed to another worksheet and asked to interpret their work. Each table group was assigned one of the three timelines and asked to mine it for historical trends that might call forth and support the development of a United Religions (UR). Each group had to determine how to go about its work, but all groups had to be ready to report their findings to the whole in 30 minutes. These reports presented group understanding forged from a synthesis of individual insight. Taken together they created a collective sense of the historical momentum calling forth and supporting something like a United Religions. Some of the noteworthy interfaith trends identified were:

✛ An increasing presence of women and women's perspectives in spiritual life and spiritual institutions.

✚ A steady increase in the migration of Eastern
faiths and spiritual practices to the West since the
first World Parliament of Religions in 1893 and
an increase in interfaith dialogue in more recent
years.

✚ A rise in meditative/contemplative traditions
across faiths and a new openness to indigenous
faiths.

✚ A growing popularity of "bottom-up" decision
making and a democratization of the world that
was not about capitalism, but about encouraging
every voice to express itself and be respected.

A MIND MAP

Building on the insights from the timeline work, the whole group
then created a mind map. The participants gathered in a semicircle in
front of a large 8' x 12' piece of white paper to map the positive
trends that could support the URI effort and the negative trends that
might hinder it. As participants called out the trends, the ideas were
recorded on the paper, creating a rich matrix of interconnected, and
often counterbalancing trends. Negative trends that emerged included
these: the increasing gap between the rich and poor, the gulf between
liberals and fundamentalists, aggressive proselytizing by some religions, and religiously motivated violence erupting in hot spots all over
the world. Positive trends included an expanding consciousness that
was able to hold opposites in tension, an increase in meditation and
silent prayer, rising social responsibility in corporate structures, and a
growing recognition of the shared values and of a universal spirit
underlying all religions. From an avalanche of individuals' ideas, the
group constructed a complex map that highlighted dominant trends,
creating another shared context for the unfolding work. The map provided insights into the UR movement's place in the sweep of the
evolving history of humanity and into the UR movement's spiritual
yearning for global wholeness. The group discussed the relative

impact of the trends and then ranked them as each person placed colored dots on the three trends they believed were most significant. The positive trends that received the most dots were these:

- The trend toward a sense of global solidarity
- The growing recognition of common values at the heart of every religion
- More positive collaboration among religions

With the mind map completed, participants reflected on the insights they had developed from the perspective of their life's work. Participants self-selected into groups that focused on business or religion or education or interfaith work. They discussed these trends with respect to their own field of endeavor or organization and what they were most proud of and most sorry about. The activity ended as a reporter from each group shared its "proudest prouds" and "sorriest sorries" with the whole group.

At the close of the day, participants shared personal artifacts that symbolized their motivation or commitment to this journey. People's faces lit up as they conveyed the significance of their artifacts using symbol, metaphor, and personal stories. Their table mates listened with rapt attention to the deep yearnings that brought each of them to the table, to this journey of cocreation. In this time of intimate sharing, the group members came full circle, returning to where they had been with the appreciative interviews that morning.

Looking back on the day, one would see that there had been no keynote speakers, no solo vision carrier seeking followers. Instead, the day had been a deft interweaving of individual reflection, interviews in pairs, cocreative work in small groups, and engagement of the whole. The underlying message was that each individual voice brings a precious and needed contribution to the collective effort of the whole. The somewhat uneasy collection of individuals that had assembled at 9 a.m. had become a community. They shared a sense of the extraordinary capacity of each individual and of the group. They created a shared history that identified the unique gifts of this moment in time to establish a foundation upon which to dream and to build. The group was eager to face the challenges that lay ahead. Though the group did not know it at the time, this journey of transformation would be played out again and again all over the world on the journey toward a charter for the United Religions.

APPRECIATIVE INTERVIEWING – A SPIRITUAL ART

Why does the Discovery phase in the AI process touch people so deeply and inspire a higher purpose and capacity? What happens in the intimacy of an appreciative interview to release such a positive flow of values, visions, and positive experiences? What happens that encourages people to reclaim a passion and a commitment? How is the divine spark kindled in people as they tell their stories? How is the listener changed? What happens when the whole community begins to create a mosaic of the diverse gifts of the assembled individuals? How does an appreciative interview evoke the best in the human spirit and build and enrich a community?

David Cooperrider has written that people often feel "surprised by friendship" (see Appendix 3) after engaging in an appreciative interview. Experience with appreciative interviews at URI gatherings over the years confirms David's perception. As people share the carefully crafted questions with their partners, a relaxed but intense atmosphere is created – relaxed because people feel valued and comfortable and intense because people are dealing with some of the most powerful and moving experiences of their and others' lives. Most people find that their answers to the questions flow naturally and effortlessly. The interviewers often lean forward, listening in earnest to their partners' replies. As people are given the opportunity to listen appreciatively to another, they see the extraordinary gifts that person has to offer and are able to reflect those gifts back to their partner in a way that often enhances both people's sense of connectedness, of their unique value, and of the powerful possibilities for cooperation sparked by the interview. People who begin as strangers usually end the interview moved by appreciation – for themselves, for their partner, and for the endeavor that brought them together. Friendships blossom and individuals become a community as they share appreciative interviews.

AI questions often ask the participants to remember valuable moments in their lives, to tell stories about those moments, and to describe their dreams for a better future. As people respond to these questions and speak from the heart about their own stories and dreams, they remember what they most admire about themselves. It is a spiritual act to speak from one's heart about things that matter and to be witnessed in these revelations by an appreciative listener. These questions evoke responses that spring from a person's inner spirit. A listener feels an impulse that honors the other and often feels an enlivened connection with the other person. Appreciative interviews invite people to take on a spiritual posture – a way to honor one another naturally and to approach one another in a holy way.

Crafting the questions beforehand is akin to the work of a midwife who helps to create the conditions for a "miraculous birthing" to occur. An intention of care and consideration is conveyed in the words of the best appreciative questions. Like a supportive friend, the writer desires to craft questions that meet people where they are, that use the questions to elicit the best of a people's past and their highest vision of a future, and that invite people to bring their ideas and experiences to bear on the topic at hand.

Well-crafted questions encourage people to speak at a deeper level about what matters to them.[2] People enjoy recollecting parts of themselves and hearing their own stories. The natural flow of one's "best self" gives one's partner an original experience that is fun and fascinating to listen to. It is easy to listen with an open heart when people are speaking authentically about what matters to them. This simple setting offers appreciation, the act of receiving another with gratitude and offering back gracious regard.

Appreciation touches the spirit of intelligent goodness that resides within everyone. Giving and receiving appreciation is one of

---

2 David Cooperrider, et. al., *Encyclopedia of Positive Questions*, vol. I (Euclid, Ohio: Lakeshore Communications, 2003).

the most healing of all human experiences. Appreciation is an honest connection with oneself and others that renews physical energy, reduces fear, and expands self-worth. Appreciation replaces the usual habits of finding fault and fixating on what is wrong; appreciation feeds the human spirit and gives it strength to fly.

The URI story abounds with people from all sectors of society and different religious and socio-economic backgrounds who yearn to fulfill their aspirations and create a world that is more peaceful, just, and harmonious with nature's goodness. Rather than wait for someone else to make the change for them, people called to the URI are taking action to be the change themselves. Appreciative interviews help people feel the inspiration of their own values and reinforce their sense of self as valuable contributors in this world by offering them an opportunity to speak about what is meaningful and to be received by others in a holy way — with appreciation, reverence, and respect.

DREAM

IGNITING THE DREAMS

AI allows people to realize that they are dreamers and that they are not alone. AI honors imagination and the precious human capacity to dream. AI methodologies help people tap into capacity so they experience the vitality and joy of their own dreams and those of others.

In June 1996, the URI was itself only a dream. It had begun as the expression of one person's dream. Its power grew as that individual dream connected with a larger global dream awakened in the hearts and minds of countless people yearning, on the eve of a new century and a new millennium, for a new world of peace, justice, and healing.

The subsequent Global Summit would be the first of hundreds of occasions in the life of the URI where people gathered together to imagine their greatest potential for making the world a better place. They were asked to *dream*. What does the world you want to live in look like? How might a vital and effective United Religions help to make that world more real? What would the UR's mission be? How about its core values? Who would belong? What kind of organization and structure would the UR have? What would it do in the world?

Again and again people came together to dream about a better world and the URI's place in it. Again and again, people contributed their visions of this transformed world and their visions of a United Religions organization that was an agent of global transformation. The more people dreamed, the more the vision took shape. The more the vision took shape, the more it summoned the hearts and minds of people all over the world to make the vision a reality. What might have initially seemed impossible became possible as people were captured by the power of their collective dreams and compelled to work together to make those dreams real.

At this summit of 55 individuals, the Dream phase began on the second day. A question from the day before was reiterated and expanded upon. Participants, meeting at their home tables, were given a series of "dream questions":

1. Put yourself 30 years into the future. The year is 2026. Visualize the United Religions you believe the world is calling for, a United Religions you really want. Visualize it as if it now exists.
2. As part of your vision, imagine the variety and types of contributions the United Religions is making to the world. List its special contributions since 1999.
3. Finally, as part of your vision, imagine the form and structure of the United Religions. Choose a good metaphor for the United Religions as an organization; for example, the United Religions is organized like a solar system, with separate planets orbiting each other around the sun, which is a symbol of the burning issues of the global or common good.

First individually and then in table groups, participants imagined the United Religions they yearned for. They jumped into lively conversations about what the organization was doing and how the world was changed because of its presence. They then had to choose a creative way (such as a radio talk show, a celebration or ritual, a drama, a work of art, or a poem) to present their vision or dream as if it were happening now.

One group developed a radio show called "Global Awareness Radio Network" in the year 2026. Each person was being interviewed on the day when all of the dreams they dreamed in 1996 came true.

Though most groups had similarly positive views of the future, one group had negative reactions to the exercise and chose to engage in difficult, confrontational discussion rather than sharing members' dreams. When the time came for the presentations, this group observed what had happened during its rather cantankerous session and realized that, in spite of the negativity, something significant and positive for the future of the UR had actually occurred. Group members realized that the truth in the experience at their table was that they had listened patiently and respectfully to one another. They had endured argument and controversy and had chosen to stay together at the table. For their presentation, members sat silently in a circle, indicating that the future URI at its best might be one where people remained in a respectful relationship no matter how severely they disagreed or how challenging they found each other to be.

The groups also presented powerful images of the future URI's form and structure. One group imagined three concentric circles — local interfaith groups, international interfaith groups, and the world's religions. Another imagined a spiritual web or internet of global interfaith relationships. Another imagined a "spiritual United Nations," serving as a source, not a resource. Another imagined the formulation of a "Bill of Spiritual Rights." Others imagined a decentralized, inclusive network or a democratic, grassroots movement; a fluid organic structure; and a change of consciousness on the planet.

The following highlights some of the participants' comments during the Dream phase.

Iva Goldman, an interfaith organizer and professor from Hawaii, said, "I dreamed of a day when rock stars and movie stars and athletes would lose their luster and teachers and nurses and mothers would become the objects of adoration and role models for our children. That day is now."

Jim Lord, an internationally recognized trainer in philanthropy, said, "I dreamed of a day when children had grandparents and parents they could ask for advice and they would heed that advice and of a day when children would be the agents of inquiry among their elders. That day is now."

Dr. Robert Muller, former Under-Secretary to U Thant at the United Nations, said, "I dreamed of a day when every time one eats one thinks and thanks first and a day when all people meditate upon awakening and sacred bells greet each new day. That day is now."

Mary Garner, a spiritual friend to many and head of an NGO in Washington, DC, said, "I dreamed of a day when the human ego would be harnessed and all aggression would be channeled into constructive energy; that we would remember that we are spiritual beings of light, love, and harmony in physical form; and that the power of that light would spread throughout the world creating heaven on earth. That day is now."

A New Star Is Born

The last dream presentation was unscheduled and a fitting grand finale. It was the dream of ten year-old Walter Gray, the son of a conference participant whose day-care arrangements had gone awry. As all the adults dreamed expansive dreams and developed clever presentations, Walter sat silently, observing and fashioning origami figures out of the colorful paper he had brought to amuse himself. When the last adult had spoken, Walter stood up and offered his dream. It began with a bright octagonal shape with a hollow center. As he slowly formed the pieces of paper into a new shape, he told this story:

> "Once the religions of the world were far apart, like this," he said, holding up a bright, flat octagonal shape with a gaping empty space in the middle. "Then something happened and the religions started coming together." He began slowly, carefully manipulating the pieces of the shape, shrinking the empty middle until it disappeared. "The religions WILL come together." He transformed the octagon into an unexpected new shape. "And once they are together, there will be something no one thought would be there — a new STAR!

It was a beautiful star, a kindred spirit to the star birth image from the Hubble telescope on the URI postcard that was created a few months before. This offering was so powerful and so resonant with deep vision and its source so innocent and unexpected that the multicolored star became and remained the symbol of the URI in the years ahead.[3]

The participants sharing dreams in pursuit of their highest visions and deepest values connected them at a heart level. They laughed, applauded one another, and enjoyed being at the center of such inspiring creativity. In the Dream phase, AI offered a process that elicited their ability to dream, to create together, to make room for the

---

3 Gurudev S. Khalsa (2002). "The Appreciative Summit: The Birth of the United Religions Initiative," in R. Fry, F. Barrett, J. Seiling, & D. Whitney (Eds.), *Appreciative Inquiry and Organizational Transformation: Reports from the Field* (pp. 211-237). Westport, CT: Quorum Books.

unexpected, and to be lifted in spirit by being witnessed by others. The Dream exercise used these natural inclinations and experiences to help the participants stretch farther, to believe even more in themselves and in the future they were imagining.

Identifying Barriers

Included in the Dream phase was an exercise to identify barriers that had to be overcome in pursuing the URI vision. The participants' insights were recorded on another large piece of paper on the wall. Comments included these:

- Structures in "churches/religions" and "institutions/denominations" are currently top down. The Top down model won't work for the UR; a new model of organizing must be used.
- The proposed name of the organization (United Religions) – while it was easy to identify it with the United Nations, it also raised problems and confusion.
- Many questions about membership, inclusion, representation, decision-making structures.
- Fear, ignorance, old habits, reluctance to change.
- Funding, funding, funding.
- The tendency of organizations (including religions and interfaith organizations) to create turf boundaries that must be honored and transcended in this initiative.
- The concept of "Great" or "Authentic" religions, the danger of excluding others, the tyranny of "The One Truth."

The Dream phase ended with participants envisioning an ideal year of engagement that would lead to an initial charter-writing summit in June 1997. Beginning with the assumption that resources were not an obstacle, the participants were invited to dream big dreams of how to mobilize people, evoke visions, engage in research, and attract funds as the foundation for gathering a global community to begin writing the charter. These dreams created a bridge into the next phase of the summit, Design.

RENEWAL

A special renewal event took place Wednesday afternoon. As one participant later remarked, the break, coming between the Dream phase and the Design phase, had symbolic as well as practical significance. It "allowed a washing away of personal agendas and suppositions so that purged of the dross, we might design with clarity." The renewal included a picnic lunch and a relaxing hike through the natural beauty of Presidio National Park. Not only did the hike provide a welcome connection with nature after nearly three days in a hotel, it also created a symbolic connection with Bishop Swing's early vision, which had included founding the United Religions in the Presidio. The exhilaration and playfulness at being outdoors was matched by a sense that the participants were walking into history. The hike ended at a musty former military chapel that had been recently vacated by the military and rededicated as an interfaith chapel and home of the Interfaith Center at the Presidio.

Representatives of the local interfaith community greeted the hikers warmly, handing each person a flower as he or she entered the chapel. The ceremony inside included offerings from 11 different wisdom traditions and silent meditation. Following the meditation, the summit participants were invited to come forward with their flowers and form a circle around a large empty golden vase. A member of the local community began an achingly beautiful song of hope whose refrain was "This is the beginning, not the end, of blessing upon blessing, my friend." The participants, one by one, silently placed their flowers in the vase. In return, each received a vial of water that had been gathered from over 20 sacred sites around the world and offered as part of the interfaith service for the UN at Grace Cathedral the year before. The last flower placed in the vase completed a magnificent bouquet that stood as sacred manifestation of the unity in diversity that underlay the URI's efforts. Each flower was glorious in its undiminished uniqueness, and yet together they created something of unsurpassed beauty. Perhaps more than any other event of the week, this simple service revealed the spiritual heart of the URI. The chapel was transfigured in the richness of this moment of transformation. We were what sought to become.

DESIGN

FINDING COMMON GROUND AND ORGANIZING TO MOBILIZE

The Discovery and Dream stages of the AI process created a community and a shared vision of the positive future the participants wished to cocreate. The third D, Design, challenged the community to articulate the common ground that had emerged from the week's work, to become more specific and concrete in its vision, and to develop plans to make that vision a reality. Beginning Thursday morning, the participants worked individually and then in small groups to identify common ground in four areas: images of organization, purpose, principles, and actions. This work led to the creation of a second mind map organized into four quadrants reflecting these four areas. The map revealed a shared desire for a new kind of organization, one that had a spiritual heart, that was nonhierarchical and broadly inclusive of all who wanted to participate, and where the people involved embodied the organization's values in their daily lives. The map was an organization more of actions than words. The map showed the importance of making a difference in the world through specific action to alleviate the gap between rich and poor, to increase dialogue among people of different faiths, and to work for peace and for justice for the entire human family.

Standing on this common ground, the group mobilized the energy and interests of the people in the room to plan for action. Based on the principles of Harrison Owen's "open space," anyone interested in convening a group to discuss and plan for a particular action was asked to write his or her proposal on an index card. These proposals were then presented to the whole group in an attempt to generate interest and help people identify what they might want to continue working on after the summit. By the end, three rounds of discussions had been scheduled with eight groups meeting simultaneously in each round.

Emboldened by the experiences of the week and given the opportunity to be heard, people trusted the bold visions in their hearts and minds. They stood up and said they had something they want to offer to this initiative. Almost all of the discussions that day led to actions that were instrumental to the birth of the URI in the months and years ahead. They included holding regional conferences in ten different locations around the world, refining a draft purpose statement that had been generated during the summit, developing funding strategies, creating guiding principles for the URI charter, creating a workbook to engage expanding numbers of people in this initiative, and staffing an office in San Francisco.

The plans and commitments emerging from the open-space sessions would be shared Friday morning. Thursday was a night to celebrate! The group shared a banquet in the very room in which the UN charter had been drafted 51 years before. People told stories and celebrated how far the group had traveled together in four days. People shared toasts, laughter, and the thrill of answering a call to express and commit to a deep purpose in their lives.

DESTINY

MAKING COMMITMENTS

On Thursday afternoon, as the group was breaking for the first round of meetings, a worker from the hotel staff dropped in to make sure the organizers remembered a wedding reception was scheduled in the meeting room that evening. They had not remembered or had not been clear about the fact in the first place. In either case, it was now instantly and painfully clear that the magnificent work – timelines, mind maps, and sheets of newsprint with colorful reports – that had created a richly nourishing womb for a week of gestation would have to be disassembled and removed immediately. Though most of the participants had dispersed to their meeting rooms, a few worked with shocked speed to strip the room bare. They left the room in mourning. The room was as naked as if no one had ever been there, and the group still had one more day to go. As the organizers discussed whether they should try to reconstruct the room in the early hours of Friday morning after the wedding reception had ended, it became clear that they could either fight what had happened or seek to claim a gift from it. The decision to claim the gift called them to abandon any heroic efforts to reconstruct the room, letting go of the evidence of the group's collective work and trusting that this work would find other ways to manifest itself positively.

The participants reassembled Friday morning in a room stripped bare. After expressing initial shock, they began to appreciate the openness and lightness of the empty walls. Because the participants carried their visions and commitments in their hearts, the emptiness seemed like an invitation not to dwell on the week together, but to focus on the creative future they wished to share. This future became tangible as they listened to the reports of plans and commitments from the open-space groups. These groups articulated an amazing array of energy and commitment to action focused in six areas: statement of purpose and principles for the charter-writing process, organization, regional gatherings and enrollment in the UR Initiative, communications, funding, and action.

The open-space groups also articulated important insights from the week: To succeed, the URI needed the participation of major religious leaders and the engagement of people at the grassroots level. In addition to people from the world's great historic religions, the URI would include people of all spiritual and indigenous backgrounds. It was essential for women to be involved in every aspect of the URI and for the URI to address issues of social justice. In his closing comments, Bishop Swing emphasized the importance of preparing to begin a new phase of the URI's life. He affirmed the importance of a grassroots URI with strong participation by women and a door open to all traditions. Also, he committed to securing a line of credit that would enable hiring a staff.

As the morning continued on toward the closing ceremony and a final meal together, the participants experienced a growing recognition that each person attending the conference had become a vision carrier for the URI. One person remarked, "I have gone from being an observer of this initiative who felt slightly embarrassed by its grand design to being a participant believer who will spread the word about it."

The group's commitment and new identity as vision carriers was made manifest in the closing ceremony. As the ceremony began, Dr. Muller had a special chair brought into the room. It was a simple wooden chair with a bronze depiction of a half-sun at its top. It was a replica of the chair used by the president at the U.S. Continental Congress in 1789. Throughout the deliberations, Benjamin Franklin had reflected on the half-sun, wondering if it was setting or rising. As the congress successfully completed its daunting work, Franklin expressed his conviction that, without a doubt, the sun was rising. The replica had been used the summer before for the presider at the first UN People's Assembly. Now Dr. Muller invited Bishop Swing to sit in the chair. As the conference participants gathered around the chair, Dr. Muller asked a blessing on Bishop Swing and the URI, recognized that everyone was charged with the sacred obligation of being vision carriers, and that this Initiative was not about one person but about all people. The bishop rose from the chair, and one by one, each of the conference participants sat in the chair and received a blessing from the group. Finally, as the chair sat empty and Dr. Muller played the chorus of Beethoven's "Ode to Joy" on his harmonica, the participants asked for one final blessing for all people and especially for those from every faith, tribe, language, and nation who would step forward as vision carriers to help make the URI a reality.[4]

During the week, a poem had been offered as one of the images for the new organization. It described the URI as a heartbeat.

I am the UR
I am a heartbeat
I am a little thing just now that points to God's
     call to everyone.
I am not an idol.
Breathing as one,
I hold the center for all to enter.
I am silence.
I am strength.
I am the UR,
I pump life sustaining behaviors into the whole world.
I stand as a daily enduring heart for the whole world.

     — Sally Mahé

In discovering AI, the URI found a process for creating an organization that reflected the values members thought the organization should embody. At the center of those values was a belief in the essential nature of interfaith cooperation that honors, and indeed celebrates, diversity and that listens to voices that are not often heard. At the same time, the process strove to a discover common vision leading to shared action for a better world. At this first summit, the participants created a tapestry that wove together the valuing of diversity — a

---

4 Gurudev S. Khalsa (2002). "The Appreciative Summit: The Birth of the United Religions Initiative," in R. Fry, F. Barrett, J. Seiling, & D. Whitney (Eds.), *Appreciative Inquiry and Organizational Transformation: Reports from the Field* (pp. 211-237). Westport, CT: Quorum Books.

summit design based on AI, silence, shared religious and spiritual practices, renewal in nature, celebration, and hospitality. This tapestry became a model to serve the URI's development over the coming years. The URI heart was beating for the first time. It would soon be pumping its lifeblood into every part of the world.

CHAPTER 3

*In place of one spokesperson, there were now
55 fully deputized vision carriers committed
to moving the URI into the world.*

URI and AI
Meet the World

THE URI'S FUTURE

The world was new for the URI following its first Global Summit. In place of one spokesperson, there were now 55 fully deputized vision carriers committed to moving the URI vision into the world. The next areas of engagement had become clear:

- Statement of Purpose and Principles for the Charter-Writing Process: a much greater and more inclusive conversation and dialogue is needed; the question of how this dialogue occurs and how the charter writing itself is accomplished are as important as the words that are written.

- Organization: establishing the organizational infrastructure to support the ongoing work of this initiative.

- Regional Gatherings and Enrollment in the URI: hosting regional "visioning gatherings" in various parts of the world; having local/regional religious and community leaders, grassroots organizations,

and concerned citizens participate in shaping the
United Religions and even planting the seeds of
future regional centers of the United Religions;
enrolling world religious and political leaders; supporting grassroots enrollment campaigns and
strategic alliances.

- Communications: build the communication infrastructure that will permit a free flow of information.
- Funding: all activities are dependent upon funding; $1.5 million needed for the coming year will
  be sought from individuals, religious organizations, and foundation grants.
- Action: sponsoring regional gatherings, networking with religious leaders, enrolling grassroots
  support, and so on, to create an infrastructure for
  action in support of ideals.

An immediate and far-reaching manifestation of this shared leadership was the creation of a statement of vision and purpose. Before
the summit, any articulation of the United Religions vision came
from a small group in San Francisco and had as its point of reference
a United Religions centered in San Francisco. During the summit,
Josef Boehle, who would become the URI's first coordinator in
Europe, had led an effort to create a draft purpose statement. Now a
global group, with Josef as convener, had committed to develop the
statement of vision and purpose begun during the summit. Among
other realizations was a clear sense that the United Religions had to
be centered in many different locations around the world. The members of the group had volunteered and, in the spirit of the closing ceremony, had the authority to refine this seminal document for the
whole. There was no discussion of a formal decision-making process.
In its place was the unspoken assumption that the document would
be adopted once the group, which used email, fax, and prayerful delib-

eration to develop and share refined drafts, reached consensus.

In less than a month, the URI had a Statement of Vision and Purpose, shown below, that would be the group's essential statement until, in a slightly revised form, it would be incorporated as the Preamble into the URI's First Benchmark Draft Charter in 1998.

The United Religions Initiative
Declaration of Vision and Purpose
A Working Document

We, people of faith, called by our respective traditions to compassion in response to the suffering of humanity and the crises which endanger our planet, wish to create permanent centers where the world's religions and spiritual movements will gather daily to engage in prayerful dialogue to make peace among religions, leading to cooperative action for the sake of all life on earth.

We respect the uniqueness of each religion and faith tradition, value every voice, and believe that our shared values can lead to cooperative action for the good of all. We acknowledge that our religious life has often divided us and has been used to justify shedding blood rather than building community. We affirm that, in spite of apparent differences of practice or belief, our faiths call on us to care for one another. We believe that the wisdom of our religious and spiritual traditions must be shared for the sake of all.

Therefore, as communities of faith and interdependent people rooted in our faith, we now unite for the sake of peace and healing among religions, peoples and nations, and for the wholeness of the earth.

- We unite to pray for peace, to practice peacemaking, to be a force for healing, and to provide a safe space for conflict resolution.

- We unite to support freedom of religion or belief and the rights of all individuals, as set forth in international law, and to witness together to the wondrous spirit of life which embraces all our diversity.
- We unite in cooperative action to bring the wisdom of our religious traditions to bear on the economic, environmental, and social crises that confront us at the dawn of the new millennium.
- We unite to be a voice of shared values in the international arenas of politics, economics, and the media and to serve as a forum for research and excellence on values in action.
- We unite to provide an opportunity for participation by all people, especially by those whose voices are not often heard.

All members of the United Religions do solemnly vow to use our combined resources only for nonviolent, compassionate action in our whole-hearted efforts to manifest divine love among all life on earth.

Another immediate outcome of the summit was hiring the URI's first staff, opening its first office, and securing start-up funding. By the beginning of September 1996, what was initially designed to be a living room in a guest apartment in Grace Cathedral's Chapter House was packed with desks, computers, phones, and a fax machine for three members of the founding staff – Paul Andrews, Mary Ellen Blizzard, and Sally Mahé. Charles Gibbs had his office and a small meeting space in the bedroom. The shower was soon a storage space for printed material and office supplies.

Bishop Swing, his diocesan house office next door to the Chapter House, had committed to raising the initial funds to support this start-up effort. He secured a line of credit and began approaching potential funders. With no formal budget, a small office, an unseasoned staff, a line of credit, and the visions articulated at the summit to guide it, the URI prepared to step boldly out into the world.

The following statement of mission and purpose emerged in those early days:

The **MISSION** of the United Religions Initiative is to bring a United Religions into being. The purpose of the URI is threefold:

- To SHARE THE VISION of a United Religions as broadly as possible, all over the world, in ways that model what the UR might become.
- To INVITE PARTICIPATION in the development of the UR vision by people of all religious and faith traditions and by people involved in spiritual, value-based movements within all walks of life.
- To GATHER REPRESENTATIVES from the religions and spiritual movements of the world to work together to create a United Religions by the year 2000.

ROOM FOR SILENCE

As it worked with the mechanics of office equipment, who would sit where, and what responsibilities each person would hold, the staff also wondered how best to keep fresh the spiritual grounding that had been so important to the development of the URI to date and had been such a powerful force at the Global Summit. One answer to this search emerged through a connection with the local Brahma Kumaris house and its director, Sister Chandru Desai.

The Brahma Kumaris, a 60-year-old spiritual movement that grew out of Hinduism in India in the 1930s, emphasizes the leadership of women and the practice of Raja Yoga for personal and societal transformation. "Traffic control" is a spiritual discipline practiced in all Brahma Kumaris' centers around the world. At regular times during the day, meditative music is played. People throughout the center pause in what they're doing for a few minutes of meditative silence — a time to recenter, a time to remember who and whose they are, and a time to refocus on the high purpose and deep spiritual values that motivate their work.

The new URI office received a timer, courtesy of the Brahma Kumaris, and instituted its own practice of "traffic control." It was not unusual in those early days for the music to come on while staff members were on the phone. Hearing the music, a staff member would invite the person on the other end of the phone to share in the silence, after which the phone conversation and all other business in the office would resume.

In addition, the staff developed the practice of beginning all meetings, including conference calls, with a brief period of silence, followed by a brief spoken prayer, meditation, or reflection. These practices were intended to invoke the active guidance of the sacred, the divine, the holy — whatever words people used to describe the source and destination of all life, creativity, wisdom, vision, courage, and joy. These practices were intended to help those participating be more aware of the presence and guidance of the sacred. Underlying these practices was the unshakable belief that the URI would succeed to the extent that it was in alignment with the deeper movement of the sacred at work in human history. A primary objective in all the work was to be as open as possible to that movement, in its wonderfully diverse expressions in different religions and spiritual traditions.

BUILDING THE NETWORK

Those early days were filled with activity, often shared with summit participants, now dispersed to their homes, mainly across the United States, but also in Europe. Sally Mahè oversaw the creation of a workbook based on the AI model, which had been so successful during the summit. The workbook was designed to engage small groups all over the world in envisioning United Religions. A URI newsletter, under the coeditorship of Paul Andrews and Rohinton Rivetna, a Zoroastrian interfaith leader from Chicago, began to take shape. A URI web site also was launched (www.uri.org).

The staff and host committee began looking ahead to the Global Summit 1997 and the beginning of the charter-writing process. The goal was to gather 200 people from a diverse faiths and vocations, from every continent; and with a mix of women and men, young and old. The main challenges were to identify potential invitees, to create a database to keep track of them, and, ultimately, to convince those who were invited that there was a compelling reason for them to give a week of their time to this exciting but largely unproven new venture.

As all this work was unfolding, the staff began to address the question of how to convene vision gatherings in different regions of the world. The expanded URI community came into play immediately. At a three-day October planning gathering hosted by David Cooperrider at his home in Chagrin Falls, Ohio, the SIGMA team, plus Jim Lord, met with Charles Gibbs to map a strategy. Building on the success of the Global Summit, they decided that a similar appreciative process, appropriately contextualized for different parts of the world, would form the basis of the gatherings.

People from different parts of the world would be asked to develop unique visions of a world they would like to live in. Flowing from that, they would be asked to imagine a United Religions that would help make those visions real. They would be asked to explore the potential mission, vision, and values of a United Religions – who would be involved; what it would do; and what its organizational structure would be. The results of these regional visioning summits would contribute to the work of the Global Summit in June 1997.

PLANNING THE FIRST REGIONAL GATHERINGS:
BUENOS AIRES, OXFORD, AND NEW YORK

An essential component of any regional gathering was to be a local hosting committee. Religiously diverse, involving men and women and youth, the committee would provide both the organizational infrastructure to produce the summits and the local/regional perspectives to contextualize the program design. The URI would provide the funding; support would come from a SIGMA facilitator and a member of the URI staff.

The central challenge was to identify potential hosting teams in different parts of the world. Since the URI had neither the resources nor the time to build such teams from scratch, the group decided to take advantage of existing relationships to build new relationships that would yield host committees. This idea of creating a network of networks would become a central strategy for the URI's development. Members brainstormed a list of ten potential hosts, covering every continent. Each was possible; none was a given.

Thus the search for people and places to host the first URI summits outside of North America. By the end of November, three host groups and three sites had been identified. The Brahma Kumaris had generously agreed to host a summit for Europe at their global retreat center outside of Oxford, UK. Josef Boehle, David Storey, and Sister Jayanti Kirpilani, all participants in the first Global Summit, agreed to serve on a host committee and to help attract the desired religious and gender diversity.

The Temple of Understanding (represented at the Global Summit by its founder, Juliet Hollister; its director, Sister Joan Kirby; and board member Allison Van Dyke) graciously agreed to take a lead in organizing a summit in New York City that would draw participants from the NGO community at the UN. Deborah Moldow, UN representative of the World Peace Prayer Society and participant in the Global Summit, pledged her support. Father Luis Dolan, who would become the URI's first coordinator for Latin America, offered the services of Associacion Intercultural Dialogo, the Temple of Understanding chapter he had formed in his native Argentina, to host a summit for Latin America in Buenos Aires.

From the SIGMA side, Kathryn Kaczmarski was selected to lead the planning and facilitation of the summits in New York and Buenos Aires; Gurudev Khalsa was to lead the summit in Oxford. Charles Gibbs accepted the responsibility of representing the URI in the planning and production process of all three.

BUENOS AIRES

On November 28, 1996 – Thanksgiving Day and a scant five months after the Global Summit and three months after the opening of the URI office – Charles and Kathryn were on an overnight flight to Buenos Aires for a three-day planning session with the local host committee. After this, Charles would travel on to South Africa and Egypt to explore possible future regional gatherings.

They took off from Miami, whose days were of deepening darkness, and landed the following morning in Buenos Aires during days of lengthening light, with summer at hand. The change of climate, the change of seasons, the change of cultures, and the change of language invited them into a deeper experience of difference and diversity. Jet lag compounded the sense of strangeness that impelled them into a swirl of meetings to meet the local host group and introduce URI and AI, to explore potential sites and dates for the regional summit, to discuss desired diversity for an invitation list, to plan the program and budget, and to discuss the next steps. They were seeking, with Father Dolan's help, to forge a mutually sensitive and respectful local/global partnership in order to plan and produce a locally contextualized, appreciative future search summit designed to bring the URI to Latin America and Latin America's voice and participation to the URI.

One of the first meetings was with approximately 20 people who were loosely affiliated with a developing Buenos Aires' chapter of the Temple of Understanding, including a Chinese Buddhist who was learning to speak Spanish, a Brahma Kumari sister, the Dalai

Lama's representative in Argentina, an indigenous woman, and a wide variety of Jews and Christians. This group was a living affirmation that, the world's diverse religious traditions were no longer geographically isolated from each other, but existed side by side in cities all over the world.

The group members were receptive to the URI vision and to the idea of helping to host a conference, but they weren't content with only visioning. They wanted to know how the visioning would lead to action. Whether a United Religions ever came into being, they wanted to use the opportunity of this interfaith conference to plan for local action.

By the end of the third day, everyone saw the potential of the 4-D design to provide a Latin American voice in the evolving global URI vision and a new energy for specific local interfaith engagement. There were clear steps to take, including these: confirming a date and site, expanding a host committee, refining the program planning, identifying a local facilitator to be part of the team, exploring a local vision of a teleconference on the final night of the summit, seeking local funding support, and beginning to develop an invitation list that reflected a broad diversity. Everyone was pleased to discover that the proposed dates called for the summit to begin on the afternoon of the Christian celebration of Pentecost, a feast celebrating the power of the Holy Spirit and unity in diversity.

All this work in early December took on a special urgency since January was summer vacation in Buenos Aires and it would be nearly impossible to accomplish much work at that time. Kathryn and Charles left believing they'd accomplished everything they'd hoped to; that URI's international conference work was well under way; and that for all that was known, team members were walking blindly, trusting that the light would appear to guide the team as needed.

BACK IN SAN FRANCISCO IN MID-DECEMBER

After stops in South Africa and Egypt, Charles Gibbs found work moving forward with great speed on many fronts. Sally Mahé had completed the workbook, which was being tested in different local communities. The staff, led by Paul Andrews, was working hard to develop a list of attendees for June and began planning for that conference. Since the Internal Revenue Service had granted the URI status as a tax-exempt 501(c)3 organization in early December, there was increasing work to be done with the Initiative's organizational structure. That work included building the first really functional board of directors. A nominating committee of Rita Semel, Gerry O'Rourke, and Paul Chaffee was hard at work on this issue. Supporting Bishop Swing's efforts to raise the money necessary to fund this year of ambitious work, Paul and Sally, with some expert guidance from Jim Lord, took the lead in convening a funding group to help shape a more comprehensive vision, thereby enabling structure for the URI's crucial work.

As all of this unfolded, the staff recognized the need to continue to internationalize the URI's effort as quickly as possible. The regional summits would be a big step in that direction, but only one step. The June summit would be another step in that direction. But everyone recognized the need to be expansive and creative in developing a multitude of ways to expand the circle of participation and the circle of those who heard about and provided input into this initiative. As ambitious as the known work was, it was simply the tip of the iceberg of what tasks lay before the URI. As Louis Dolan would later remark, "The URI didn't really have any time to grow up. It was born as a teenager."

> *Even though the staff often felt overwhelmed, they also shared the belief that they were being carried by the creative spirit of the universe — which would ultimately make a United Religions happen — if it was to happen.*

By the time Charles Gibbs and Gurudev Khalsa made the trip to Oxford, the effort in Buenos Aires had moved forward on many fronts. The host committee had expanded. The dates of the conference were set, as was the site, the Centro Cultural Recoleta, a former convent founded in 1720 and now a center for the arts. It was huge but intimate, with plenty of white walls for work space, windows, high ceilings, and courtyards, transmitting an incredible spirit of creativity and creative energy that would be a gift to any conference. The host committee had developed a large and diverse list of invitees and an invitation letter had been written and translated into Spanish. Marita Fontanarossa was selected as the local facilitator, and Kathryn Kaczmarski had added a Spanish-speaking colleague from SIGMA, Jon Levitt, to the facilitation team. Both Marita and Jon would receive their grounding in the URI by attending the conference in New York City, Marita as a participant and Jon helping with facilitation. The team continued to grow.

If the Buenos Aires trip opened the door to an interaction between the URI, AI and a new culture (or as the URI would soon discover, new cultures), and language, the planning trip to Oxford would call for a different kind of acculturation and provide an extraordinary opportunity to ground the URI even more firmly on a spiritual foundation. The trip to Buenos Aires had seen the URI seeking a site and a hosting group on a continent where interfaith work was new. The host committee Luis Dolan had offered was a group, like the URI, in its infancy. The group had been challenged to work in a new language and culture in order to build commitment and organizational capacity among people who were new to interfaith work and to the URI.

OXFORD

In going to Oxford, the group was assured of a wonderful site and a strong organizational infrastructure, both offered as a gift by the Brahma Kumaris. The group would be working in English with many interfaith veterans, four of whom had previous URI experience in a culture rich with interfaith work. The planning group would include Marcus Braybrooke, Chairperson, World Congress of Faiths (WCF), Director of the International Interfaith Centre (IIC), and author of

Pilgrimage of Hope, a chronicle of the development of the interfaith movement from the first Parliament of the World's Religions in 1893; Josef Boehle of the International Association of Religious Freedom (IARF) and the IIC; Lynn Henshall, a Brahma Kumaris' volunteer who would handle the detail work of invitations and registration; Sister Jayanti Kirpilani, Director of Brahma Kumaris Europe; Sister Maureen Goodman, Programme Coordinator, Brahma Kumaris London; Natubhai Shah, Chairperson; Jain Academy, UK; David Storey, WCF; and Celia Storey, IIC. Their primary work would be developing a theme, a program, and an invitee list appropriate for the European summit.

Beginning with Bishop Swing's meeting with representatives of international interfaith organizations at the United Nations in June 1993, the URI had regularly sought the counsel of existing interfaith organizations. The Oxford context would present new opportunities and challenges in this important area. How could the URI appropriately recognize, honor, learn from, and yet not be limited by the history and effectiveness of existing interfaith work? How could the URI seek counsel and engender cooperation, but still have the freedom to follow the calling to create something new in a new way? Speaking from his perspective within the World Congress of Faiths, David Storey would contend that it was difficult enough to find support for existing interfaith efforts without creating more competition for limited human and financial resources. Marcus Braybrooke would contend that while unequivocally supporting and celebrating existing efforts, it was clear that far more work was to be done than was being done; thus, every new effort was welcome. While no one had the answers, everyone was clear that cooperation with and among existing interfaith efforts had to be an important part of the Oxford summit – and, indeed, of the URI's work globally.

While Oxford in January and the big stone manor house that housed the Global Retreat Centre were numbingly cold, the welcome Charles and Gurudev received from the Brahma Kumaris was as warm and inviting as early summer in Buenos Aires. Though they learned that Lewis Carroll had created *Alice in Wonderland* on the grounds of this manor house, that fact seemed of less note than the positive spiritual energy that flowed so palpably. Group meditation and teaching were part of the centre's rhythm, occurring twice a day, and periodically meditative music would play throughout the house, calling everyone into silence.

Building on the foundation of spiritual energy in the centre, the planning committee began and ended each session with silence. In this environment, it was easy to reflect on the spiritual power, known in many ways through diverse traditions, that called each person to interfaith work. It was important to acknowledge that the group was moving into the unknown, which brought risk and fear and a need to trust deeper spiritual wisdom that would guide the group and the infant URI.

Deliberating on the purpose and focus of the summit, the group decided to weave together visioning work with attention to some specific focal points, such as poverty, the environment, values, peace, and a global ethic. Following much discussion, the group settled on a theme, "Developing the United Religions Initiative," and sketched out a format following the 4-D design. *Developing* struck everyone as a wonderful verb/metaphor to attach to this initiative because, like a photographic print, the URI would become clearer and more well-defined over time.

Later it was discovered that the tentative dates the group had set included the observance of Passover and Orthodox Easter. Where the idea of beginning the Buenos Aires summit on the afternoon of Pentecost had seemed appropriate, having this summit conflict with Passover and Orthodox Easter did not. Scheduling and diet are two of the most delicate issues in interfaith work. It is easy to offend unwittingly. It is as extraordinarily difficult to develop a deep and practical sensitivity to these concerns, which is essential if one wishes to offer genuine hospitality.

On the final day of its meeting, the planning committee was graced by a visit from Dadi Janki, one of the Brahma Kumaris' most revered elders. Dadi was part of the first group of women who renounced a regular life to live in the new community that Brahma Baba founded in 1936. She had lived and worked in that community until, in her 60s, she felt called to leave India to begin founding Brahma Kumari centers in other parts of the world. Dadi went to England, where immigration laws required that she remain for five years before returning to India. Though she spoke no English, she faced the challenge of this separation and began work that led to the establishment of centers in 63 countries! The great courage and sacrifice required for Dadi to leave India and begin this new phase in her and the Brahma Kumaris' life were a clear inspiration for the URI.

REGIONAL SUMMIT MEETINGS

These two planning meetings, just over a month apart, resulted in the URI taking a large step forward. The first Global Summit had expanded the URI from a small group in San Francisco to 55 people (many of them outside the Bay Area, a few of them outside the United States). Subsequent planning meetings had established leadership teams producing URI summits on two continents. The URI had begun to engage new cultures and new languages and to learn new practices in order to ground the work spiritually. The URI had begun to ask how to extend visioning work into practical engagement that would be a down payment on the type of daily interfaith work the organization sought to bring into being around the world. Seeds for future growth had been planted in South Africa and Egypt. Planning for the New York City summit was on the horizon. A site at Stanford University had been secured for the second Global Summit. Invitations had been sent to an extraordinarily diverse group of people all over the world. Program and production planning had begun. A newsletter and a journal had been published. Some funds had been raised; the line of credit drawn down. No budget or formal decision-making structure existed. The group decided on each possibility as it presented itself. The URI was on the move. Charles Gibbs, reflecting on this stage, thought, "We continued to grow and deepen and, by

the grace of God, to move further and further down the road toward
the creation of a United Religions, which would be a tremendous gift
to the world and help shine a bright new light into human history."

April came quickly. When Charles Gibbs and Gurudev Khalsa,
along with Mary Finney (a new addition to the SIGMA team)
returned to Oxford for the regional summit, the cold and snow of
January had turned into the blooming daffodils of April. After a day
of preparation, the planning team relaxed as 45 conference participants from 12 countries and 14 religions (including 4 Christian
denominations and a range of professions, including journalism, education, theology, interfaith dialogue, business, and religion) were welcomed by the Brahma Kumaris. The team held its collective breath
when time came to begin the summit.

DEVELOPING THE UNITED RELIGIONS INITIATIVE
SUNDAY, APRIL 13 – THURSDAY, APRIL 17, 1997
GLOBAL RETREAT CENTRE, OXFORD

DISCOVERY

As we gathered after tea, everyone had already been greeted by a
written welcome and a statement of support from Sanford Garner
and the URI Washington, D.C. group. Now they were welcomed in
person by Sister Jayanti, Charles Gibbs, and Natubhai Shah, who was
already calling for the establishment of a URI infrastructure in
Europe. Marcus Braybrooke did a masterful and inspiring job placing
the URI in a general historical context and in a context defined by a
quote from Mahatma Gandhi:

> *I will give you a talisman. Whenever you are in doubt or when the*
> *self becomes too much with you, apply the following test: Recall the*
> *face of the poorest and the weakest man whom you may have seen*
> *and ask yourself if the step you contemplate is going to be of any*
> *use to him. Will he gain anything by it? Will it restore him to a*
> *control over his own life and destiny? In other words, will it lead*

to Swaraj for the hungry and spiritually starving millions? Then
you will find your doubts and your self melting away.

After this rousing call to reflection and action, Sister Manda, head of the retreat center, finished the welcomes with some house rules and a gracious offer to try to meet any needs that arose during the conference.

After an overview of the group's time together and the AI process and conditions for success, the participants moved smoothly into the opening of paired appreciative interviews, followed by mutual introductions in table groups. Once again, this process transformed a group of diverse individuals, most of whom were new to the URI, into a community with a high vision of what might be possible through the URI. The first session ended with a brief time of silence and with a sense of great promise for what was to come.

Monday morning began before breakfast with an optional meditation led by Sheikh Gamal M. A. Solaiman, formerly head of the largest mosque in London and now Professor of Islamic Law at the Muslim College in London. He read passages from the Koran in Arabic and then translated them into English. He allowed a space of silence for meditation. He finished with the story of a thirsty man in the desert who came across a well. There was no bucket, so he took off his shoes, climbed down into the well, and drank his fill. As he climbed out, he saw he had been joined by a dog so thirsty that it was eating the damp sand around the well. Seeing the dog, he grabbed one of his shoes, climbed back into the well, filled the shoe with water, and raised it up for the dog to drink. At this act of compassion, God spoke, saying, "Because you have gotten water for the dog, all your sins are forgiven."

After breakfast and brief self-introductions, the participants continued their work of discovery. Because of time constraints, the planning group had decided not to engage in the timeline exercise. Instead, a good part of the morning was spent creating a mind map of the trends supporting or opposing the creation of a United Religions. The brainstorming session was energetic and far-reaching. Once the participants finished, they filled the remaining time voting with colored dots to identify the trends they believed were most noteworthy. The top seven were as follows:

- The search for spirituality outside religion
- The confusion of information with wisdom
- Polarization and the search for a middle way
- The search for global ethics — common understanding within religion
- An increasing interest in religions
- The feminization of religion
- The belief that the mystic way unifies religions

DREAM

Following lunch, the participants imagined themselves celebrating the 30th anniversary of the creation of the UR in 2027. What did the United Religions look like? What had it contributed to the world? What were its core values? What barriers had been overcome to create it? People answered these questions individually; then they created a shared vision in small groups and planned a creative presentation of their vision to the whole group. The energy level rose throughout the afternoon, as people let their imaginations and hopes soar.

The evening presentations were wonderfully inventive and expressive of the most exalted visions of a world at peace. Sacred lands (such as Jerusalem) are owned by no one, but maintained by a United Religions trusteeship with free and open access for all people. Hunger was eradicated and all children grew up free from violence and prejudice. In the midst of these high visions, there was plenty of humor and lots of laughter. People went to bed weary from a long and challenging day, but energized by the shared visions of the future they wished to create together, ready for a good night's sleep, but eager for the morning and the opportunities it would bring to move the work forward.

DESIGN

Tuesday began early with an optional guided meditation led by Sister Sudesh, head of the Brahma Kumaris' work in Germany. Her meditation was yet another part of the enabling climate the Brahma Kumaris created at their retreat center. That environment, the wonderful contribution they made in bringing people to the summit, and their network around the world were tremendous gifts to the URI. They were wonderful partners with SIGMA and the San Francisco crew for this summit as well as the overall initiative.

After breakfast and a sacred opening, the group created more common ground by offering insights and questions from the work so far.

Insights included the following:
- The UR is a moral forum.
- The UR is a network.
- In the UR, authority comes through values.
- The UR values different paths to the same goal.
- We gain new energy through crossing boundaries.
- We become more deeply rooted in our own faith through contact with other religions.
- We practice respectful collaboration.
- The UR will not be an organization, but a practice.
- We will relate from the core spirituality in each religion.
- The UR must have a clear vision of goal and achievement.
- The UR will practice empowerment through small organization centers.

Questions included the following:
- where to draw the line in relation to different roles – political, moral, and so on
- on what level to operate – cultural-organization, soul-movement, spiritual-mission

- how to effect genuine peacekeeping, bridge building, deeper solutions
- how to represent the voices of minority religions
- how to dialogue with external and internal fundamentalism
- how to embody prophetic boldness and pedagogical wisdom
- how to learn about and include agendas of all religious groups in all cultures and nations
- how to make UR self-sufficient so it lives up to its best values
- how to revive spiritual life of the disaffected half of the world's population
- how religions can motivate people for the welfare of society
- how the rights of the earth and the environment will be represented
- how the UR balances being a movement and an organization
- how to include women's experiences and views on religion
- how to build on what existing international interfaith, religious, and other global organizations are doing
- how to relate to the structures/leaders of religions (leaders of synods)
- how to be omniscient but not omnipotent

Following this exercise, the participants were invited to consider convening open space groups for discussion and planning in areas to which they were passionately committed. Twenty-three people came forward with topics that represented the breadth of hopes and concerns that had emerged from the common ground of people's dreams and their insights and questions. One open-space session ran the balance of the morning. A second followed lunch and ended in time for the attendees to enjoy two hours of free time before dinner. Both open-space sessions and the free time were filled with energetic engagement as people imagined how they might pursue their deepest commitments to a better world through the emerging United Religions.

Jehangir Sarosh, a Zoroastrian and head of the World Conference on Religion and Peace's UK and Ireland chapter, led a sacred opening to the afternoon open-space session. He walked into the room with an armful of flowers, which he distributed randomly to half the people in the room. Those with flowers were clearly pleased. Those without just as clearly wondered why they hadn't received flowers. "This is what I want you to do for the next five minutes," Jehangir said. "If you have a flower, find someone who doesn't. Look that person in the eye, and hand him or her your flower, saying, 'What you are, I am. What I am, you are.' When someone hands you a flower, look that person in the eye and repeat, 'What you are, I am. What I am, you are.'" At the end of five minutes, no one cared whether they were holding a flower. The participants had something far more precious than a flower – a profound and appreciative experience of their magnificently diverse and shared humanity. People were what they sought to become.

An early vision of the charter signing in June 2000 included millions of people engaging in pilgrimages all over the world as they joined together to celebrate the birth of this new organization, which brought with it such hope for a new, more peaceful and just chapter in human history. As a foretaste of those pilgrimages, the participants began Wednesday morning with a half-hour meditative walk through the lush English countryside. As they walked, many people had the thought, "Why do they have to wait until June of 2000 to have walking pilgrimages?" During the morning check-in, one of the participants said she felt those pilgrimages taking place as the group walked this morning, adding, "This morning I felt this feeling as though I was marching with thousands and thousands of people."

Following one more open-space session that morning, the balance of the day was devoted to each group sharing its discussions and plans. Plans emerged for Bright Light, a women's group that would meditate each day at noon for the good of humanity; for a steering committee to guide the URI development in Europe; for a conference for young people to engage with the URI vision, with possible funding from the European Union; for a group to create an interfaith collection of prayers and meditations about love of nature and the earth; for a women's group focused on a new kind of interfaith education for children; for a group "healing vessel" based more in intention and question than on knowing; and for dialogue with Islam, recognizing that the strongest prayer is listening.

There was discussion about the belief that all aspects of the United Religions should be based on commonly held spiritual values embodied in the people who lead its work, about the belief that the URI should have a highly visible council of elders who serve in humility, on the importance of teaching and practice to aid in the individual and group transformation necessary to create a positive future for humanity, about the importance of hospitality, and about the need to find ways to engage the fundamentalism within and the religious conservatives without.

It was pointed out that hundreds of millions of people know only the violent face of religions and spiritual traditions and not their riches. Such people are waiting for a place to invest their spirits. If the URI is grounded in repentance, humility, and hope, it can be a magnet to attract these people, a collecting agent to call out the best in all of them. Thus, it was apparent that the URI needed to be transparent to the hope that is within all people and to be a positive reference point for the world.

Some attendees put the URI in the context of the extraordinary interfaith work already going on in the UK and wondered how mutual learning might best occur. Others saw the URI as part of a spirit-led worldwide movement working for renewal in all areas of human endeavor and stressed the importance of letting the energy flow, honoring what the group in Oxford was doing even though these people were part of something much larger. There can't be too many faith-based organizations, provided that energy is shared energy. An embryonic interfaith living community was important.

There was discussion of the potential charter signing in June 2000, with an insistence that it should be a "We the people" charter. There was further discussion about the rich possibilities represented in pilgrimages all over the world that would be visible signs of the desire of religions to be agents of world peace. People talked about money – about the importance of having it and of using it wisely. Someone suggested that local leaders of United Religions should stay home rather than travel to a headquarters and cautioned against building up a large bureaucracy – only a few of those running the UR should be on salary; the rest should work on a voluntary basis in order to avoid greed.

The afternoon session ended with extraordinary energy as people realized the boldness and scope of their shared vision and proposed projects, which had been spread like so many seeds onto the expectant soil of a world yearning for a better future. No one knew how many of those seeds would be nurtured and bear the intended fruit, but that uncertainty seemed less important than the participants' vision of a bright new world and how they might cooperate to make that new world a reality.

Anticipating an evening with invited guests coming to hear about the group's experience with the summit, attendees finished the afternoon session early and headed out to the sunny grounds that extended down to the River Thames. Some engaged in animated discussions growing out of the day's work. Others walked pensively around the grounds. Still others gathered on the lawn overlooking a bend in the river for 30 minutes of paneurhythmic dancing led by Leon Moscona, a Bulgarian expatriate mystic-esoteric. It was a glorious time with energizing movement that flowed into a closing benediction: "May the peace of God and the pure joy of God live in our hearts forever."

After a quick dinner, an evening presentation was held for an invited audience of people interested in interfaith work. Dadi Janki began with a powerful and straightforward teaching, stressing that the work of unity is a common core for the Brahma Kumaris and the URI and that the Brahma Kumaris were ready to serve if the URI needed help.

As Dadi finished, Marcus Braybrooke took over and was a gracious and humorous emcee. He gave the bishop a wonderfully affirming introduction, and the bishop gave a stirring presentation of his calling into the URI vision and process. Charles Gibbs followed with a sense of the URI's current activities and aspirations. Then four members of the conference – Szabolcs Sajgo, a Roman Catholic priest from Hungary; Charanjit Singh, a Sikh educator from the UK; Annie Imbens, a Roman Catholic feminist scholar from the Netherlands; and Jehangir Sarosh, a Zoroastrian interfaith activist from the UK – gave their insights into what the URI meant to them. People moved to the dining room for refreshments and appreciative conversations aimed at engaging the guests in some of the work the group been doing all week. Both summit participants and guests were energized by the evening. More seeds were sown. The URI circle was growing.

DESTINY

As some people had to leave early, the summit dwindled in numbers, but not in energy on the final morning. Those who remained shared a few final hours of reflection and commitment.

Leon Moscona offered a vision of the URI as a river of life, with countless tributaries joining together. The organization would find its path itself and grow to embrace millions, even billions, of people in its own way. Josef Boehle noted that humility and patience were required for the URI to have influence within major religions and that St. Francis of Assisi and Swami Vivekananda were exemplars.

Andrea Zaki Stephanous, from the Coptic Evangelical Organization for Social Services, the largest NGO in Egypt, saw the URI as a platform where different religions would come together to present and share their treasures. He stressed that the URI must be built on the spiritual ground of a common understanding of peace, justice, and equality among the world's religions, especially the marginalized and oppressed religions, whatever they may be in whatever country. He urged the organizers to look at the practical side of the URI, which would make a concrete difference in people's lives.

Bishop Swing, who had joined partway through the summit, said, "I have no authorship in the URI. I see myself as a catalyst. You are all the author of the URI. I've heard more truth today than I've ever thought. My vision of what the URI will be is like a cloudy day, where the clouds part for a moment and you get a glimpse of blue. Then they close and it's gone, but you know you've seen the blue. The holy spirit of God will accomplish this around the world." Patrick Hanjoul, a Roman Catholic priest from Belgium, who would one day become chair of the URI's European Executive Committee, replied, "I've been waiting to hear that."

Ari Van Buuren offered, "I have two images of the URI: a shining light and disappearing salt. We must abide in what we have been sharing here." Sister Maureen Goodman observed, "Spirituality doesn't belong to anybody; it belongs to everybody. When I first heard about URI a year ago, I was skeptical; but then, in January, I met with people who are at the heart of it, people who wish to live by spiritual values within their faiths. They inspired me. If we keep this effort fresh and alive, it will succeed. The seed planted will bear good and abundant fruit."

For the closing ceremony, the participants formed a circle around a large central candle surrounded by four glass bowls of water and 40 small floating candles of different shapes and colors. Sister Jayanti and Natubhai Shah lit the central candle. Then one by one, people moved to the center of the circle. There they selected one of the floating candles and lit it from the central candle. Holding this light, each person offered a statement of personal commitment to carry forward the work of the summit and a word of hope, prayer, or thanksgiving and then placed the floating candle in one of the bowls of water. The spirit of holiness and beauty filled the space. After the last person had placed a candle in the water, everyone joined hands and sang a couple of songs. People were what they sought to become. Then each person took a candle from the water to carry the light home. After thank you's, the Brahma Kumari hosts gave everyone a sweet and a Global Retreat Centre T-shirt. The large central candle would travel to New York City; then to Buenos Aires; and, finally, to Stanford.

Following lunch, the organizing team met to debrief. They were all quite pleased with the conference and asked questions about how to support what needed to happen next. The newly constituted European Coordinating Committee would need to develop a sense of the initiatives that were most important for it to support and/or initiate and of the resources necessary to carry out that work so the organizers could plan how to attract those resources.

The organizing team raised the important question of how to identify and prepare people to carry on this Initiative, as it would become impossible for a few people from San Francisco and Cleveland to be everywhere at once. The group wondered what would qualify a person to be a spokesperson for the URI, as opposed to someone speaking about his or her personal convictions about and commitment to the URI, and how the organizers would prepare people for that role, as well as for AI facilitation.

The Oxford summit had answered several key questions about the URI's work: the URI vision and a belief that every voice mattered in developing it to maturity were magnetic; the AI methodology was supple enough to adapt to local conditions and still retain its amazing power to create community, elevate vision, and lead to action; intentionally grounding in the spirit, inviting authentic and inclusive offerings from different traditions, and offering optional early morning meditation experiences were powerful fuel for the deep work of the summit.

Organizers came away from Oxford with a sense of accomplishment beyond anything they had expected. They also possessed a firm belief that the accomplishment flowed not from their efforts, which had been considerable, but from some deeper spiritual rhythm of "the sacred" moving in and through human history. The URI vision was a magnet that carried great power, attracting people of vision and commitment. It seemed likely that the URI would soon outgrow the small, relatively costly conference model and would need to find economical ways to take its vision to much larger groups. Based on the energy and vision generated in Oxford in two days, the staffing and funding challenges for the URI were going to expand exponentially.

During the last night in Oxford, the organizing team learned that the manor house that housed the Global Retreat Centre had been requisitioned by the Royal Air Force during World War II. The building's windows had been boarded up to seal in all light. Behind those boarded-up windows, aerial reconnaissance photographs were received, analyzed, and then used to launch the D-Day invasion that marked the beginning of the end of Hitler's death grip on Europe. In the excitement of that evening, it seemed providential that this same manor house was launching what everyone there hoped would be an equally historic movement to alter the course of human history.

URI SUMMIT – ST. VARTAN'S CATHEDRAL (ARMENIAN ORTHODOX), NEW YORK CITY, NY, USA SUNDAY, APRIL 27 – TUESDAY, APRIL 29, 1997

DISCOVERY

Ten days later, at 12:45 p.m. on Sunday, April 27, the candle that had burned during the closing ceremony in Oxford was rekindled in an opening ceremony for the second regional summit at St. Vartan's Armenian Orthodox Cathedral in New York City. Earlier that day a team that included Kathryn Kaczmarski and Jon Levitt from SIGMA; Marita Fontanarosa from the Buenos Aires Host Committee; Joan Kirby, Monica Willard, and Deborah Moldow from the New York City Host Committee; and Charles Gibbs had transformed a basement meeting room into a setting for a URI conference. Joan had brought 11 nylon banners with symbols of different religions painted on them. Marita, Joan, and Charles hung the banners, while Kathryn and Jon put up overview material and Monica and Deborah covered the tables and set out materials. With the set-up complete, the organizers reviewed the agenda for the summit. Having worked hard to condense an appreciative future search into two-and-a-half days, the organizers wanted to make sure people knew their parts so not a moment would be wasted. This completed, the organizers prepared to greet people as they arrived for lunch.

Approximately 50 people attended the summit. After an opening prayer, greetings from Oxford, and a lighting of the candle, Joan Kirby gave a welcome and offered her sense of the objectives of the conference, which ranged from strengthening the interfaith movement to creating actions to support the URI. Juliet Hollister added her welcome, including a brief history of the Temple of Understanding and its place in the effort to create a "spiritual UN." Charles provided a brief history of the URI and placed this conference in the context of the journey toward a charter-drafting summit in June. Kathryn and Jon gave an overview of the conference and the AI process, including some conditions for success, and introduced the opening appreciative interviews. Almost immediately, animated conversations filled the room and spilled up the stairs and out onto the plaza in front of the cathedral as all sorts of unlikely-looking people energetically engaged in getting to know each other.

After an hour, the group reconvened for introductions in table groups, followed by introductions to the whole. This process evoked wonder and an atmosphere of excitement as interviewers offered stirring stories on behalf of their interview partners, presenting the group's extraordinary diversity. There were men and women, young and old, religious leaders, members of the NGO community at the UN, media and business leaders, the founder of an interfaith seminary, scholars, and on and on. There was a rich religious diversity — Christian, Baha'i, Sikh, Native American, Unification Church, Unitarian Universalist, Muslim, Buddhist, Wiccan, Jew, Jain, Brahma Kumari, and Rissho Kosei Kai.

The energy ignited by the interview and introduction process was then channeled into a timeline exercise that created a shared historical context for the group and filled the rest of the afternoon. Following a closing ritual, participants left expressing appreciation for the day and looking forward to tomorrow. They had arrived at 9 a.m. to a somewhat dreary basement room and, at the end of the afternoon, had left a room filled with extraordinary and positive energy, with walls covered with the road map of where they had come from and where they were going.

The summit opened the following morning with a Native American smudging, a ritual of purification and invocation of guidance, led by Betsy Stang. Though no one knew at the time, in the years ahead, Betsy would be a leader in bringing indigenous peoples into the URI and in developing a URI presence at the UN and would become a member of the URI's founding Interim Global Council. The Very Reverend James Parks Morton, dean of the Episcopal Cathedral of St. John the Divine and longtime interfaith pioneer, followed the smudging with prayers from the Book of Common Prayer. Brief reintroductions were held to incorporate newcomers and attendees continued their work of discovery with an interpretation of the timelines they had created the previous afternoon. The group reports identified and amplified many of the trends that had been identified in San Francisco the previous June.

Noteworthy global timeline events and trends included these: writing of UN Charter, growth of microcredit concept, worldwide depression in the '30's, mass movements of populations, increasing gap between first and third world, assassination of great ones, but some great ones are still walking among us, geometric shift in the world's population toward youth since 1950, demise of the Soviet Union, suffering people everywhere, increasing voice of the marginalized (Rigoberta Menchu), and Soviet/U.S. freeing of two whales trapped in the ice as a symbol of a new way of being between nations and of being on the earth.

Noteworthy interfaith timeline events and trends included the following: the need to acknowledge God, validation of the human/Earth community, the growing role of women, the growing strength of religious NGO's, catastrophic events (Holocaust, etc.), the rise of intolerant religious fanaticism, an increase in interfaith activity, eastern traditions moving west, and adopting Native American traditions and practices into Christianity without acknowledgment.

Noteworthy religion/faith community timeline trends included the following: feminization of religions, emergence of sacred texts, founding of new religions/spiritual movements, growing awareness of indigenous traditions, growth of global consciousness in human religious experience, oneness of God / oneness of life, human experience of travel and exchange among cultures, and social justice and peace work.

As the participants finished the morning session and prepared for lunch, Rabbi Joseph Gelberman, founder of an interfaith seminary, offered a blessing over matzot that was at each table. A wonderfully gentle and open spirit, he introduced the blessing with the story of a vision he'd had. In the vision, he was addressed in Hebrew as "Blessed one." When asked who he was, the speaker responded, "I am Adonai, your God. I am Eloheinu, the God of all people. I want you to change the prayer of blessing that acknowledges God for bringing bread from the earth. I want you to say that humanity, with God's help, brings forth bread from the earth. I will help, but you must bring in the harvest." And so it would be with the URI, Rabbi Gelberman observed that God would help, but that we must bring in the harvest. The rabbi finished his blessing by offering a single word, borrowed from Henry David Thoreau, as guidance in thinking about the UR – "simplify."

DREAM

Where the Oxford planning team had eliminated the timeline exercise from the Discovery phase in an effort to allow ample time for open-space sessions, the New York planning team had elected to accomplish the same goal by eliminating creative table group presentations from the Dream phase. Instead, they planned to go directly from table group work to the creation of a mission map, designed to share specific dimensions of people's visions of a United Religions. In both cases, the hope was that the adaptation of the basic 4-D design would not disrupt the balance of individual, small group, and whole group interaction and the balance of right brain and left brain activity essential to building a truly cooperative and creative effort.

The adaptation seemed to have worked well in Oxford. As the afternoon session of the second day began, the organizers were about to see how the New York team's adaptation would work. The participants gathered in table groups for an hour, dreaming about what a United Religions might be, focusing on four areas: 1) who the people are, 2) what the form is, 3) what the values and principles are, and 4) what the action is.

Most groups began in individual silent reflection and then erupted in an outpouring of hope and yearning and vision. When people finished sharing in table groups, they formed a semicircle around an 8' x 8' expanse of white paper divided into quadrants reflecting the four areas of dreaming and began to build the map. Some of the offerings were as follows:

> **WHO:** all about inclusion; ordinary people; meaningful inclusion of youth, voluntary groups, secular people, grassroots; men and women of faith communities who believe and uphold the fundamental teachings of their faith communities; atheists
>
> **FORM:** stew or salad?; circular relationships; mutuality; many, many centers; AA model — supported by contributors, no hierarchy; organic form; wheel going around a hub; decision making by consensus; council of elders; family of God; don't exclude those who don't acknowledge God (Buddhists, etc.); Executive Branch necessary to accomplish actions; not real-

estate heavy; common mission statement; rooted in grassroots

VALUES/PRINCIPLES: open; evolving; nonexclusionary; celebration of diversity; sanctity and value of all human life; call to moral values; respect for sacredness of Earth; nonviolence; dialogue; celebration; compassion; forgiveness; openness; patience; not right/wrong, but differences (we're all right); we are all God's chosen people; faith in positive nature of humanity; adoration and prayer; non-proselytizing; action-oriented; justice; mercy

ACTIONS: advise global institutions to forge a new enlightenment of the soul; UR as "activated soul" of UN; socially conscious advisory board; acts to eliminate social injustice; ensures equal access to resources; redefines news in a positive light; cross referencing of sacred texts and oral traditions as a resource; mediating disputes according to core values; clearinghouse for existing actions for global good; web site; pray together; conversations with conservatives; celebration — music, theater to witness how we are together and yet distinct; celebration of Holy Days; growth through attraction, not promotion; bioethics; cooperative preservation of sacred sites; collective library of religious music, tapes, CDs; educational programs at all levels

MISSION: The longer people worked on the mind map, the more connections emerged with June's Global Summit and the summit in Oxford and the more people raised ambiguities and apparent oppositions: openness and inclusion versus the need for guiding and limiting parameters, nonhierarchical structure versus the need for a strong central body to accomplish an action agenda, God language versus language of

values/principles that is more universally accepted,
and the need to have sympathetic conversation partners early in the process of creation versus the need to
include all voices.

Although the ideas were still flowing freely, Kathryn finally had to
end the mission map exercise in the interest of time. Near the end of
the exercise, one person commented, "What a wonderful way to start
a global organization – to go around the world asking people what they
imagine it might be." Another startled the group by saying, "I don't see
how an organization that looks like that (decentralized, no hierarchical,
consensual) can do that (be an agent of effective, focused local and
global action)." Though no one knew it at the time, the URI would
spend the next three years seeking an answer to that question.

After receiving instructions for the open-space work that was to
follow, the group took a midafternoon break. The participants
returned to a bell of mindfulness, rung by Lyn Fine, a member of
Thich Nhat Hanh's global community, to invite them into silence
when reconvening after breaks. These moments of silence, like the
Brahma Kumari' traffic control, were powerful reminders of the need
to regularly recenter oneself through deep spiritual connection and a
compelling vision of the future. If these people were to bring in the
harvest, they had to remember to connect with the creative power at
the center of all that is.

Coming out of the silence, the group heard an enticing array of
18 challenging topics that clearly brought forward major themes from
the Discovery and Dream work: respect for Earth and all her creations; UR mission statement; advising global organizations – UN,
World Bank, IMF; living up to highest ideals; spiritual consciousness-
raising; concrete follow-up – interfaith retreat; inclusive interfaith
group to dialogue and pray together to build community and go out
and address social issues; using Alcoholics Anonymous as an organizational model; subject-by-subject cross-reference of sacred texts and
oral traditions; forging a new enlightenment to touch the soul of the

earth; mechanics of representation at a UR; interfaith celebrations in the public forum to witness how we are together in the most positive creative productive light; educational programs in schools; practical steps to begin the UR; mobilizing for social justice; interfaith initiative on Lower East Side; interfaith peace zones; interfaith networking.

These topics were quickly scheduled into three rounds of open space, which would take the group through lunch the next day. An energetic opening round generated powerful momentum moving into the final day of the summit and resulted in a proposed mission statement for the UR:

> We, as people of faith, desiring to lift all humanity to its highest level through fostering understanding and respect of the diverse faith communities and uplifting moral values that promote family, peace, education, economic and social justice, and protection of the environment, do hereby come together as the United Religions.

This statement would take its place in the midst of an assortment of mission statements over the next three years before the global URI community would finally give its assent to its chartering statement of purpose.

This second day of the summit ended with a Sufi Zikr, a wonderful movement and chant to remember Allah and to recall who one was before the soul adopted the body to be present on the earth.

The last day began with two sacred offerings. First, following ancient tradition, a Hindu leader blew a conch shell to call everyone into prayer. He then chanted verses from the wisdom of the Vedas. Second, a Buddhist monk led the group up out of the basement, around the plaza, and back to the basement on a mindfulness walk intended to help people ground themselves fully in each present moment.

The remaining two rounds of open space filled the morning. During lunch, Charles Gibbs met with 15 people who had expressed an interest in representing the vision of this summit at the global gathering at Stanford in June. He explained that decisions about who would be invited would be based, at least in part, on the need for gender and religious diversity.

After lunch, the group heard reports from the 18 open-space groups. The group that focused on "Respect for Earth and All Her Creations" asked that the United Religions organizational structure include subdivisions — one devoted to nature and native spirituality. Group members pledged their support of the Earth Pledge and the Earth Charter and committed to circulating the UN Values Caucus' statement about Earth-based values, to bringing sacred Earth values to other meetings and caucuses, and to writing a column on Earth matters for the URI newsletter.

The group that focused on "Mobilizing for Social Justice" proposed that the URI be understood as "you are I," which would lead to the realization that "we are one." Group members defined justice as ethical fairness, an even start for everybody, and an equal start for every baby. They recognized that injustice can be a group experience and asked how to mobilize to combat injustice. They proposed the experience of consciousness raising that comes from standing with the oppressed and stressed the importance of being grounded in spiritual values to sustain faithful witness. They arrived at no decision on the best strategy for moving forward, but affirmed the importance of working within existing legal and political systems.

A third group focused on "The Mechanics of Representation for URI." They noted that the originating vision of the UN model of representation had not been enthusiastically received. Existing religious groups seemed to have more to lose than to gain by being part of such a group; for instance, being bound by decisions they strongly disagreed with. This group proposed an alternative vision. Why not invite those who were interested in participating, whether or not they were official representatives? Group members wondered how the URI's work would be taken back to constituencies and implemented. Finally, they proposed an organizational form. There should be a parliamentary section with a legislative function and an executive body with a core staff whose responsibility was implementation and management of programs. Also, there should be a council of elders and sages, as well as vital youth participation. They proposed more regional meetings to develop truly representative and widespread participation.

Following these reports, which were filled with a deep sense of connection and commitment, everyone shared a closing ceremony. Gathered in a circle around the central table holding the bouquet created the first day and the URI candle, attendees began with a Sikh breathing, chanting practice based on the mantra "Sat Nam," which means "Truth is my identity" and honors the true self of the other. Joining hands, one by one, each person formed a completed circle saying the words, "Hand by hand we make this circle." After a smudging, each person offered a word of prayer/intention. Peace, love, justice, commitment, joy, and vision rose like offerings of incense. A few more prayers and a grand round of thanks followed. Charles Gibbs handed the central candle to Luis Dolan, who handed it to Marita Fontanarossa to carry to Buenos Aires. The New York Summit ended in gratitude and with a shrinking circle as one person after another left after greeting each person remaining in the circle.

The reaction to the conference was overwhelmingly positive. Once again, organizers had created a tapestry that wove together valuing diversity – a summit design based on AI, silence, shared religious and spiritual practices, celebration, and hospitality. Though being in the middle of New York City and missing the renewal in nature that had been so nourishing in San Francisco and Oxford, the participants had shared a strong focus on the importance of valuing Earth and Earth-based traditions. Attendees had created a space where a profound community could dream and plan together. Seeds were planted that would bear fruit for a long time to come.

The day after the conference, the last day of April, Luis Dolan, Kathryn Kaczmarski, Jon Levitt, Marita Fontanarossa, and Charles Gibbs met at St. Emeric's Catholic Church to finalize the agenda for the Buenos Aires conference. Eleven days later the candle would be lit once again, this time to inaugurate the first URI conference in Latin America (at Centro Cultural Recoleta in Buenos Aires), where spring in the Northern Hemisphere would be transformed to fall in the Southern Hemisphere. Expected participation was 73 people (including a UN representative) from 19 religions and denominations, with a nearly even distribution of men and women and one person from Brazil and three people from Peru.

URI SUMMIT FOR LATIN AMERICA
CENTRO CULTURAL RECOLETA, BUENOS AIRES, ARGENTINA
SUNDAY, MAY 11 – WEDNESDAY, MAY 14, 1997

DISCOVERY

At 2:30 p.m. on Pentecost Sunday, May 11, the candle that had burned during the closing ceremony in Oxford and at St. Vartan's Armenian Orthodox Cathedral in New York City sat on a white pedestal in the center of the meeting room of the third regional summit. Three timelines stretched around one end of the room. The by-now customary SIGMA flip chart pages giving the overview of the conference, conditions for success, and so on were taped to the front wall and folded up so the information couldn't be read ahead of time. The eleven Temple of Understanding flags bearing symbols from different religions, which had traveled from the New York conference, decorated a good deal of the remaining wall space. Packets containing all the conference material in Spanish lay on the tables.

Seated at the tables was an incredibly diverse group: men and women, old and young, people in varied styles of dress, clerics, psychiatrists, architects, teachers, social workers, lawyers, doctors, Buddhists, Muslims, Christians, Hindus, Baha'is, devotees of Sai Baba, Brahma Kumaris, people of indigenous spirituality, and a pastor from the Metropolitan Community Church in Buenos Aires – the United Religions in microcosm.

Luis Dolan, deeply moved to be introducing the URI to Latin

America, welcomed those attending and assured them that they were essential to the growth of this exciting initiative. Luis told them they would be listened to, so they must speak their deepest hopes and give voice to challenges they believed needed to be faced. Charles Gibbs, speaking through a translator, recounted the URI's brief history and spoke of his hope that the people of Latin America, as represented by those attending this summit, would be full partners in the creation of a United Religions.

At the end of his remarks, Charles told the story of the candle from Oxford and how Marita Fontanarossa had received it in New York to carry to Argentina. Marita came up and lit the candle. With some assistance from Jon Levitt, she then led the group through an overview of the conference and gave them instructions for the opening interview. The moment she stopped talking, people began pairing up and the room erupted in conversation. The moment was electric, and clearly the real beginning of the conference. Soon people were dispersing in pairs, already engaged in animated appreciative interviews.

An hour later the rounds of introductions, both at the tables and to the whole group, revealed the extraordinary diversity of participants and the myriad ways they were active in the world. The audience was attentive as the introductions proceeded. By the end, it was abundantly clear that AI had worked its magic once again and a group of strangers wondering what they'd gotten themselves into had become an animated, energized community eagerly awaiting what was next.

What followed, as in previous group settings, was Kathryn's explanation, given through a translator, of the timeline exercise. The timeline worksheets were distributed for people to mull over overnight; they would begin with that exercise the next morning. The formal session ended with a young Jewish couple, the woman visibly pregnant, singing two beautiful Hebrew songs *a cappella*. It was another of the "this is it" moments to hear Argentine Jews singing in Hebrew to an extraordinarily diverse Latin American group, standing in front of the SIGMA flip chart overview sheets in Spanish!

One of the undercurrents that emerged was how alienated the indigenous people felt from the mainstream community. In a private conversation with Charles Gibbs, Don Valentin Moreno, an elder of the Toba tribe, spoke in a straightforward and humble way about how grateful he was to be in attendance and to have the opportunity to speak from his experiences as an indigenous person about the extraordinary prejudice, oppression, and cruelty his people continue to endure.

Two indigenous women, Haydee Milimay, a Ranquel whose name means "Golden Condor," and Rosalia Guittierez, of the Kolla tribe, offered their cautious hope that they would be able to share information about their traditions. The women believed there was a great deal of value in their traditions but that those traditions weren't respected. Rosalia talked about how she could barely speak her native language; her grandparents had had their tongues cut out so they couldn't teach the language to their children!

The wounds of the indigenous people were unspeakably deep. Their present fears of being pushed beyond the brink of extinction seemed justified. Their presence at this conference was accompanied by a mixture of fear and hope about whether they would be welcomed and heard. Charles attempted to reassure them about the URI's efforts to create a safe space for each person to share what was most important to him or her. Charles shared the story from the Oxford conference, of how, in an open-space group (Espacio Abierto), a woman was able to tell a Muslim sheikh that she was afraid of him. A powerful silence followed. Then she saw the sheikh reclaim his gentleness and felt herself reclaim her power. From that moment, they were able to have a genuine dialogue about matters of profound personal value.

At the end of this story, Rosalia said, "So we have to take the risk ourselves. I have an important exam on Wednesday, and I was thinking about not coming back tomorrow so I could study. But now I think it is more important for me to be here." Though no one could have known at that time, Rosalia would go on to be an important leader in the URI's efforts to include indigenous people as full and valued participants; she would also be elected to serve on the URI's first Global Council.

By the end of the evening, people were engaged. And clearly, that engagement was frightening to some. To borrow an image from the Hebrew scriptures, people were indeed on holy ground, and they had to stand, shoes off, in awe of each other as people made in the divine image, or hold within themselves the fullness of Buddha nature.

The second day began with a meditation led by Luciana de Souza, a Brahma Kumari from Brazil; the lighting of the central candle; and the hanging of a UN flag alongside the banners of different religions. The participants went to work immediately filling in the timelines. A few people went straight to the timelines and began working; others stayed at their tables. However, after about 20 minutes, everyone was at the timelines, transcribing detailed notes, drawing pictures, cutting and pasting from organizational publications, and adding typescripts of original poems.

The assassinations of John Kennedy and Martin Luther King were placed on the global timeline, along with a mention of the mothers of the disappeared, marching in the Plaza del Mayo here in Buenos Aires. This event was clear evidence that, though the dark age of the generals was a decade and a half in the past, it was still a powerful force. There were stories of atrocities committed against the indigenous peoples and their fear of extinction. The host committee already had plans for a public display of the timelines that would include an invitation for people to add to them.

The wonderful energy and sense of community continued after the morning break. The Table groups moved into the interpretation of the timelines and presentation of the report-outs, which noted many of the themes common to similar reports from Oxford and New York. But there was clearly an Argentine flavor to these reports. For instance, the Dalai Lama's visit to Buenos Aires in the early '90's was extremely important, and events related to Tibet were strung throughout the timelines. Black Friday on Wall Street was a prominent event, as was the Mexican Revolution and the fall of the Austro-

Hungarian Empire. Attendees had an awareness of and a deep thirst for interreligious dialogue and cooperation. It was noted that the first Muslim arrived in Argentina near the turn of the century. The Stonewall riots and, many years later, the establishment of the Metropolitan Community Church were clearly important to at least one conference attendee.

DREAM

After a quick but enjoyable lunch, the group moved into dreaming. Group members spent a couple of animated hours working on their dreams and presentations, dispensing with the break. The most memorable moment of the presentations came when Chiru Chiru, an indigenous man whose "accepted" name was Santos Estrada and who wasn't supposed to use his indigenous name, said, "I don't need to dream. As I sit here in this group filled with love, I experience what I would dream for."

The day had been a tremendous success, in large part because the host committee had done an extraordinary job creating and supporting a climate of open and profound connection and sharing. The people attending were eager to use this opportunity to its best advantage. Several expressed their desire to see something continue after the conference. The day ended with a prayer by a Muslim man and song by a Muslim woman.

BRAINSTORMING

Following a meditation led by a woman who practiced Tibetan Buddhism, the group gathered in front of a blank mind map divided into quadrants: Values and Principles, Actions, Who, and Form. This brainstorming exercise was intended to get as many ideas as possible on the map without detailed discussion. The activity had worked well in New York, even without the rich dreaming that had preceded it here. The group started slowly, tentatively, and then there was an eruption of energy—a sea of waving hands, people talking over each other, people debating one another's additions to the map. Afterwards someone commented that this exercise had been typical of Argentines – no one listened to anyone!

Highlights from the Mission Map

VALUES AND PRINCIPLES: unity in diversity, equality among men and women, respect for life, solidarity and hope, truth, justice, peace and harmony, respect for differences, brother/sisterhood, knowledge, awareness of one universal God, love of the name of God, compassion, freedom of religion, coherence between belief in God and personal life, free investigation/research, strengthening of faith, ethics, peaceful coexistence, openness to all expressions of spirituality, wisdom, one God named in different ways, human dignity, piety, freedom, commitment to fulfillment of basic needs of all people, unity with nature, charity, moral values, noninterference in governmental affairs, equality of participation

ACTIONS: mediation in conflicts, education on points of connection between religions, education for peace, promotion of inclusive, non-sexist language, promotion of spiritual development, consultation about ethical issues, share praise/adoration

WHO: all people of goodwill irrespective of religion, race, color, ideology, gender, sexual orientation, culture, social economic status, age, disabilities, todas/todos, children, no political power, all those who agree to the URI's basic values (and those of their own religions), people who are committed spiritually, mentally, and pragmatically

FORM: forum of children, world parliament of
religions, traveling libraries with workshops, lectures,
and information about URI, foundational actions
that highlight values, pluralistic and democratic, circular structure with regional forums, different forms
of artistic expression, assure that everyone is heard,
organizations by areas of interest of people willing to
serve, promote education about spirituality in schools

DESIGN

After the break, the group began the open-space time, taking to
this exercise immediately. The participants proposed 14 topics, which
were scheduled in three rounds, with the third one being held the following morning. After lunch people launched into the first two
rounds. The groups formed quickly and worked with great energy.
The only complaint was that from time to time, the noise level in the
room made it difficult for people to hear each other.

The day ended with a song about experiencing the peace the
world could not give. The conference had been an extraordinary event
so far, with many important seeds planted. Suddenly, only a half day
was left.

The opening prayer was a simple song – Shalom, Salam, Paz. It
was followed by a brief reading from Mother Teresa and then the
passing of a sign of peace, which was wonderfully free and warm as
people greeted and began to say good-bye to their new friends.

During the three open-space groups that morning, people once
again sat well into the break, talking and listening earnestly with one
another. A group on religious estrangement included Muslims, Jews,
Christians, and indigenous people. This may have been the first time
such a diverse group sat down together to discuss how to overcome
the estrangement between them (or to borrow from the words of

group's convener, "how to come to know each other") so they might come to love each other.

The largest group discussed coming to know each other through experiencing each other's praise and devotion. Members' obvious enthusiasm left them unwilling to settle for abstract possibilities. Early in the session they began making specific plans for the future.

The reports that followed the three open-space rounds revealed an inspiring breadth of passion and depth of commitment to moving forward the cause of interfaith cooperation through the URI. People reported on making plans for children's education, sharing experiences of the sacred, doing works of social compassion and justice and tearing down barriers that separated people, and establishing relationships of mutual appreciation and trust.

As the conference drew to a close, it was clear that enormous causes of division existed among the different groups present and that some of the conversations about those causes had taken place within like-minded groups in the hallways during the breaks. But it was also clear a climate of relationship, safety, and trust had enabled some of those conversations to move from the hallways among like-minded people back into the room among diverse groups. That phenomenon happened and would continue to happen to the extent that we came to love and trust each other enough to share our version of the truth with an openness to the truth of others.

The closing ceremony, scheduled to end at noon, went on until nearly 1:30. The indigenous people spoke first, at last having the opportunity to tell a little of their stories. These people yearned for their stories to be heard and wanted to hear the stories of others so people might come to know each other, respect each other, and be able to work together honestly for a better world. Their plea was all the more poignant because so many indigenous tribes were facing extinction in Latin America.

Following their offerings, a rabbi led the group in a Hebrew song. Then the Muslims led a song in Arabic and offered a prayer of gratitude for what the URI had begun and for the success of its future endeavors. Then a Sai Baba devotee led everyone in the traditional Hindu closing "Loka samastha sukino bavantu" (May all the people, in all the world, be happy). Finally, everyone shared the Roman Catholic song from the previous day: "God is love. God is goodness. God give us that peace that the world cannot give." The group sang standing in a large irregular circle, holding hands. At the end, a round of La Paz Este con Nosotros (Peace Be with Us) erupted and the group began a spirited line dance.

Finally, Marita and Charles blew out the candle, which Charles was given to carry to San Francisco for the June Global Summit.

THE THREE REGIONAL SUMMITS RECONSIDERED

In one month, April 13–May 13, the URI had held three successful regional summits. Though the URI's main office was still in San Francisco, the URI itself would never again be merely a San Francisco initiative. In a small but essential way, the URI now belonged to the world. It had begun to be multilingual — to be shaped by the beliefs, life experiences, and world views of a diverse cross-section of the human community. The organization had taken an enormous but tiny step toward realizing an essential goal: that the URI would belong to everyone but be owned by no one.

Much of the wisdom that emerged from these regional assemblies would be carried to the second global summit by representatives. The story of two representatives is important in the development of the URI. Among those who gathered in New York City to express their interest in attending the global summit on behalf of the New York City gathering were Deborah Ann Light, a Wiccan, and Taj Hamad, a staff person for International Religious Foundation, the interfaith arm of the Unification Church. These two people would bring religious diversity to the global assembly. In addition, one was a woman and the other was a native of Sudan. There seemed to be every reason to invite them — every reason except fear of the consequences. It was easy to imagine the press getting wind of these people's involvement, with headlines reading: "WITCH AND MOONIE AT URI

SUMMIT!" And that would be the end of the URI. But the staff realized that once you caved into such fear, once you caved into prejudice against one group by others, you lost something precious. The vision of a door wide enough and a table big enough that anyone who wanted to walk in, sit down, and join in the work of interfaith cooperation for a better world was free to do so. The Moonie and the witch were invited, and it was a great victory.

What made that victory and so many other victories possible was the opening of the people's hearts and minds that AI encouraged. Since its first summit, the URI experienced again and again what happened that morning. Before the interviews, people were a group of individuals with varying degrees of curiosity, skepticism, excitement, and uncertainty. By the end of the interviews, people were a community of diverse individuals eager to work on a common task. That was an even greater victory, one that would carry the URI forward in ways it could scarcely imagine.

CHAPTER 4

*P*eople who attended the summits
had their dreams listened to
and valued.

CHAPTER 4

Growing Appreciative Genes

W

e gather here at Stanford to begin to live into the questions that a United Religions inspires. More important than initially arriving at a right answer is the quality of 'living into the questions.' The future of the United Religions is in direct proportion to the quality of living into the questions. The spirit that prevails in our living together here is the fountain from which any wisdom will flow. The religions of the world will not finally gather because of our intelligent proposals; the religions of the world will only come together because of our compelling spirit. Have you come here to be clever? In time, that could be helpful. But if you come here because a spirit of colossal energy is being born in the loins of the earth, then come here and be a midwife. Assist, in awe, at the birth of a new hope. We intend to live into the questions. Life comes before a charter.

— Bishop Swing's Opening Remarks to the
1997 Global Summit at Stanford

THE FIRST YEAR

In its first year, the URI vision was like a highly charged magnet attracting people. The vision lived in the hearts of the people who attended the first summit, many of whom renewed their initial commitments and remained active in the URI. Joseph Boehle, a doctoral student from Germany who was studying in England, convened a group to refine the purpose statement and the words of the preamble. Sister Joan Chatfield, a Catholic Maryknoll sister based in Hawaii, investigated the use of the origami star as a symbol for the URI logo. Jennifer Peace, a graduate student in Comparative Theology in Berkeley, California, explored the role for youth in the URI. Charles Gibbs formed an office with four core staff and, together with the SIGMA team, worked with people in different countries to host three regional gatherings in Europe, North America, and Latin America. The regional gatherings (rooted in AI processes and cofacilitated by Charles Gibbs, local leaders, and SIGMA staff) increased the reach of the URI across the world.

Bishop Swing inspired funders to support the work and extended an exhausted line of credit from $200,000 to $500,000. An interfaith board of directors in San Francisco was appointed, and, with guidance from David Cooperrider and collaboration with the SIGMA team and the URI staff, a grand plan was mapped out to launch a cocreative process anchored by yearly global summits. The purpose of the plan was to develop a charter that would be signed in June 2000. Simultaneously, work would go forward to build worldwide commitment by promoting an interfaith call for peace that would receive global attention and invite hundreds of thousands of people to participate and eventually enroll in the URI.

One vision called for 6 million people to sign the charter by June 2000. Another called for worldwide interfaith pilgrimages to herald the birth of the URI. Everyone was thinking big. The turn of the millennium lay ahead, visions and questions abounded, and answers were scarce. But June 2000, the date for the URI to be born, was fixed! Determination and boldness defined the path ahead, as did trust and the spirit of service to the vision.

The second, third, and fourth URI Global Summits took place during the last week of June in 1997, 1998, and 1999, respectively. Each of these summits gathered between 100 and 200 people from all parts of the world. To include more and more people, each year the organizers invited some who had attended previous summits and enriched the mix with people new to this growing global dialogue. Men and women came from more than 40 countries; from a multiplicity of faith and spiritual backgrounds; from various sectors of society; and from a range of ages, including a significant number of young adults.

URI participants came together at these Global Summits to make the vision of the URI real. Long before the official birth of the URI as a global organization, increasing numbers of people joined the movement and soon saw themselves as midwives preparing for a great birth and the life that would follow. At each of the Global Summits, an appreciative process that recapitulated a form of the 4-D methodology was created and shaped with care to meet the prevailing needs, questions, and conditions. Each year participants described feeling exhilaration, transformation, and the joy of friendship. They shared a deepening conviction that dreams that had once seemed impossible now seemed possible because they so often found themselves, on a small scale, being what they dreamed of becoming.

The effective result of employing a finely-crafted appreciative process for each of these Global Summits was an expanding community based in trust that was rooted in consistency between espoused values and lived values. The process supported the values people believed in and shared. People who attended the summits had their dreams listened to and valued. Their visions, professional expertise, and talent in song, dance, poetry, meditation, drumming, prayer, and hospitality were woven into the growing URI tapestry. At these global gatherings, people experienced being appreciated for whom they were, working in cooperation with others who were often very different from them, making friends, and having the time of their life living into their own vision of being what they wanted to become. Reverend

Heng Sure, head of the Berkeley Buddhist Monastery, who was new to the URI in 1997 but would become a member of the URI's Interim Global Council, later recalled this experience:

> Paul, a Yale-educated Episcopalian; Zeenat, a Muslim feminist scholar from India; and I, an American Chinese Buddhist cloistered monk, formed a trio. Almost every night we would meet. What happened? We talked about issues and our religious beliefs. Zeenat said to me the second night, "I can't believe that I am talking to a Buddhist. What you are saying about your religion I have never heard in my religion. I need to know more about it. I am fascinated by the idea of the No Self. I don't understand how we have such a spiritual affinity with one another."
>
> The three of us put together a play. We were all chipping in, the three of us completely merged. We found ourselves brainstorming and giggling and behaving kind of like frat boys on a night out, having a great time.
>
> We invented a Peace Corps in China where interfaith youth would surround a factory that was polluting and chant for the people in the factory to turn from greed to virtue. Zeenat imagined she was interviewing shepherds in India. Someone had asked a shepherd to cut his flock back but the shepherd had said no because it was dishonest and against the teaching of his God. We were interpreting ethics in real-world scenes. We had a great time playing like we were 12 years old. The URI gave people a chance to meet in that pure way.

JUNE 1997 GLOBAL SUMMIT: CHARTERING THE UNITED RELIGIONS

Exactly one year after the first URI gathering of 55 people at the Fairmont Hotel in San Francisco, 200 people from 40 countries and dozens of religions and spiritual traditions came together at Stanford University for the second URI Global Summit. The conference was housed in the cloisterlike Lagunitas Hall. A central courtyard with ancient oak trees and a green lawn dotted with round picnic tables was enclosed on three sides by dorm rooms and on the fourth by a large dining room transformed into a meeting hall. Sixteen banners, each painted with a symbol signifying one of the great religious or spiritual traditions of the world, and one banner with a circle representing "all the religions not known and still to come," waved each day, framing the open center where participants felt welcome and met one another with ease.

The banners were an impromptu creation of Diana Dane, one of the 65 valiant volunteers, many of whom gave a week of their time and enfolded the summit participants with an extraordinary hospitality. In months prior to the Summit, an amazing team of volunteers had been assembled and organized by a URI staffer, Paul Andrews, and Carey Craig and John Hamilton, conference production professionals brought in to assist with the summit.

As delegates arrived, many weary from the rigors of international travel, volunteers greeted them at the airport, helped with their bags, transported them to Lagunitas Hall, helped them find their rooms, and offered assistance in myriad ways throughout the week. The power of hospitality permeated the week and brought to the URI one of its most meaningful lessons – that the door to cooperation is opened by a hospitality that creates a safe space where all people, no matter their backgrounds, feel comfortable.

During the week, Bishop Swing offered a visionary note on the value of hospitality:

We could start out with an ever-expanding community of interfaith hospitality – a United Religions
independent of religious institutions, but constituted
to provide and promote hospitality in a world of
interactions between peoples of different religions; a
United Religions structured for eating and education,
for children and the elderly, for the marginal and the
leaders (not so much that the UR would make pro-
nouncements, but would gather people who would
make announcements). The UR would facilitate
finding a moral voice and facilitate common action in
the face of urgent human need. All facilitation would
be based on hospitality in service of peace among
religions.

On Tuesday night, the experience of hospitality would be extended and deepened as local hosts welcomed summit attendees into their
homes for dinner.

DISCOVERY

The theme of the summit was "Chartering United Religions –
Building Worldwide Commitment." Special meaning was given to the
word chartering. It signified the work of writing the words of a charter and the work of daily interfaith cooperation that would ground
those words in lived reality. The vision called for a URI charter to
include a purpose or mission statement, an organizational design, and
an action agenda. The charter was imagined to be a document with
enough muscle to provide the necessary legal foundation to establish a
global nonprofit organization and enough soul to touch people's
hearts and elicit their involvement.

The focus of the summit was to generate the plans and commitment to extend the URI's vision into new parts of the world and to
engage the work of writing a charter through the collaborative efforts
of the participants. The plan to accomplish this work had been

painstakingly developed through the cooperative effort of the URI staff and the SIGMA team, with new additions Godwin Hlatshwayo, one of David's graduate student's from Zimbabwe, and Diana Whitney, a leading practitioner of Appreciative Inquiry, and in consultation with the URI's board of directors.

In the meeting room, the summit's purpose was represented by a large, colorful mandala on white paper entitled "Chartering the United Religions." The organic circular form was defined by the 15 symbols signifying the world's great religious and spiritual traditions and held within it three circles: Organization Design, UR Action Agenda, and Mission and Values. These circles were embraced by the words *Building Worldwide Commitment.* The mandala manifested this stage of the birthing process: to reach out to people of all faiths in an open and inclusive way in order to create a hospitable space where all people who felt called could cocreate the mission and values, the organizational design and the action agenda for the new organization.

The 4-D process was again used to create the conditions and framework for this diverse gathering to begin to answer an array of questions. How could a world of different voices and good ideas be harmonized to create a charter? How would the ideas and values of

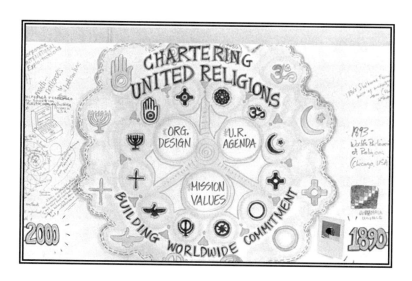

such different people find consensus in the simple and elegant language of a charter document? Were experts needed? How would they participate? How would the work begun by this group of 200 be used to inspire an even broader level of participation?

During the Discovery phase, delegates took part in appreciative interviews that asked them to share stories of their experiences in innovative, boundary-crossing organizations; to imagine the elements of an ideal charter; and to envision a worldwide action that could effectively manifest the URI to the world. As had by now become expected in the URI, the morning of interviews and introductions had created an energized and focused community ready to work together.

In the afternoon of the first day, the entire group built a shared history by creating a vibrant timeline relevant to the URI, rich with colors, words, artifacts, and images. This shared history revealed points of connection, but also points of potential controversy, such as gender equality and homosexuality, explosive issues in many religious communities. The road to the URI's charter would be exhilarating and challenging.

THE POWER OF DREAMING IN LARGE NUMBERS

On the second day, the Dream phase called people to dream possibilities in each of the core areas of the charter – Mission/Values, Organizational Design, and Agenda – and in building worldwide commitment for the United Religion vision. After initial work on all these items in table groups, participants carried their table's best dreams into new groupings focused on just one of the core charter areas or on building worldwide commitment. Using the collected dreams of the table groups, these new groupings shaped a collective vision of the future of the United Religions in their designated area.

Later, in astonishment at the abundant expertise and spirit of the people in the room, the groups summarized their dreams in a variety of presentations. People who had arrived as strangers two days before took up the microphone to present their group's work to the assembly. The microphone traveled from a Sufi scholar to a college physics student; from a female Hindu guru to a New York stock broker; from a 17-year-old singer to a visionary author; from an Irish Catholic priest to a computer wizard from Silicon Valley.

Diana Arsenian, a specialist in graphic recording from the Grove International Consultancy, Inc., had volunteered her expertise in depicting in words and images what people said at the same time they were saying it. As people spoke, Diana, who had also created the central mandala, quietly astonished the group with her creativity. Using colored markers and pastels, she transformed an 8' by 20' expanse of white paper into an intricate mural entitled "Chartering the URI." This mural was vibrant with images and words that reflected the essence of the visions of the people in the room.

With the mural complete, Masankho Banda, a dancer and peacemaker from Malawi, picked up his drum and closed the Dream phase by leading everyone in a song: "Let loose the spirit, let loose the joy. With one another, sister, and brother. Let loose the spirit, let loose the joy." As people sang and responded to the beat of the drum, they began to dance, clap hands, and greet each other with joy. We were what we sought to become.

The Global Summit in 1997 was electric with people's excitement, soaring creativity, and inspired commitment. One vision saw 3,000 peacekeeper volunteers bussed to a strife-ridden area for prayer, mediation, and provision of basic needs. Another imagined an international interfaith bank that offered microloans to groups doing interfaith work for peace. One group raised the vision of a 24-hour global cease-fire as a gift to the new millennium. One man proclaimed he would commit his hands, his feet, and his heart and even live on the streets, if it came to that, in order to help make these visions real.

LIVING INTO THE QUESTIONS

The visions elicited in the Dream work were captured for the charter, as each group was asked to identify specific questions and issues it believed should be addressed in its charter area. Each group formed key questions and identified priority items. Rather than being discouraged by the abundance of questions and the absence of answers, groups were energized by the long list of fascinating questions. Here are a few of them.

MISSION/VALUES: How will the URI be owned by all the people? How can we best move toward generating peace among the peoples and cultures of the world? How can a URI continually and effectively invite others (including minority religions) to a common space to celebrate, to persist in building the URI?

ORGANIZATIONAL DESIGN: How, if at all, will membership be defined? How will the URI work with other interfaith and like-minded organizations at local and international levels? How will decisions be made locally and globally? How will the decision-making mechanisms interact?

ACTION AGENDA: How do we define, defend, and promote religious rights? How will the URI distinguish itself by the way it lives out its life in the world? How will the URI incorporate meditation, prayer, worship, and indigenous practices into its culture?

BUILDING WORLDWIDE COMMITMENT: How might we support communications region-to-region and globally, especially incorporating effective communication among indigenous people? How can the URI mobilize the resources needed to make it a viable organization? How will information technology be harnessed by the URI?

Some witnessed the power of these questions and the empowerment of having so many questions as the agenda. A delegate commented, "These are not merely questions. They are the agenda of tomorrow. They are the exciting, irresistible invitation to each of us to abandon prejudgment and stubborn refusals to deeply hear each other. These questions are the program and the means to make that leap of faith with each other that will move humanity and our earth into a new era of reconciliation and hope."

Underlying all of these questions was a fundamental question also raised during the week: *Will we recognize the mystery of this possibility? Will we be open to its opportunities?*

Raising questions, sharing questions in conversations across continents, and using questions as a gateway into the unknown (and framing the next step in the process) became the "URI way."

As the URI and SIGMA staff and participants realized that they rarely had answers to the questions that accompanied each new set of challenges, an organizational ethos of "living into the questions" evolved. When they were frozen by an Everest of unknowns and no one knew for certain where to begin, they took the next step by living into the questions as they engaged with others in appreciative inquiry.

They often felt as if they were building the plane while flying in it. The flight demanded courage and trust that with the support of the creative source of the universe, the human efforts pouring in service into this initiative would bear good fruit. It required an openness to acknowledge that often the fruit was something no one could predict. In the URI, people learned to relish questions and grew familiar, if not altogether comfortable, with moving forward together into deeper and deeper unknowns. As they discovered the future together, lines that separated leaders and followers blurred, opening up more opportunity for innovative answers to emerge. It is hard to recollect how they resolved question after question, but then as now, they discovered answers as circles of people applied their skills and ingenuity to the issues and moved forward.

INVITING THE PUBLIC

The 1997 Global Summit established a tradition of welcoming the participation of the local community at a public forum midway through the summit. The appreciative spirit of inclusion and participation spilled over in the desire to open up the summit experience and share it in entertaining ways with others. The public forum was not just entertainment, but a sincere invitation to the hosting community to engage in the issues and high points of the gathering. The public forum that year, which saw the group leave its comfortable cloister for the sacred space of Stanford Memorial Church, included interfaith blessings from the elders, an overview of the URI by Bishop Swing, different perspectives about the summit from delegates, song, meditation, and a mini-appreciative inquiry that invited the public to pair up and offer to a partner their visions of a better world.

The evening culminated in an elegant Peace Prayer Ceremony, which was adapted by Deborah Moldow and Sally Mahé from a ceremony the World Peace Prayer Society used for the nations of the world. Delegates representing 16 different faith traditions proceeded down the aisle, each carrying a banner with the symbol of his or her faith tradition. One by one they walked up the steps into the sanctuary and turned to face the gathered community, holding their banner in front of them. As the first banner was displayed, a reader intoned, "The Baha'i people." The community answered, "May the Baha'i people live in peace. May peace prevail on Earth." Religion after religion continued to pray for peace, until the ceremony ended, "May the Zoroastrian people live in peace. May peace prevail on Earth." Like the public forum, this ceremony became a Global Summit tradition.

A mini-appreciative interview was included as part of the evening. Those attending were invited to find a partner and share with each other how they envisioned the world becoming a better place because of the United Religions. They recorded their answers on "dream sheets," which were later adapted and used all over the world. The "dream sheets," which were collected at the global office, reflected the core work of the URI at this stage of its development. Evoking dreams and visions was the URI's essential work in 1997. Dreams and visions preceded the words of the charter and the structures for the organization. Here are some of those early dreams:

> My dream is that we all learn to listen. Stories are the least threatening way to share; dogma is threatening.
> — Ron Dexter, Santa Barbara, CA

> I dream that people of all religions see people of other religions as their brothers and sisters, all as manifestations of God. Let the spirit of peace, love and wellness prevail; let enmity be forever banished.
> — Carl Goldman, Los Altos, CA.

> I dream that URI keep spiritual values at its heart and as its guiding force.
> — Sister Maureen Goodman, Brahma Kumaris, United Kingdom

> I dream this movement will catch fire in grassroots as well as leadership areas and result in a more compassionate global population.
> — Sister Elizabeth Hagmaier, San Francisco, CA

> I dream of the joy that we feel as we look around the table and see our whole family gathered in mutual respect.
> — Linda Morrow, San Francisco, CA

> I dream that the URI will create an atmosphere in which all cultures may become more contemplative, passionate, vital and loving.
> — Spiritual Life Institute, Crestone, CO

I dream that the next generation of children are brought up to see the United Religions way as a way of life.
— Charanjit Ajit Singh, Middlesex, UK

I dream that the UR will give the world new stories, new images, new energy, and new flights of fancy. This must be the gift from the religions to the nations.
— Malcolm Stonestreet, UK

I dream of a monthly interfaith prayer meeting held at our Friend's meetinghouse for our spiritual neighbors to join us and chant with us prayers of universal peace, praise, and thanksgiving.
— Helen Huber, Salford, PA.

Design: Research and Development Action Plans

On Thursday morning, in the spirit of self-organization, participants selected specific areas for research and development they wanted to accomplish in the coming year, found others who wanted to do the same, and proceeded to outline a year-long research and development plan in preparation for drafting the charter the following June. Each group used a round paper template nearly large enough to cover its table, colored markers, ribbon, glitter, and construction paper to organize its discussion and document its plans. The colorful templates, each one a unique expression of the R&D team that created it, included a statement of the R&D task, research questions, possible pilot projects, timetables, and names of people with whom to consult. One group, afraid there was an overemphasis on thinking and discourse as the preferred ways to work together, proposed that its R&D group would focus on "other ways of knowing" and explore the power of sign and symbol, story and movement. By the end of the day, 20 groups had self-initiated a range of action research projects to advance the charter-writing project and to advance worldwide commitment.

One group decided that the most important action step would be to "hold the space that holds us." Members dedicated themselves to the soul of the URI – to the renewal of people in mind, heart and body and to remembrance of sacred wisdom and reverence for the sacred Source of all life. An immediate gift this team gave the assembly was a "silence stone" to use at each table. At any time, anyone at the table could take the stone, hold it, and maintain silence as the group carried on its discussion. In addition to silence, the holder of the stone offered his or her prayerful intentions for the well-being of the group. This R&D group also convened an international retreat day several months later, with different gatherings connecting briefly by phone. A thrill rippled across the telephone lines when one group after another joined the brief conference call and greeted one another in peace and love. This small but powerful moment was part of an ongoing effort to maintain a sense of global connectedness when people were united in purpose but separated by distance.

DESTINY

On the last day of the Global Summit, each R&Dgroup presented its template and committed to contribute a "possibility paper" or another creative product in the next several months as a resource for creating the first draft of the URI charter.

The reality that the URI was being cocreated and co-owned by people from different cultural and faith backgrounds was manifested in the passion and commitments of the diverse community of people who left Stanford that year. When the dispersed community became aware of a law severely limiting religious freedom that was awaiting the signature of Russian President Boris Yeltsin, an informal letter-writing campaign was spontaneously organized. Here is an excerpt from one of the letters:

Dear President Yeltsin,

Especially in this global age and this time of transition in human history, it is imperative to encourage and not repress diversity. Participants in the United Religions Initiative, myself very much included, believe that humankind is reaching a precarious point in history, a time when we need every available source of spiritual wisdom in order to perceive and understand the nature of ourselves as spiritual beings, the nature and will of God, and therefore our human purpose as part of the Creation.

Mr. President, please use your powers to safeguard this necessary religions diversity and spiritual wisdom as a guiding force in your country and in the world.

Anthony Willett
Participant in the June 1997 UR Summit
Consultant in International Rural Development
and Conservation

By the end of the summit, most of the delegates had committed to work with the R&D groups they had formed during the week. Some R&D groups went home to further develop the statement of purpose; some chose to develop guidelines for particular action agenda items dear to their hearts; some went to explore organizational designs; some went to plan a collective global action to build worldwide commitment that would bear to the world the news of the URI's birth. People left feeling the joy of being connected to the URI in ways that recognized their gifts and gave voice to their dreams and abilities. Glimpses of wisdom and guidance from the delegates helped to light the way.

We build a road and the road builds us.
— Dharma Senanayake, Sri Lanka

Let us practice local authenticity and global solidarity,
— Godwin Hlatshwayo, Zimbabwe

We must find what resonates rather than detonates.
— Sister Joan Kirby, New York

The tribal neo-pagan traditions must not be marginalized or excluded. We are your beginnings, your ancestors in the human creation of all religions.
— Phil Lane, Canada

Out of conversation, compassionate expression, and deep listening comes inspired action.
— Diana Whitney, New Mexico

It is not about being right, it is about being.
— Brother Wayne Teasdale, Illinois

URI is building bridges rather than walls. Let us include youth and build a commitment for the younger generation to take up peacemaking.
— Mario Fungo, Philippines

During the week, it became clear that people wanted the URI to be an effective, globally connected organization. Further, it was to be decentralized, inclusive, locally self-organized, and focused on action. People had imagined an organization that looked like a tree with a broad horizontal spread of roots and branches; that looked like the cosmos, with thousands of stars circling and radiating light one star to another; that looked like a human body, with all parts operating interdependently to produce a healthy body. At the end of the summit, the community shared an enthusiasm and a trust that a different kind of organization, one that would honor the hopes for new ways of organizing that people had expressed at the regional gatherings, was on its way.

In his closing remarks, Bishop Swing noted, with a wistful grin, that the URI had made great progress during the past year. At the end of the first Global Summit, the URI had been $50,000 in debt. Now the organization was $400,000 in debt. That is growth! With that sobering news, humorously presented, as another dimension of the challenge of the group's dreams, Bishop Swing deputized the gathering to go out and be the URI:

> We have come together for one week to work toward the creation of the United Religions. Our hearts have been opened. We have witnessed overwhelming outpourings of commitment. You are all deputized in the name of the URI to go back to your homes and get to work.

Reverend Heng Sure felt the power of these words and the bishop's general approach profoundly:

> My Master teacher had just passed away two years earlier. I did not need another shurfu — another teacher — so I was watching rather cautiously. Who was Bishop Swing? What am I into? What is this all about? Is he the leader? Is URI his thing?
>
> And what I saw him do early on is what I have seen him do consistently, which is step back from the center. He did not own it. He said, "That was my dream. If it's your dream, it flies." This is only going to go if there is resonance, if there are kindred spirits seeing this vision the way I do. Then we have something.

I think because of that everyone saw room for themselves — to come in, to explore. We weren't following Bill Swing; we were walking side by side into a space that was inviting, that was full of promise and unexplored. The same thing held true at the very last moment of that summit. People were being introduced and thanked. The bishop was introduced. It was again his moment to come forward and receive applause and ownership, but he stepped back into the circle and held hands and merged into the group. And I thought, "Now there is the mark of this leader. That is somebody worth following. He is not here for the fame. He left the center of the circle open."

As people dispersed to different parts of the world, they carried with them the phone and fax numbers and email addresses of their R&D team members. The participants did not know exactly how they would forward their plans and give shape to their excitement, but they left the summit eager to pursue the new relationships they had made, trusting that their work in the year ahead would play a part in the development of the United Religions. As a surprise on the last day, a woman from Oakland, California, who had heard about the global gathering, gave a handmade doll dressed in a multicultural outfit to each delegate as a remembrance of the week.

As one delegate departed, he exclaimed, "the UR is an organization that we can create ourselves!" Walking to the final meal, Robert Aiken, an eminent Buddhist scholar, shared these words, which he said he would have offered into the Closing Circle if there had been time. The words are a gatha, a Buddhist vow in poetic form:

> "Holding hands in a ring I vow with all beings to ease the pain in the ring of breath around the world."
>
> —from *The Dragon Who Never Sleeps*

A sign that the URI was getting more and more real came at the board debriefing a few weeks after the summit. As the meeting began, Ravi Peruman stood up. "Before we begin," he said, "I need to ask my Christian sisters and brothers on this board a question. Do you believe that I am going to go to hell because I'm a Hindu?"

For long, painful moments, no one dared breathe. Ravi broke the silence. "You don't need to answer, because I know you don't believe that. But you need to know that for many Hindus around the world, that is their experience of Christianity." He went on to describe abusive, unethical conversion practices he had been told about. He finished, saying, "The URI I dream about will change that. It will help us get to the day where you value my faith for me as much as you value your faith for you."

Also after the summit, Reverend Heng Sure and Sally Mahé created a photo journal to serve as something of a family album for the participants and to give them a way to show the URI story to other people. In addition to the pictures, was a spare text that guided newcomers to the URI in this way:

What Can I Do?

Our minds have no limits; be creative, begin where you are, use wisdom and compassion.

MEDITATE AND PRAY: in whatever way you wish, individually or in community. Include the URI vision in your prayer and meditation.

REACH OUT: Share and explore the URI vision with friends. Get to know at least one person from another faith or cultural tradition. Reach out and appreciate people in new ways.

ACT: Begin to make the URI a reality in your community. Dream about what's possible. Explore local interfaith activities.

> CONTRIBUTE: Financial contributions show com-
> mitment. Every donation from two cents to 2 million
> dollars is welcomed to sustain the URI's vision and
> work into the future.
>
> CONNECT: Let the URI know who you are and
> what you are doing, even if it seems like a little thing.

In the ensuing months, the URI staff followed up with the R&D teams and assisted in various ways as diverse projects began to bloom. As the projects expanded in all directions, one colleague remarked that this job was like "trying to stuff a mattress into a pillowcase!" In addition to work moving forward out of the office in San Francisco, Luis Dolan was now working as part-time coordinator for Latin America; Josef Boehle was working as part-time coordinator support-ing the efforts of the steering committee that had emerged from the Oxford summit; and Godwin Hlatshwayo would soon become the part-time coordinator for Africa.

Appreciative genes that defined the URI in 1997 and carried for-ward into 1998 were based on the value that every voice mattered. Early on, Bishop Swing had articulated this essential democratic value that guided the fragile new life of the URI:

> An initiative that yearns for a United Religions is not
> one person's genius or copyright. The seeds for a
> United Religions have been planted in the hearts of
> people of goodwill throughout the world — among
> inestimable numbers of people of all religions, spiri-
> tual movements and ethical practices. These seeds have
> been growing for 100 years, these seeds will come to
> full bloom."

The exhilarating and tedious chartering process became a central focus for the next year. It included hundreds of people in the process of transforming their visions and ideas into viable organizational structures and action agenda guidelines. It was work inspired by the value Bishop Swing had stated —that the seeds for this initiative had been growing in people's souls for a long time. The time had come to enlist the people and channel their creative energy toward the creation of a charter.

IN SEARCH OF A NEW ORGANIZATIONAL DESIGN: THE CHAORDIC MODEL

Three months later an unexpected resource materialized to assist the Organizational Design R&D team's efforts. Barbara Marx Hubbard, a visionary thinker in the area of conscious evolution and a member of the R&D team attending to Organizational Development, discovered a kindred spirit whose words and wisdom about creating organizations seemed to match the genetic code of the URI's emerging body. Dee Hock, a former banker and founder of VISA, International, had retired 15 years earlier and had devoted his attention to studying organizations and exploring how organizations might operate in new ways to accomplish their purposes; satisfy their employees, stakeholders, and customers; and do no harm to the earth.

Dee was pioneering a visionary concept he called "chaordic organizing." This new approach intended that organizations replicate more of nature's way of being and depend on core principles, self-organizing interdependent parts, and freedom that allowed for unlimited diversity of expressions. Dee recognized that command and control management in organizations did not work and that given virtually unlimited access to information via the Internet, people were essentially free to create what they wanted and connect with whom they chose. He realized that organizations could no longer be led successfully by a central authority that set policy and gave directions for others to carry out. Leaders in these new "chaordic" organizations would not control decision making nor try to manage people's work.

Instead, they would exemplify the core values of the organization in their daily life, serve the purpose of the organization, and strive to create a climate that encouraged appropriate shared decision making that inspired people to work together for common purpose in a multiplicity of personal and unique ways.

Chaordic is a fusion of two words, *chaos* and *order*. Chaordic organizations embrace order by holding fast to core values and shared purpose and principles; they embrace chaos by honoring and encouraging unlimited expressions, as people act in pursuit of shared purpose and principles. This new way of organizing focuses attention on people's sense of their own core values and relies on self-organization of personal initiatives, decentralization of decision making, and the inclusion of many voices representing diverse interests. Dee explained that chaordic organizing encourages organizations and corporations to pattern their actions in ways that depend on life-giving principles shared by all. As organizations are able to incorporate specific principles and live them in a daily and enduring way, they achieve their purpose, help people renew their sense of meaning, and heal rather than diminish the environment. A chaordic organization exists to serve the creative energy and resourcefulness of the human spirit. Dee believed that, given certain circumstances and the liberty to try, ordinary people would consistently do extraordinary things. "Chaordic" patterns of organizing intended to create just those circumstances.

The vision underlying a chaordic organizational design draws upon a spiritual quality in people. The vision honors the essence of each person to live into his or her fullest capacity and highest service as a human being. The synergy of values was clear. As had happened when the URI met AI, the founders recognized that they had been blessed to discover a partner who brought vision, theoretical brilliance, and practical experience to help the URI travel with greater confidence and wisdom down the road that had been intuitively selected. The Chaordic Alliance joined the journey of the URI and AI, in the flight of trust that was headed toward the birth of the charter.

The R&D team, including Bishop Swing, dedicated to organizational design, asked Dee and his staff at the Chaordic Alliance to lead them in a process of creating an organizational design for the URI that would follow chaordic patterns and principles. An organizational design team was formed that included participants from the 1997 summit: Reverend Heng Sure; Phil Lane, a Native American leader; Avon Mattison, Head of Pathways to Peace; Barbara Marx Hubbard, head of the Foundation for Conscious Evolution; Carol Zinn, a sister of St. Joseph and senior staff with Global Education Associates: Godwin Hlatshwayo; David Cooperrider; Nahid Angha, director of the International Association of Sufism; Bishop William Swing; staff from the URI, and staff from the Chaordic Alliance.

By the time the organization design team first met, the URI had moved out of the guest apartment it had long since outgrown at Grace Cathedral into offices housed in a remodeled hospital ward in the Presidio. This move connected the URI with the bishop's initial vision of a UR in the Presidio — with the work to transform a former military base into a civilian peace center and with a mission of healing.

The team met for three days every three months for two years. During that time, they led the development of the preamble, purpose, principles, organizational concept and structure, action agenda, and bylaws for the URI. Like the San Francisco host committee that worked on the first Global Summit in 1996, this group chose to intersperse discussion with meditation and silence and deepened its sense of what it meant to act in service to the URI. The team grew to appreciate its role as servant in preparing the useful first drafts of the documents that others would be able to react to and improve upon. Instead of reverting to a command-and-control model, the group was encouraged by the models set by its members to be in a servant leadership role with the rest of the URI community. With his usual jocularity, Bishop Swing led the way by enthusiastically and unrelentingly offering, one after another, his always "improved upon" purpose statements for the team's approval, only to have the team again and again reject his offerings and say, "Not yet. The purpose statement is not there yet, Bill."

The organizational design team could see that Dee's philosophy and development strategy brought an indispensable gift — namely the *chutzpa* and expertise necessary to create an organizational structure true to the URI visions and values that could act with authority on the world stage and was in accord with California law as a nonprofit membership organization. The design team flung itself into intensive discussion around drafting a preliminary statement of purpose and a list of principles. The team was also concerned about creating an organizational concept and structures for decision making that would resolve membership questions and governance issues and provide the basis for relationship among all the parts of the organization.

During the early days of imagining a UR charter, it became clear that a small group of people could draft a charter quickly and efficiently. The challenge would be to have broad ownership of that charter. In response to this challenge, the URI decided to go more slowly in writing the charter so far more people could be included in the process. With the formation of the organizational design team and the power and scope of Dee's vision it quickly became clear that the team ran the risk of becoming that small group writing the charter, hoping everyone else would accept its work. The value of inclusion was at stake at this juncture, as was the concept of chartering that called for inviting and honoring many different voices in the creation of the URI charter. In this context, the team discussed the need for its thinking and its preliminary work to be fully transparent to the URI community. The team committed itself to a process that would include the voices and input from the greater URI community as it went along in its work. The work would be slower, but the means would be consistent with the type of organization the team was seeking to create.

Not surprisingly, at this juncture, the URI board and several members of other R&D teams challenged the decision to bring on Dee and his team to help design the charter. They feared doing so would undermine the trust built up in a process that was already under way — that it would take the power out of the hands of the whole and place it in the hands of a small group. They had serious questions about the large amount of money the URI was going to pay the Chaordic Alliance and were angry that the decision to enter into a contract with Chaordic Alliance had been reached without any consultation with the board. It would take years for the wounds of this moment to heal fully, but even in the woundedness, gifts were discovered – a new focus on more inclusive decision making that would lead to more and more global input into key decisions and the ability to move through the controversy and claim the extraordinary gifts the Chaordic Alliance had to offer.

The vital question was how to integrate the gifts and expertise of the Chaordic Alliance with the developing work and at the same time include the URI community in real and relevant ways in developments toward the writing of the charter. As months passed, the design team's contributions were accepted because its ideas were valuable, because communication with others outside the design team was well maintained, and because a deep level of trust had been carefully nurtured between the URI staff, the URI board of directors, the SIGMA team, and the URI extended community. To support this bedrock of trust, notes were taken at every organization and design meeting, summarized, and made available to the URI community. Preliminary drafts of the purpose and principles as they were emerging were shared with the R&D teams, and input from the extended URI community was brought back into the organizational design meetings.

By December 1997, it was clear that an additional gathering was needed before the next summit in order to bring key R&D efforts together, to introduce Dee and the work of the organizational design team in a comfortable setting, and to attempt to transform the various research into a coherent draft charter. In March 1998, a special "working retreat" was called for key R&D team members; URI Board; and staff from URI, SIGMA, and the Chaordic Alliance. This mini-summit, held at a simple and homey retreat center, started with appreciative interviews and focused on integrating the multi efforts of many people, including the efforts of the organizational design team, to produce a draft charter that could be offered to the global assembly of URI participants at the fast-approaching summit in June.

Diana Whitney, Diane Robbins, Amanda Trosten-Bloom, and Gurudev Khalsa contributed their expert leadership as professional consultants. The interactive group processes they designed for this three-day "retreat" skillfully maintained the focus on inclusion and synthesis. At this gathering, individuals self-selected their primary area for work. Some groups summarized vast amounts of material and created an inspiring summary set of action agenda guidelines; another team scrutinized and improved the words of the Preamble; another task group went round and round discussing different proposed purpose statements and finally whittled their choices down to three versions of one statement. A list of key principles, which had been a primary contribution of the design team, was approved and rewritten in a more elegant and simple style. This retreat gave the participants a chance to work in depth to understand the principles and how they served as the fundamental beliefs that would guide the organization's structures, conduct, and decision making. Here are the principles the group approved:

Key Principles of the URI

PRINCIPLES OF RELATIONSHIP:

1. We share a profound respect for the sacred.
2. We listen and speak with respect to deepen mutual understanding and trust.
3. We give and receive hospitality.
4. We address conflict through a practice of healing and reconciliation, without resorting to violence of any kind.
5. We seek and offer cooperation.

PRINCIPLES OF ORGANIZATION:

6. The UR welcomes as members all who subscribe to its Purpose and Principles.

7. The UR honors, encourages, and depends on local expression consistent with our purpose and principles.

8. All members have the right to organize in any manner, at any scale, in any area, and around any issue or activity that is relevant to and consistent with the Purpose and Principles.

9. Deliberations and decisions are to be made openly, are to reflect diversity fairly, and are not to be dominated by any single view or interest.

10. Authority is vested in and decisions are made at the most local level that includes all relevant and affected parties.

11. Every part shall surrender only such autonomy and resources as are essential to the pursuit of the Purpose and Principles.

12. The financial support of the United Religions shall be broad-based and reflect the diversity of its members.

13. Each part of the UR has primary responsibility to develop financial and other resources to meet its needs and secondary responsibility to share financial and other resources to help meet the needs of all other parts.

14. The UR maintains the highest standards of integrity and ethical conduct, prudent use of resources, and fair and accurate disclosure of information.

15. The United Religions is a bridge-building organization and not a religion.
16. The UR is committed to organizational learning and adaptation.

Going into this presummit chartering conference, the work of the dispersed R&D teams had constituted one track going forward. The work of the organizational design team constituted a second track. A major goal of the conference was to merge this work into one track that everyone shared. The result would be a preliminary draft charter offered to those attending the upcoming Global Summit for their review and refinement before being sent out to the broader URI community for its review. At times, the work to effect this merger was excruciatingly difficult as people struggled with the feeling that the work of a movement that had valued every voice was being hijacked by an expert. At other times, it was filled with grace, as moments of clarity and mutual valuing emerged. The results of this struggle were the preliminary draft charter and a far deeper experience of community. The participants had struggled mightily together. They had hurt, been hurt, expressed their hurt, and swallowed their hurt, all in service of the high vision they served. The foundation of mutual respect and deep listening that AI had helped create was what saw the group through this challenging moment. It was not the last time this foundation would be tested before arriving at a final charter.

The "Preliminary Draft Charter" was sent out with an invitation, and registration materials for the 1998 Global Summit. The draft included a history of people's contributions toward the charter since 1996. Its opening words echoed the values of inclusion and participation in its creation:

United Religions Draft Charter
An Invitation to Participate

As we approach June 1998, we move toward the creation of the first draft of a United Religions Charter, which will establish a United Religions organization in June 2000. Our vision of including the diverse voices of the world's religions and spiritual communities in the process of creation is beginning to be realized.

Unlike some documents that are presented as finished products, the URI Draft Charter is intended to be lived and changed. It reflects the best we know at this time. It comes to you in a spirit of humility. Many more spiritual and cultural perspectives are needed to make our vision brighter, clearer, and more compelling. We invite you to bring your voice to this process.

In addition to the introduction, the draft charter document also included homework for the delegates.

We ask you to reflect on how you and others might be able to experiment with this document in the coming year — to reflect on the questions it raises, the use of language, its strengths, on things that might improve it, things that might be missing, and how it might guide URI development in your area.

As you read the Draft Charter, please keep in mind the following questions:
- Can you hear the voice and values of your tradition speaking through the words of this Draft Charter?

- To make the UR not just a dream but a living
  reality, what ideas in this Draft Charter inspire
  you, compel you to be part of its existence?
- What questions does the Draft Charter raise?
  How do you imagine field-testing these questions
  and issues in the coming year?
- Discussion questions raised in prior conversations
  are included in each section. Please feel free to add
  your thoughts to these inquiries.

As this work on the charter moved forward during the year, the URI continued to develop in many other ways. Its board was expanding and becoming more diverse. In different parts of the world, the vision was attracting enough interest and commitment that people asked for guidance about how to organize. They hoped for answers from the San Francisco office. Instead, they were invited to share in the questions.

Also coming out of the 1997 Global Summit at Stanford was the vision for a 24-hour cease-fire at the turn of the millennium. The vision had electrified the group. Paul Andrews was given the responsibility of developing the vision into a possible project. Discovering that December 31, 1999, was a Friday, the holy center of the week for Muslims and the beginning of the Jewish Sabbath, Paul proposed that the project be expanded to 72 hours to include the whole weekend, which would also include the Christian Sabbath and days when most faith communities gathered. This notion won universal acceptance, but it was about the only thing that did. As Paul reached out to peace activists around the country and around the world, he quickly discovered all sorts of objections to and modifications of this stunning idea, not unlike what the bishop had encountered when he first shared the URI vision. Also not unlike what the bishop first encountered, Paul also found vast support for the core compelling vision of transformation. He spent the year exploring the issues as deeply as possible and creating a vast network of contacts.

VISION GATHERINGS IN SOUTH AFRICA, VENEZUELA, AND KENYA

In October 1997, the URI held a visioning gathering at Wilgespruit Fellowship Center just outside Johannesburg, South Africa. In April, the 1998 URI held a similar gathering in Caracas, Venezuela; in May, another gathering in Nairobi, Kenya. Each of these gatherings used the pattern developed the previous year, involving local hosting committees and an AI conference model. A stunning example of the community-building power of this methodology came in Nairobi during a regional conference for 60 men and women, young and old, representing 14 faith traditions from 8 East African countries. Two days into the conference participants began coming to Charles Gibbs during breaks and commenting: "I am a Muslim and I was afraid to come here because I thought I would have to sit down with a Christian." Or "I am a Christian and I was afraid to come here because I thought I was going to have to sit down with a Muslim." Both Muslims and Christians continued, "But I conquered my fear and came. And I'm glad I did because I did have to sit down with a Christian/Muslim and I discovered that it wasn't so bad. Yes, we have differences. But we want the same kind of future, and I believe we can work together.

Two-and-a-half years later, Charles Gibbs would pay another visit to Africa, where he would see firsthand some of the fruits that had grown from that conference. In Kampala, Uganda, he met with representatives of 12 URI Cooperation Circles whose work included interfaith dialogue, education, AIDS prevention, economic development, and conflict transformation. Cooperation Circles were interfaith groups organized locally or around an issue. They were bound together by the URI's charter and had autonomy in organizing their own activities to make the charter a living reality. Among the plans to emerge from the meeting was the development of conflict transformation workshops that would provide training of trainers for all 12 Cooperation Circles, that they might be more effective in creating peace cells in their local communities.

In Addis Ababa, Ethiopia, the local Cooperation Circle inaugurated the first URI office outside San Francisco. The members have been a consistent force for interfaith peace building during the war between Ethiopia and Eritrea and have recently engaged in peace education for young people, but that is getting too far ahead in the story.

GLOBAL SUMMIT 1998 "LIVING INTO THE UNITED RELIGIONS INITIATIVE"

From June 21–26, 1998, 208 delegates from 5 continents, 38 countries, and 32 faith traditions, 14 indigenous communities gathered again at Stanford University. This year the summit had to move to more spacious dormitory facilities on the Stanford campus in order to house all of the guests. Nineteen delegates came from Africa: from Ethiopia, Kenya, Rwanda, Burundi, South Africa, Ghana, Sudan, Uganda, and Tanzania. Fourteen came from Latin America and the Caribbean, including Trinidad, Venezuela, Argentina, Brazil, and Mexico. Nineteen came from Asia, including Pakistan, India, Indonesia, Thailand, Vietnam, Malaysia, and Japan. Over 100 came from North America, many of them originally from other continents; and twenty came from Europe, including Romania, France, England, the Netherlands, and Germany.

Many of the volunteers from the previous year returned to offer the same abundance of hospitality and care to delegates as in the previous year. Hospitality included meeting delegates' flights and, in some cases, greeting delegates with a fresh rose! Dietary needs were given careful attention, and a snack lounge stayed open day and night. The spirit of appreciation that characterized so many of the formal sessions during the week flowed in the mundane actions too. The production team and the volunteers created an atmosphere of graciousness, as they had the previous year.

Late Sunday afternoon, after delegates had arrived and settled in their rooms, drummers filled the air with expectant vibrations as they summoned the delegates to the opening ceremony. Guests from North American native tribes prepared to open the week with sacred ceremony. Phil Lane and Rosalia Gutierez offered a traditional prayer, chant, and smudging ritual and gave thanks to the land, to the original people who lived in that part of Northern California, and to those who still abide in its history. Prayers were asked for the protection of the participants and guidance in the work that lay ahead.

A large tent had been constructed in a dusty field near the residential halls. It had several entries that allowed for pleasant breezes. More than 200 chairs had been set up inside in several concentric circles that left a large opening in the center. In the very center was a simple table, set with flowers and a candle that had traveled to regional conferences across three continents. There was no podium or raised stage. As people spoke, they walked to the center near the little table, took the microphone, and had to turn in order to face people seated in the circle around them. Even though this felt awkward for some people, most agreed that the room setup proved to be a powerful bearer of the vision itself. The URI was indeed a community of equals, dynamic people from around the globe who sat together in a circle — a circle with an open, modest, and sacred center. The summit was conducted in English. A few delegates needed translation; individual translators were provided for them.

Around the perimeter of the tent, sturdy 4' x 8' white foamcore boards were secured, each identifying a different workstation: Preamble and Purpose, Principles and Organizational Design, Action Agenda Items, Global Cease-Fire Project, Regional Development, and Circulation of the Draft Charter. A lively mural, another product of Diana Arsenian's genius, was a focal point in the circle. One of the aims of the week was to collect the stories that would be told in this setting. The focal mural reflected this intention. It was a map of the world entitled "The URI Story Unfolds." Photos of many of the participants and their memorable quotations that had been collected during the last year were placed on the world map, reflecting back to the participants' images of themselves — the beautiful, powerful, and committed individuals who were the URI.

For five days, delegates immersed themselves in storytelling,

reflection, sacred practices, and celebration to deepen their relationships and to strengthen their commitment to move the URI from
vision to action. Each day held a rhythm, alternating large group plenary gatherings and smaller break-out work sessions devoted to different topics. In the plenary gatherings, everyone participated in
sacred practices offered by participants from different faith traditions.
The participants told stories of ideas and projects in their regions,
and the assembly was able to respond and offer input into the unfolding work. Gurudev Khalsa served as the master of ceremonies "under
the tent" for plenary sessions and led the team of facilitators in
adjusting the plans and processes for the week. (See Appendix 2 for
the worksheets from the 1998 Global Summit.)

> It was a collection of diverse dynamic people – a fabulous
> group of powerful beings. I learned the value of silence in
> organizing folks towards something profound.
>
> – Joe Hall, Banana Kelly, Bronx, New York

The first day focused on " Discovering the Whole." The day was
devoted to stories that shared the development of the URI up to that
point and an explanation of the major conference themes. The first
morning was given to appreciative interviews that connected the
major questions and topics that would receive attention that week
with people's life experience. The appreciative interview worksheet
reminded everyone "that this week people will simultaneously be 'living into the United Religions' as they relate to one another in a spirit
of trust, openness, and love."

The participants engaged the whole of the draft charter on the
first day. On the morning of the second day, "Living the Charter,"
delegates self-selected into groups working in one of three areas:
Charter Preamble and Purpose, Charter Principles, and Global Religious Cease-Fire – 72 Hours of Peacemaking. The afternoon began
with the leaders of the respective R&D teams, who had done their

"homework" in the past year, offering summaries of their findings and being honored for their extraordinary voluntary efforts. Inspired by these presentations, participants were free to continue the morning's work and/or to form groups centered around URI action agenda items, the organizational design concept, or additional areas of compelling interest. In this spirit, participants formed several new groups. One group was made up of young people who wanted to explore a multicultural and interfaith service project for young adults. This meeting created the seed that would grow into the Interfaith Youth Core. Another group gathered impassioned delegates from Pakistan and India, motivated by a moment of high tension between their two countries, to develop an Indo-Pakistan Dialogue Forum that would offer a small but valuable step toward resolving historic hostilities between India and Pakistan.

Each group was led by a skilled facilitator. Groups met in small rooms in the surrounding dormitories, out under the trees, or sitting around picnic tables near the dining hall. Every group had a full agenda to accomplish. One group focused on charter preamble and purpose. With Josef Boehle's indefatigable care and Diane Robbin's perseverance and adeptness, they dug, word by word, into the meaning of the preamble. They faced the daunting task of reconciling many diverse statements of purpose in an attempt to achieve consensus on one statement they could propose to the entire assembly by the end of the week.

The group that focused on the 72-hour project struggled mightily with whether it should be called a "cease-fire" (a negative action that was beyond the URI's capacity to engineer) or a time of peace building. By the end, they reached an uneasy agreement to call the project a 72-Hour Cease-Fire. They proposed a call for three-days of focused peacemaking at the turn of the century — a time to reject the use of violence in the name of religion and to plant new seeds of peace in the world and in local communities. Proposed activities included groups of spiritual leaders witnessing for peace in zones of conflict, 72 hours of continuous prayer and meditation for peace, and local interfaith dialogue and cooperative action for peace. By the end of the summit, participants would commit themselves to work with global and local spiritual leaders and other peacemaking groups to carry this plan forward.

By the last day, the task groups had placed the results of their work on the big boards around the periphery of the tent. The tent's perimeter had filled more and more each day; as a result, by the end of the week, each workstation was spilling over with the creative results of the groups' labors. A new purpose statement had emerged to replace all previous drafts; the list of 19 organizational principles had been refined to 16; summaries of the action agenda were reaffirmed; the plan for the Ceasefire – 72 Hours of Peacemaking – continued to move forward; and participants were developing regional plans for living the preamble, purpose, and principles and, spreading the URI vision on five continents.

On Friday morning, in an effort to get a sense of the meeting about the results of the week's work, participants were asked to walk from station to station to read the results of each group's work. They were asked to place green dots on the ideas they favored, yellow dots on ideas they questioned, and red dots on ideas they opposed. A sea of green dots emerged, with a few yellow dots and red dots for the new proposed purpose statement:

Proposed Purpose Statement

The purpose of the United Religions is to create a safe space for spiritual partnerships in which the people of the world pursue justice, healing, and peace, with reverence for all life.

The 4-D design elements were not as explicit at this summit as they had been in the two previous ones. However, Discovery, Dream, Design, and Destiny processes were woven into the flow of each of the activities to create a steady rhythm of inquiry and positive engagement for people. For example, in the task group focused on charter principles, David Cooperrider elicited people's engagement by preparing a set of appreciative questions for the task group to use as they reviewed the set of 16 principles that had been put forward by the organizational design team.

The worksheet directed group members:

> To envision the principles of organization we truly believe in and want to work toward. As a group, review the Draft Charter Principles in terms of their priority of importance to the URI's future success. Pick out three to five principles you would like to work with as a group to hold up as priorities.

> The following step asked the group to imagine that "…it is 2020 and to imagine what is happening that lets people know that the URI is bringing these principles to life in real ways."

For many, the experience of this Global Summit was like trying to keep one's head above water in a beautiful but fast-flowing river. The sacred practices and ceremonies at the beginning of each morning and afternoon session provided moments of calm on the still shore before the participants leapt anew into the swirling currents. Stories in plenary sessions from the different regions revealed the glory of diversity as the participants witnessed different styles, different voices, and different perspectives of the people of the world living the URI into being. Task groups pressed forward the work of the draft charter and the plans of the 72-Hour Project. A banquet and a public forum celebrated the high points of the week. Throughout, a sensitive balance was maintained between holding fast to the planned schedule and allowing adequate time and space for the unexpected to intervene. Sometimes the unexpected was particularly challenging, as when one participant interjected into the plenary session a passionate demand for religious communities to stop persecuting homosexuals and to support their rights. Many of those attending agreed with the sentiments. Many disagreed. What made the action polarizing was not as much what was said as how and when it was said. The summit planners had built into the agenda many opportunities for people to speak to and with others about concerns they held passionately. Many had taken advantage of these opportunities to address a broad range of issues, from nuclear disarmament to the plight of Tibet to the rights of women and children. The primary concern about this gay rights statement was not that it challenged some people's beliefs, but that it had been one person imposing his will on the whole. One of the gifts of this difficult moment was that it raised issues of how the URI could and would speak on controversial issues that it is still dealing with today.

At this summit, the hard work of crafting words and disagreement over them could have easily impeded the successes of the task groups and fractured the gathering that, for the most part, was still very new to the URI. The content for the year ahead was slowly revealing itself in the revised words of the newly approved Benchmark Draft Charter and the developing ideas for the 72-Hour Project. However, the true gift of this summit for the URI was that the spirit of inclusion remained vibrant; everyone was a part of the process of creation. The sharing of stories and perspectives with people from around the world who were different, yet dedicated to the same cause, the use of Appreciative Inquiry in the work groups as a vehicle to engage people, the emphasis on positive rather than critical engagement with this information, and the opportunities to listen with respect to all the voices assembled – all were experiences that were woven like strands shining golden throughout the fabric of the week,

At the end of the summit, the URI's identity was clearly rooted in growing regional participation. The URI began to recognize itself as one body with many strong parts, as people from five different continents – Africa, Asia, Europe, Latin America, and North America – shared their commitment, vision, and concrete plans for the steps needed to bring the URI to life in their part of the world. Dedicated to an inspiring vision and a mission, these people from different religions and regions were beginning to cocreate the URI with an impressive array of commitment and action.

1998 SUMMIT AFTERMATH

Following the 1998 Global Summit, the task was to keep the community intact, growing in number, involved in circulating the draft charter and participating in its final development, and planning for the 72-Hour Project. In addition to the completion of its charter, the URI community was looking toward December 31, 1999 – January 2, 2000, the turn of the century and the millennium according to Western calendars, as the moment in history when URI groups would first exercise their muscles and lead a global collective action for peace that would impact millions of people across the planet.

TAKING THE URI INTO THE WORLD

As she was leaving the summit, one delegate asked, "How shall we be spiritual partners for one another? How shall we help each other?"

Would the delegates stay in touch with one another? How might they help each other in the years ahead? What would the delegates do when they got home to keep the URI alive in their hearts and to invite others to share the vision? Why was it important to the birthing of the URI to spend one full year engaging people across the world in developing its charter? How would the coordinating staff actually accomplish that? How would the 72-Hour Project gain acceptance and inspire people to bring their own ideas to this possibility? How would the URI staff serve as the heart for this growing URI body and offer consistency, spirit, and direction to all of its stakeholders in order to lead the community in these next steps? And given a financial debt approaching $600,000, how would the URI's new Director of Philanthropy, the Reverend William Rankin, help the organization reverse its journey of heading ever deeper into debt and begin a long climb toward solvency and sustainability? As dreams called for boundless and often costly initiative, the balance sheet screamed for fiscal discipline before the URI vanished into a black hole of visionary indebtedness.

A central wall at the URI office in San Francisco had become the locus of attention for carrying the spirit of the 1997 Global Summit forward. After the 1997 Global Summit, the dream map that had brilliantly captured the powerful dreams for the URI as a new organization hung in the URI office as a reminder of the visions that were fueling the R&D task groups and the regional gatherings that continued that year. After the 1998 Global Summit, the focal piece from the summit, "The URI Story Unfolds," with photos and quotations from the growing URI global community, became the new focal piece in the URI office. The URI story, now being told by many new voices from many more countries and faith traditions, was, in fact, unfolding across the continents of the world. The 1998 summit blossomed with stories of how the different regional groups were going to realize the vision of the URI in their homelands. The groups had returned to their continents invigorated by the hope of the URI, ready to spread the news and enroll others, to help circulate the draft charter, and to mobilize people for the "millennial event." The URI game plan that was catalyzed at each of the Global Summits in 1996, 1997, and 1998 was to call more people to the vision by inviting them to join their dreams with the URI's vision and to bring their own initiative and creativity, values, and effort to the task of giving life and birth to a new organization that would make their dreams real.

The changes to the preliminary draft charter that had been affirmed by the delegates at the summit were made, creating the First Benchmark Draft Charter, which was taken to a graphic artist for final copy and design. The designer used the star logo created by Walter Gray in 1996 as the cover design and, with Sally Mahé and Charles Gibbs, created a Draft Charter package that included a letter of Introduction, the Draft Charter divided into five sections (each with questions for discussion), and a feedback form. All respondents also indicated their name and contact information and whether they wanted to help in the birth of the URI in the coming year. Ten thousand draft charters were printed in soft, dignified blue tones, and the plan for worldwide distribution was implemented.

From June 1998 until June 1999, thousands of people across the world would be introduced to the URI by being invited to read its draft charter and to respond to it. More than 30 delegates from the 1998 Global Summit, some from every continent, volunteered to serve as charter trustees and agreed to help circulate the draft charter. A major task of the next year would be to enlist these volunteers and others to help broadly circulate the URI draft charter around the world, engage increasing numbers of people in conversations about it, gather input, thank the contributors, study the responses, incorporate changes, and craft a second draft of the charter to be revised at the Global Summit 1999 on the road to signing the charter in June 2000.

The letter of introduction to the charter package opened by inviting readers to become dreamers.

> **Imagine a world…**
> …*where there is peace among religions;*
> …*where people from a diversity of religions and spiritual traditions and from all sectors of society gather at common tables all over the world to pursue justice, healing, and peace with reverence for all life;*
> …*where there is a United Religions, an inclusive, decentralized organization, a spiritual partner of the United Nations, where local actions are connected to form a global presence, where the wisdom of faith traditions is revered, where the deepest values of people are respected and put into action for the good of all.*

The introduction reemphasized that the URI needed every voice. Values, appreciative perspectives, and practices that had guided the URI to that moment were restated in the body of the introduction.

> Now the UR needs you — to share this draft widely, to offer input freely, to create the global awareness of the possibility. The birth of the UR depends upon the involvement of people from all sectors of society and

from a great diversity of cultural and spiritual perspectives. The draft charter is far from complete. It will go through extensive development and revision between now and June 2000, when people all over the world will sign it giving birth to the United Religions Initiative. Your participation is needed now to prepare for this birth. Together we are the UR.

At this time, the URI draft charter consisted of five sections. An introduction provided a brief, elegant definition of each section to help people understand the spiritual intent of the charter:

PREAMBLE – the call that inspires us to create the UR now;

PURPOSE – the clear statement that draws us together in common cause;

PRINCIPLES – fundamental beliefs that guide structure, decisions, and conduct;

ORGANIZATIONAL DESIGN – a way of organizing that enhances cooperation and magnifies spirit;

ACTION AGENDA – early thinking about UR action in the world and proposed projects.

Each section of the draft charter had a different origin and history. The preamble had originated as the URI declaration of vision and purpose following the first Global Summit in 1996. The purpose statement was new and had been recently crafted by the working group at the 1998 Global Summit and approved by the rest of the delegates. The set of 16 principles of organization had originally been developed by the organizational design committee, substantially revised by a key gathering of R&D leaders prior to the summit, and affirmed by the 1998 summit delegates. The organizational design had been developed only so far as to summarize the vision of a United Religions that was inclusive, nonhierarchical, decentralized, and self-sustaining; where the resources were to be shared and decisions made at the local level; where local initiatives were to be connected to one another for global impact; where spiritual leaders of all faith traditions were to be revered; and where the deepest values of people were respected and put into action for the good of all.

A summarized version of the action agenda topics with a short introduction had been revised and approved. The topics were: Rights and Responsibilities; Sustainable, Just Economics; Ecological Imperatives; Nurturing a Culture of Healing and Peace; Sharing the Wisdom and Cultures of Faith Traditions; and Supporting the Overall UR Agenda.

The questions that accompanied each section were an essential element of the draft charter. They invited readers to connect the values stated in the words of the document with their own. For example, in responding to the statement of purpose, the first questions were: "When in your life have you been part of something that reflected the values expressed in this vision? What difference did it make in your life? In your community?"

The draft charter was warmly invitational and aimed to elicit appreciative conversations that tapped people's values based on their lived experience. Rather than being a finished product, the URI charter reflected the best that was known at the time. It was a starting point from which to test, to learn, and to grow. Not only did people all over the world study the draft charter, many used it as the best guidance to date on how to *be* the URI. Even as the charter was evolving, it created a framework to guide the self-organizing development of the URI community.

In the coming year, responses to the draft charter from all over the world were received and suggestions were studied and tallied. Summaries of the responses were reported to the organizational design team. In addition to fine-tuning the words of the preamble, purpose, and principles, the organizational design team set to work after the 1998 summit to create a conceptual design for the organization that would meet the criteria that people all over the world had established.

DEVELOPING THE ORGANIZATIONAL CONCEPT: COOPERATION CIRCLES ARE BORN

Dee Hock's ideas for a chaordic structure had seemed like the right match all along, but now it was time to put the theory and the Preamble, Purpose, and Principles (PPP) to use to create structures that would define the whole and the parts of the URI and to define the set of relationships that would connect and govern them. The organizational design team had been imagining groups of people who were locally established and able to organize in any manner, at any scale, in any area, and around any issue or activity that was relevant and consistent with the PPP. Participants at the 1998 Global Summit applauded this model that demanded adherence to the PPP but that also allowed each group to have maximum freedom to live the URI in its own uniquely expressed ways. The chaordic model spoke of these smallest or most local units as fractals, groups that replicated each other. Each group would act in accord with the PPP, but also was free to self-organize their work and grow and manage their affairs in pursuit of the URI purpose as they saw fit. Other organizations experimenting with chaordic models had named these local units alliances, councils, or chapters. None of these names felt right for the URI.

In the fall following the 1998 summit, at a meeting marked with laughter, silent meditation, brainstorming, a wall full of possible names, and a roundtable discussion, the design team unanimously agreed to name these local autonomous entities Cooperation Circles (CCs). The team remembered that every URI gathering had taken place at round tables where people sat in circles and that a circle was understood to be a powerful form, especially among indigenous peoples, for it represented nature's life cycles and nature's interdependence. Even though the purpose statement was still under construction and the final words had not been approved, the notion of cooperation had withstood the test of time and continued to stand out as the URI's central action.

With the name settled, the team went on to address the simple rules that would define CCs. To ensure viability, CCs would be required to have a minimum of seven (7) individuals (that might include associations or organizations as well). To ensure a minimal level of faith diversity, at least three (3) of the Circle members must be from a different religion, spiritual expression, or indigenous tradition. It was decided that, according to the principles governing autonomy and self-organizing, CCs would have the freedom to choose their own name, to define their unique purpose, to translate United Religions documents; to raise, spend, and give away funds; and to decide their own action agenda and act in ways consistent with the PPP.

The organizational design team envisioned that a CC would have the opportunity to join with other CCs, not to create a massive power base, but to provide for coordination and mutual support. The team decided that if a minimum of three CCs wanted to join together, they could become a Multiple Cooperation Circle (MCC). To extend this freedom further, the team decided that if MCCs wanted to join together for similar purposes, they could; as a result, Multi Multiple Cooperation Circles (MMCCs) came into being. These constructs were intended to create the organizational structures that would enable unfettered creative development and provide channels for communication, for the selection of trustees to the Global Council, and for other work essential to maintaining a global organization.

Having established this concept, the design team set about designing CCs in an effort to understand how they might function and what the relationships among them might look like. Team members set to work creating their own CCs. Members were armed with 14" white tagboard circles; a guide sheet that assigned different colored dots to represent different faith traditions and to distinguish between individuals, organizations, and associations; and plenty of different colored dots, pens, and markers.

First, the creators imagined a specific purpose for the CC and then determined individuals, associations, and organizations they wanted to be part of a CC dedicated to that specific purpose. Team members then used the colored dots and markers to create a model of the CC on the tag- board circle. The model included the graphic representation of membership and a written expression of purpose and manner of governance consistent with the PPP.

One person proposed creating a CC that would encourage youth and elders in a neighborhood in San Francisco to share stories from their faith traditions. The creator decided who might participate in the group and added different colored dots to symbolize participants who came from a variety of traditions: Russian Orthodox, Muslim, Jewish, Hindu, and no faith. The creator knew some of these people already and was imagining what might happen if they came together to start an intergenerational dialogue.

Soon the design team had created a dozen or more model CCs and placed them on foamcore boards. As the team marveled at the diversity and unique expression of each CC, members began to speculate about why a CC might want to establish a bond with another CC and why the two might want to join forces and become a MCC. The team spent hours fleshing out this model, creating new CCs, developing MCCs, evolving MMCCs, until everyone knew the design concept from the inside out. This knowledge came with equal measures of delight in the relatively simple concept the team had created and uncertainty at the myriad questions the team could anticipate but had no answers to. Living into the questions can be intimidating at times. The design team was encouraged to move into the unknown by Dee's foundational belief that members should aim at creating something that was "good enough for now," trusting that they would see far enough ahead to be able to go forward and in going forward, would find enough answers to help them see still farther. The team often took refuge in a principle about commitment to organizational learning and adaptation.

When the organizational design team first explained the concept of CCs, MCCs, and MMCCs to the board, its members saw an artificial array of alphabetic jargon that evoked sterile institutionalism more than the warm human organization they had worked to create. Radical faith was needed to trust that these terms were going to be useful and not lead the cherished URI vision and its spiritually devoted people into an incomprehensible bureaucracy. To help shift the initial reaction, the team had developed an exercise that called people to create their own CCs. With this exercise, the abstract became concrete and people began to see the incredible potential in the concept. The design made CCs the heart of the URI and granted CCs essential freedoms and responsibilities – the freedom for each CC to give life to the URI purpose in its own way and the freedom to connect that gave each CC the right to join with other CCs in a sustaining way to coordinate efforts and realign decision-making processes. The joy of these freedoms emerged as people made their own circles. As they made model circles, using colored dots to signify members and describing in their own words the unique mission of their CC, they realized they could make their dreams come true! They could construct a simple structure that would give their vision wings and allow it to work and fit with others like it. These locally initiated and diverse CCs were bound through their commitment to the values declared in the URI charter.

People easily took to the hands-on activity of designing their CCs. As people applied the simple rules that gave integrity and definition to CCs, they felt the joy of their creativity. This hands-on activity saved the URI from drowning in a conceptual sea of CCs, MCCs, and MMCCs and gave individuals a positive way to understand the concepts and become a creator of a CC.

Almost immediately this model was introduced to the entire URI community in the URI newsletter, which had a circulation of about 7,000. The entire mailing list was invited to experiment with creating CCs. The headline read "Imagine Yourself Being a Part of the UR – an Invitation to Create a Cooperation Circle – a CC." The article reminded the reader that from its beginning, the URI had been a vision and an invitation. Now people were invited to imagine how a local group, a CC, might take root where they lived or around a particular interest. How might such a group spring into being from an individual's passion, creativity, resourcefulness, and determination? The URI invited people's CC designs, both to spark their imagination and to provide input to help the design team envision how these circles might work when each one shared the imprint of the PPP. What would happen when hundreds, thousands of self-organizing CCs determined their own destiny and their relationship to one another as members of the URI?

A powerful symbiosis occurred in these months. As the form and function of CCs was being discovered and the structure of the URI as a global organization was emerging in a real way, the 72-Hour Project was developing a global community of commitment that channeled the URI's organizational vision into cooperative action for peace around the world. Although the birth of the United Religions as a global organization with member CCs was still a year-and-a-half away, people on every continent were manifesting the URI vision as they planned an action or a program for peace that would take place at the turn of the millennium. The 72-Hour Project provided an experiment and experience of how the URI might change the world. All people, regardless of rank, faith background, or sector in society, were invited to initiate a peace action of any scale. While actions could take place at time prior to the millennial weekend, the impact of diverse groups acting as one would be spotlighted from December 31, 1999, to January 2, 2000. As the URI geared up for another Global Summit in 1999, the URI community and hundreds of others were already planning for how they would usher in a twenty-first century of peace as part of the 72-hour collective global action.

GLOBAL SUMMIT 1999
STANFORD UNIVERSITY, PALO ALTO, CALIFORNIA
JUNE 20–25

Hard-won fiscal accountability, a debt approaching $700,000, and a budget shortfall, required that the 1999 Global Summit, originally planned to include over 200 participants, to be scaled back to 100. As the summit approached, regional activity, including consultations in Asia and Africa and a historic summit in Itatiaia, Brazil, continued to spread the URI presence and practice around the world. The organizational design team continued to process input from around the world, pushing the next draft of the PPP and Action Agenda near completion. The 72-Hour Project was on the horizon, and the URI was on schedule to give birth to the United Religions organization on June 26, 2000.

To keep to that schedule, much work was still needed on the organizational structure and governance of the URI. The Global Summit 1999 (again at Stanford University, June 20–25) called for key leaders from every continent to come together to strengthen their sense of connectedness, to share their experiences over the past year, to engage with the CC concept, and to explore how the governing body of the URI would be established and how it would function.

Each year since 1996, the Global Summit planning and facilitation had been increasingly shared by SIGMA consultants with URI staff and leaders from around the world. Leading up to this Global Summit, global planning teams worked through phone calls and emails to plan different parts of the summit — sacred practices and opening/closing ceremonies, the program; the public forum, and so on. This group gathered a day early, bringing together a world of expertise and harmonizing it in service of an inspiring and inclusive summit.

DISCOVERY

On Sunday evening, people were startled when they walked into the summit meeting space. The focal mural was an 8' by 20' map of the world. It had no names, only continental and island boundaries. And the Southern Hemisphere was on top. People were momentarily confused before they recognized what they were looking at. The recognition was followed, especially for participants from the Southern Hemisphere, with broad smiles. The image of the world from this fresh upside-down perspective was a powerful reflection of the URI's effort to create a new vision of the world.

The Summit opened with a simple ritual organized by Sister Laetitia Borg, a Franciscan sister from Addis Ababa, Ethiopia, who had led the planning team responsible for sacred practices and the opening and closing ceremonies. For months before Sister Laetitia arrived at Stanford University in June 1999, she had been sharing questions and conversation via email with the team of facilitators. She had been hard at work creating a magnificent opening ritual meant to renew the foundational values imbedded in the words of the charter. Sister Laetitia's own light, wisdom, and artistry would shine through this simple ritual.

Now the summit convened with table groups receiving a 10" by 16" symbol hand painted by URI members in Ethiopia. Each symbol represented a core value, such as integrity or joy or trust. Following a brief discussion of the values, a person from each table carried his or her group's value card and placed it on a wall — where all the cards were assembled to create a mural that rerooted the assembly in the basic values it cherished.

A few months earlier, Sister Laetitia had called upon the world-wide URI community to pray for Ethiopia and Eritrea because hostility had broken out again along their border. She mentioned that the

URI vision was spreading in her warring country. As fighting became heavier along the border, Laetitia wrote:

> *We appreciate the way the URI is growing and raising awareness that what the world needs now is peace, dialogue, and respect for all that is life. An Ethiopian Muslim friend of the URI is cooperating with us to get the URI message out to Islamic groups. We hope to send this friend to Muslim groups in Djibouti so that a URI presence there may be truly established as a light of peace.*

What had been only a vision in 1993 was now a reality being lived around the world and shared in stories and messages flashing across email lines. The vision was becoming real as people from different faith backgrounds drew upon their respective values and deep wisdom to work together for peace and justice where and when they were needed.

Once the values mural was completed, people were asked to place colored dots representing their geographic and/or spiritual home on the world map. The map was soon glimmering with different colored dots that mirrored the diversity and geographic spread of people in the room. The simple exercise engaged the participants at their core. One man from New Zealand couldn't find his island on the big map. This omission reinforced the experience that people from his part of Oceania remained unseen and uncounted on the world stage because they were overshadowed by the massive size and populations of their Asian neighbors to the north. The map reinforced the picture that the URI was not located in one central place, but belonged to the spread of colored dots now beginning to light up the world map.

Monday morning opened with the assembly reading together the PPP of the proposed second draft of the charter. A profound hush accompanied the reading. People allowed the words and what it meant to be in this gathering of people from different cultures, professions, and faith traditions who shared these same convictions to sink into their being. The assembly of 100 people read the preamble in unison that began with the words:

We, people of diverse faiths, called by our values and traditions to compassion in response to the crises that endanger our earth community and to the rising hopes of humanity, wish to create a permanent forum where we gather in mutual respect, dialogue, and cooperative action to foster peace and the flourishing of all life.

Members of the URI board of directors took turns reading the purpose and the principles. The thousands of unique voices and shared aspirations that had poured into these words in the past few years were represented in this communal reading. The PPP were not just words on a page; they were symbols of the cherished hopes that fueled the determined actions of people across the world. The reading evoked a sense of profound respect and gratitude.

The URI sought to promote enduring, daily interfaith cooperation; to stop religiously motivated violence; and to create cultures of peace, justice, and healing. The URI utilized two unique processes for producing positive change — a new "chaordic" structure and appreciative inquiry philosophy and processes. The common value in these two powerful tools for organizational change was the spirit of inclusion; everyone who was committed to the same core values was welcome to join the process. All voices were valued and could find a place in doing the work. There was no limit to what people might do given the opportunity to try and the encouragement of trustworthy friends. Was this vision too incredible, too visionary, too ungrounded? Was the URI attempting to be upside down in a rightside up world? Could it work? Where were the army of "experts" and the leaders from the clerical hierarchies from the different faiths who could undertake the responsibility of peace building and stopping religiously motivated violence and, with their expertise, prestige, and money lead, train and educate others to solve the problems too?

How would the new URI organization fit with the preexisting expectations and patterns of decision making that guided most non-profit organizations? How would the URI community be challenged to sustain its core values and vision once it was born? And if the URI was able to act with a new "from the ground up" mentality and a consciousness that welcomed all people, what unprecedented things might result that could renew life and give respect to the earth and all living beings?

At the Global Summit 1999, the URI community gathered to renew its original intent to be the kind of organization that was not controlled by people "at the top" or that looked to "central headquarters" for directives and sustenance. The URI was still discovering itself, and its identity was being defined in the lived experiences and stories that kept emerging as clusters of self-motivated, locally grounded groups of people drew meaning from the same PPP and learned and grew together.

Following the reading of the PPP, the participants leapt into the appreciative interviews, which served to deepen the already profound sense of connectedness and to focus the week's work. Building on the interviews and introductions that followed, various URI leaders from around the world told stories about the interfaith work that was occurring back home. Marites Africa, a Roman Catholic laywoman from the Philippines, told stories about home gatherings in small villages across the Philippines and about the Peacemaker's Circle in Manila, where people from a broad diversity of religions came together weekly to share silence, meditation, and dialogue.

Mary Page Sims, the wife of a retired Episcopal bishop from North Carolina, eloquently told about the enthusiastic response URI received as she spread the word in the Carolinas and about how her group had evolved into a community of committed friends. Prafultabai Jaintilal, a Hindu from Mozambique, reported that the President of Mozambique had attended a recent URI meeting in Maputo and that local people looked to the URI's work to bring positive change and stability to the social structures in Mozambique after long years of war.

André Porto, interfaith activist and staff member of Viva Rio, the largest NGO in Brazil, told about the recent URI gathering in Itatiaia, Brazil. The gatherings had brought together diverse people from

Brazilian society and people from other Latin American countries to celebrate existing efforts; to explore new visions of interfaith cooperation; and to begin to heal ancient wounds as they danced, sang, dreamed, and prayed together.

Livina Gill, a social rights advocate from Lahore Pakistan, compared the URI to a building:

> The URI is like a building that is made with rocks, bricks, cement and water, and iron. Rich people and poor build it together. Just as with wood and water a building cannot be complete, neither can the URI be complete until all kinds of people in the world (religious, social, political, men, women, young, and old) are a part of it. If the URI is working in the same way in 30 years, it will become a huge and splendid building where people will gather from all over the world and get an education for peace and justice, love, hope, faith, human rights, unity, and equality with one mind and soul
>
> — Lavina Gill, Lahore, Pakistan.

Discovery through storytelling continued into the second day in small groups. As people listened to each other share significant anecdotes about their interfaith work, others in the group, with copies of the newly revised draft charter in hand, listened to the stories for ways in which the person was already living the URI PPP. Then people discussed what they had heard. Somewhere in this swirl of engagement, Nestor Muller offered a rule he had learned from a wise teacher: "If I am in a group of eight, I must listen seven times and speak once." This rule helped deepen awareness that the quality of deep listening was essential to authentic community.

Design

After reconnecting with the PPP in this way, it was time to create CCs. Armed with cardboard circle templates, markers, and colored dots and buoyed by each other's enthusiasm and some confusion, everyone began to create CCs. Lively discussions erupted as people engaged with one another. Many made CCs of actual groups they belonged to or groups that they wanted to initiate. Circles, each with its own colorful array of members, its specific purpose, and its self-determined form of governing process, popped up everywhere.

In addition to the authority to create CCs, the organizational concept also gave CCs the means to connect to other CCs to form MCCs. The challenge at the summit was to understand the positive energy and opportunity this freedom offered. The planning team had designed a "simple" exercise to dramatize the way CCs could be drawn together by some common purpose to form MCCs. With their newly created cardboard circle templates in hand, summit participants were led outside to a grassy hillside and given directions, resulting in far more confusion than clarity. In that moment of frustration, it seemed as though chaos might triumph completely over order and two years of work would dissolve.

Miraculously, people found their way into two long lines, facing each other on the grass. They began moving silently and slowly in opposite directions, holding up their circle templates so the templates could be studied by those passing by. Though the plan had called for people to view all the circles in an orderly fashion and then seek out those they were most interested in connecting with, something else happened. With stunning swiftness, people began to recognize potential colleagues, and clusters formed out of the chaos. Circles geared to interfaith education found each other. Circles attending to ecological issues talked about how they might connect after the summit ended. A large gathering congregated to talk about peace building and another to talk about women's issues. People naturally and easily gravitated to others who shared similar interests. They made connections, found new friends who shared similar ideas, and exchanged email addresses.

They experienced the freedom to connect in a way that was natural, fun, and practical. And they created a demonstration of why and how CCs would cluster into MCCs far more powerfully than the planners had ever imagined, precisely because it happened in spite of, not because of their best plans.

As a finale to learning about the organizational concept, the entire assembly was invited back to the grassy lawn and taught a simple dance. They laughed and felt the flow of themselves – circles in motion, moving and connecting in a free-flowing manner, dynamic, alive, and beautiful.

The Global Council

Another unfinished part of the charter would define the legal body charged with the responsibility for sustaining and nurturing the URI principles and for managing the business of the URI. The organizational concept proposed that when the URI was established as a global membership organization, a majority of its trustees would be selected by the CCs. The plan was that every CC would be given one vote and that three trustees from each of seven geographic regions of the world and one nongeographic region (CCs that came together around an issue rather an a location) would be selected by CCs in their region to serve on the global council. A next step in the destiny of the URI at this juncture was to give further definition and meaning to the role the global council trustees would play in the organization. Would the global council act like a traditional board of directors? Would members adequately represent the interests of people in their regions? How would the global council be both wise and spiritual, practical and representative, a leader and a servant?

The original URI board of directors, who had served since 1996, had been appointed by Bishop Swing. It had been expanded by a board nominating committee, who had selected additional members, but its members still came from the San Francisco Bay area. As a step toward more global representation, the organizational design team had proposed (and the board accepted) a plan to create a global

Transition Advisory Group (TAG) to work with the board between the 1999 summit and the signing of the charter in June 2000. In the early days of the summit, regional groups had met to select representatives to serve on this TAG.

On Thursday, the delegates at the 1999 summit were asked to bring their eyes, ears, and voices to deliberate about the global council. They were invited to participate in a "fishbowl" exercise to offer up their highest visions for the future global council and to witness the forerunner of this council, the combined board and TAG, in action as they discussed their personal visions for the global council and the pressing questions they were currently working on.

To begin the exercise, each table group was invited to hold a mock election, selecting one of its members to represent the table at the "global council." As part of this exercise, each group was asked to answer these questions: "What is the highest purpose of the global council? What will its highest service look like?" Following discussion and elections, each new "trustee" took a seat in a circle in the center of the meeting room in full view of the entire assembly. Each person in the circle of people in the "fishbowl" began by sharing the visions and images of the global council that had emerged from his or her table's discussion. The images included the following:

- The council listens with humility and embodies the best in spirit and deed.
- The council is a carrier of trust.
- The council is an exemplar of the PPP and maintains a strategic perception of the good of the whole, safeguards the whole, and activates the power of the whole.
- The council manages change and holds and creates a positive consciousness about change.
- The council is the nexus that facilitates communication to enable and connect all parts of the URI community.

- The council inspires spiritual citizenship.
- The council translates world service into an inner attitude where true intention flows from the heart.
- The council is a shepherd gathering its flock, not a policeman.
- The council remembers that with all its idealism, everyone has a saint and a sinner within and stays aware of the likelihood of power domination.

This expression and discussion of "highest visions" transitioned into a meeting of the board and TAG, as members of both groups replaced the first "mock council" and took their seats in the "fishbowl" inner circle. Rita Semel, chair of the board, began by "getting practical" and giving a report on the cash flow of the URI. She spoke of URI's relative financial health and commented that she was nervous about the high costs looming in the coming months. Other trustees offered comments about what it felt like to be a trustee at the time. One person suggested, "We don't need to be decision makers for the parts of the URI, but we will be decision makers for the whole. And any part can say, 'We're not ready for that yet.' " Another person commented that he looked forward to failures within the council because those experiences would prepare the group for the fertile possibilities. Another member observed that not all organizational experts were from the United States and to beware of too much organizational development jargon and institutional language. Another member questioned, "Are we as trustees decision makers, advisers, or vessels?"

The power of this moment was that everyone in the room could see that the members of this group were human beings, no better or worse than anyone else. Each person had commented that he or she felt somewhat inadequate to live into the highest visions for the global council that had just been described. This juxtaposition of exalted visions with acknowledged human limitations deepened trust and strengthened the bond between board members and nonboard members, reinforcing the power of transparent conversations to inspire and to reduce human tendencies to react with doubt, suspicion, and critical judgment of others.

The Reverend Wesley Mabuza, a theologian and veteran of the antiapartheid struggle in South Africa, said afterward that he had come to the summit from his homeland with a heavy heart because he believed it was impossible for people to set up governing structures that used power appropriately. He said that the morning's expressions about the global council lightened his spirit and rekindled his resolve to believe again in the power of people to do what seemed impossible and that he would not give up on the processes for positive change taking place in Johannesburg.

As this exercise drew to a close, the group was asked to provide a "sense of the meeting" relative to the key elements of the proposed draft charter. They gave broad assent to the preamble, principles, organizational design, and agenda for action. But they gave broad disapproval to the proposed purpose. Trying to make sense of a wide diversity of often conflicting input, the organizational design team had changed the statement significantly from the previous year. While some thought it was an improvement, others believed the process had been betrayed. And nearly everyone believed they were still a long way from having a statement that would include and energize everyone. Many people volunteered to be part of an email dialogue to develop a definitive, broadly accepted purpose statement.

URI's agenda in the coming year, 1999–2000, embraced a worldwide 72-hour collective action for peace; the approval of numerous URI CCs on every continent; the mobilization of people all over the world to plan local URI charter signing ceremonies; continued work to affirm the final revision of the charter; a large URI-led delegation to the Parliament of the World's Religions in Cape Town, South Africa, in December 1999; and preparations for the Global Charter-Signing Ceremony and Summit 2000.

The closing ceremony took place on the lawn that had witnessed the miraculous emergence of order from chaos and a closing banquet the night before. The ceremony was led by Donald Frew, an elder in the Wiccan spiritual tradition, and Betsy Stang, both from the United States; Rosalia Gutierrez, from Argentina; and Salvador Quishpe, an indigenous leader from Ecuador. The participants gathered in a large circle around a redwood sapling. One by one people were smudged with sage. People had been asked to bring to the summit sacred waters and earth from their homeland. The offerings of earth were now mixed together. The offerings of water were added to a basin holding water from the 1996 service at Grace Cathedral. Each person took some of the dirt and some of the water and sprinkled them on the redwood, dedicating it as a peace tree. Blessings were offered that as the redwood sapling would grow into a mighty tree, the URI would grow into its highest vision and be continually nurtured with the "sacred water" poured into it by people from all parts of the world.

CHAPTER 5

"I would like to support your 72 Hours Project. I am specifically interested in the Prayer Vigil and offering blessings to spiritual neighbors..."

– His Holiness The Dalai Lama

The Birth

1999: LOOKING BACK, LOOKING FORWARD

When, in June 1999, the sun set on the URI's fourth Global Summit, a long, successful journey lay behind and an improbably long journey lay ahead on the road to June 2000 and the birth of the United Religions. It would be a year of extraordinary challenges, accomplishments, and surprises.

Following the vision of the 55 people gathered at the Fairmont Hotel in June 1996, the URI had developed a presence on every continent and had engaged thousands of diverse voices in developing a draft charter. The URI had held four global summits, six regional conferences, and countless smaller consultations and speeches and had engaged people over the Internet, thereby generating many local projects and organizational partnerships in just over three years.

The fourth Global Summit had overwhelmingly approved the preamble, principles, and organizational design of the charter; had selected members of a global TAG to begin an active transition from a Bay Area board of directors to a global council; and had enthusiastically endorsed the 72 Hours Project, which would mark the URI's first effort to organize a globally initiated, locally implemented action.

Along the way, the URI had raised nearly $3 million and accumulated nearly $900,000 in debt. By July 1999, the debt had been reduced to $400,000 and the URI had a pledge base of $750,000 committed for 2000.

Yet there was little time to celebrate these accomplishments because the pages were already flying off the calendar, bringing the 72 Hours Project at the turn of the millennium and the June 26, 2000, charter signing ever closer. An enormous amount of work was to be done.

The preamble and principles had received overwhelming approval, with only a few suggestions for improvements, most notably strengthening the language concerning the environment and including justice wherever peace was mentioned. However, reaching agreement on a statement of purpose seemed much farther away. A meeting toward the end of the fourth Global Summit had demonstrated just how far.

Thirty people from different faith traditions and different parts of the world had self-selected because they cared deeply and passionately about the purpose statement. They sat in a circle to address the question "What is most important to you about the purpose statement? What must be in the purpose if you are to be able to find yourself and your community in it?"

One of the first people to speak was an Anglican bishop from Canada, Michael Ingham. Bishop Ingham answered, "As a Christian, as an Anglican, and as a bishop, I must have God in the purpose statement. If God is not there, I can't find myself in the purpose." This clear and powerful statement was spoken from the bishop's heart. People listened carefully to what he said. After Bishop Ingham's statement, the group listened as person after person expressed what was most important to them. Sitting opposite Bishop Ingham was the Venerable Jinwol Lee. When his turn came, Venerable Lee spoke powerfully and movingly from the depth of his tradition. He said, "What is most important to me about the purpose statement is that God is not in it. As a Buddhist, if God is in the purpose statement, I cannot find myself there."

In some ways, it was a small moment – 30 people sitting peaceably in a room, speaking from their hearts and listening intently to each other. Yet they saw before them the sort of religious opposition that has polarized people throughout history, often leading to estrangement and violence. The group could have easily quit in the face of such seeming polarization, but it did not. Over the years, people had been working on the charter. Immersed in the valuing and visioning practices of AI, they had developed a commitment and a community. The commitment was to create a table large enough so that anyone who wished to share in the work, regardless of tradition, could take a seat. The community was a group of people from diverse religions, spiritual expressions, and indigenous traditions who had come to see in each other sisters and brothers who shared similar values and wished to work together to make the world a better place. The strength of the commitment, the bonds of community, and the discipline of deep listening and creative imagining imbued by AI demanded that the group find a way through this seemingly intractable opposition. As had happened so many times in the URI's development, the participants were called to approach a seemingly solid brick wall in the belief that, even though they could not see it, a door would appear for them to walk through. And so they journeyed on.

Refining the Purpose Statement

Weary of the struggle but caring deeply about the outcome, many in this group asked to be part of the process that would move the URI forward from the summit, hoping to create a purpose statement that would be approved by the board of directors and would have the assent of the global community. Three years before, a small self-selected group had left the Fairmont Hotel and successfully developed the "Declaration of Vision and Purpose: A Working Document." But the group working on the purpose statement was no longer dealing with a working document. And these people did not have the freedom they had had three years earlier to embrace diverse viewpoints by expanding the text. All agreed that the statement needed to be concise, memorable, and essential. But not everyone agreed on how concise or what made a purpose statement memorable or what was essential. And the clock was ticking.

Some believed that ending religious violence was essential. Others believed that, instead of positing a goal that was essentially negative (the elimination of violence), the purpose should articulate a positive goal – creating peace on earth, which some thought should be spelled Earth. After all, Earth was a planet. One never referred to "mars" or "venus." Some were content to view the URI's work from a human perspective; for instance, working for the good of humanity. Others, led by a deep concern for the whole community of life on Earth, often coming from a group holding Buddhist or indigenous world-views, believed a great deal of damage had been done because humanity considered itself apart from the rest of the biosphere. These people believed that the purpose had to address the good of all life, not simply the good of humanity. Some wanted God to be central to the purpose. Others could not find themselves or their tradition in the word *God*.

In the summer of 1999, it became clear that nearly every issue that people cared passionately about was focused on the statement of purpose. Over the preceding two years, different people had felt alternately elated and defeated by the statements of purpose; but the ones who, at any moment had felt defeated, had always known that only exhaustion would prevent them from having their say in the next round of discussions. The URI was now rapidly approaching the point when there would be no next round. According to the organizational design timeline, the text of the PPP, and the whole charter had to be approved by February 2000. At that point, the discussion of the United Religions' purpose would be closed, at least for a few years. This created an urgency and a sharpness to the process that would test the URI community to its core. At the same time, people remained hopeful and committed, as this banner from the URI's email server indicated: *The Purpose of the United Religious Initiative is currently in the process of Joyful, Inclusive, and Inspired cocreation!*

As daunting as it was, the task of settling on a purpose statement formed only a small part of the work required to finish the charter and bylaws. While many organizational questions had "good enough for now" answers, others were still unanswered; further, the bylaws to translate these answers into a legal structure were largely unwritten. The URI community and, in particular, the organization design team excelled at designing CCs, but wondered about their legal rights and responsibilities. The URI community and, in particular, the organization design team had imagined how to create the first global council but lacked clarity about precisely how its members would be selected in a manner that gave voice to all, honored local autonomy, and ensured that the full diversity of the community would be represented. The URI community and, in particular, the organization design team anticipated that a CC might violate the PPP, but struggled with what to do about it. The URI community and, in particular, the organization design team eliminated legal language that was not absolutely necessary and incorporated noble words and imagery from the Iroquois Constitution created by the Iroquois Confederacy in the northeastern part of North America thousands of years ago. While the emergent URI possessed a principle that said, "We are committed to organizational learning and adaptation," organizers recognized that it did not save them from the practicality of articulating a comprehensive legal framework consistent with both the governing law of the state of California and the preamble, purpose (even if it wasn't yet finalized), and principles of the United Religions. And the clock was ticking.

With work on the charter and bylaws under way, the staff also had to plot and implement a membership strategy. Designing model CCs on cardboard templates energized participants, but would these people be energized enough to go home and create living, breathing, acting CCs? Would participation in the URI's creation lead individuals, organizations, and associations to affiliate formally with the URI? What about those who had never heard of the URI? How were they to be reached? And then there was the work (both the mundane and that which demanded tremendous creativity and sensitivity) of designing, printing, and distributing the charter and application forms for CCs and affiliates.

Also, on the final day of the fourth summit, a sizable majority of the participants had expressed a strong desire to keep the I in URI when the charter was signed. For three years, organizers had imagined that the URI would give birth to the United Religions. Now they were contemplating having the URI give birth to the URI! Among the reasons given: United Religions seemed presumptuous, United Religions Initiative sounded appropriately humble; important to maintain the emphasis on "initiative," only through the initiative of committed people all over the world would the high vision of the charter be realized. Among the challenges: How do you change your mind after promoting such a clear goal for three years, and how do you generate excitement about the birth of a new organization if you're talking about the URI giving birth to the URI?

In early November, the URI's board of directors and the TAG were to meet for the first time for two days. The revised charter and draft bylaws had to be finished by late October, along with budget for 2000 (which had yet to be developed) and other key pieces of work so members could review them before the meeting and, hopefully, make decisions. But making decisions even presented a challenge. The board had the legal authority to make decisions on its own and the legal responsibility to stand behind those decisions, especially the ones involving money. The TAG represented the future of the United Religions and its rootedness around the world. To include the TAG as voices only with no vote would have been a violation of the spirit of the URI. How did the board and the staff deal with those issues?

THE 72 HOURS PROJECT

And the 72 Hours Project loomed large. Though scaled back considerably (see following display) because of finances, it both challenged and blessed the URI's relatively small organization. For nearly two years, Paul Andrews consulted with potential partnering groups in different parts of the world, gaining a wide range of advice and generating a broad base of interest. Sarah Talcott, a college intern, came on to assist in communicating with groups planning 72 Hours actions. The 72 Hours vision had evolved through two Global Summits. Now the challenge was to transform interest into commitment and to unite that commitment into a major project of global proportions at the turn of the millennium. The blessing in this challenge was that each moment was a vivid reminder of why the URI community was engaging in the hard work of building an organization and why they were doing it in a manner that placed a high value on local expression.

"72 Hours: An Interfaith Peace-Building Project of the United Religions Initiative"
A selection from the brochure

AN INVITATION...
   You are invited to join with people of faith from around the world to participate in an unprecedented act of interreligious global cooperation – 72 hours of interfaith peacebuilding at the turn of the millennium as a living pledge to a new and more hopeful future for all people.... The purpose of the 72 Hours Project is to bring into being a whole new level of global interreligious cooperation, to commit together to a culture of cooperation and peace, and to create a gift of hope for the generations that will follow us.

WHAT PEOPLE WILL BE DOING...
"We will be out at the Nevada nuclear test site to witness for peace. ..."
   – Bishop Thomas Gumbleton,
      Roman Catholic Bishop of Detroit

"We are planning a five-day retreat, including prayer, meditation, and local actions. ..."
— Swami Satchidananda, United States

"I would like to support your 72 Hours Project. I am specifically interested in the Prayer Vigil and offering blessings to spiritual neighbors. ..."
— His Holiness The Dalai Lama

"We will invite our centers around the world to take part in the Peace Vigil. ..."
— Sister Jayanti, Brahma Kumaris
(5,000 centers in 68 countries)

"We will offer prayers during the 72 Hours. ..."
— Dr. A. K. Merchant,
National Spiritual Assembly of the
Baha'is of India

"I will communicate with all 5,000 Sacred Heart sisters on five continents and urge them to join. ..."
— Sister Joan Kirby, Executive Director,
Temple of Understanding

"I will offer prayers during the 72 Hours. ..."
— Dr. Seyyed Hossein Nasr,
Islamic scholar

"We really appreciate your concern for peace in the world. ...The Chinese Christian community will join in this call. ..."
— Dr. Han Wenzao, President,
Chinese Christian Council

"We are calling on physicians around the world to promote the idea of 72 hours of nonviolence at the end of the millennium. ..."
— Dr. Wade Aubry, San Francisco

YOU CAN MAKE A DIFFERENCE
Achieving global peace can seem unimaginable. And yet when people act together, there is no limit to what they can accomplish....

As the 72 Hours project vividly illustrated, the URI had become an organization that belonged to people all over the world, yet was owned by no one. Months before the charter was signed, there was a living, breathing URI that would find its vivid manifestation for three days at the turn of the millennium. But the turn of the millennium was many months away in the immediate aftermath of the Global Summit. In the months ahead, as people around the world prepared for their acts of interfaith peacebuilding, it was the responsibility of the board, the TAG and the staff to consider the "sense of the meeting" that had emerged on many issues at the summit and, on behalf of the whole, to translate it into language and decisions that would guide the development of the URI over the coming years. The success of this undertaking would require and test the best listening skills and the deepest sense of trust and accountability to the whole that had developed over the previous three years. Success would require the guidance of the spirit – the divine spirit, the spirit of Buddha nature, the spirit of wisdom, the spirit of vision, the spirit of courage, the spirit of humility, the spirit of risk, and the spirit of trust.

As late summer turned to fall in the northern hemisphere, the staff and the Board also turned their attention to preliminary planning for the birth of the United Religions (or URI) at a global charter Signing and Summit in June 2000. With summits held each summer for three years at Stanford University, organizers assumed the charter would be signed there. But over the summer, the possibility of holding this historic event in Pittsburgh, Pennsylvania, was put forward by Bishop Swing. The hope of new sources of funding in Pittsburgh, a growing group of locally influential people committed to leadership roles in helping to produce the charter signing and summit, the symbolic importance of Pittsburgh as the city in the United States with the most bridges, and the pressure that had been growing over the years to move the URI global gathering out of San Francisco's Bay area led to a decision in October to hold the event in Pittsburgh. With that decision made, an already stretched staff took a deep breath and started planning in earnest.

On top of all this was an operating budget to fund and a $400,000 debt to retire. The work of raising that money was yet another challenge. Blessedly, it was the first challenge to be met with extraordinary success. As the organization and design team met in late July, Bill Rankin was called out of the meeting to take a phone call from someone with a recent inheritance who had read a URI newsletter and was having trouble finding an organization interested in hearing about her desire to make a donation. As a result of that conversation, in mid-August, the URI received a check for $1 million! Going into what promised to be the most demanding year of its brief existence, the URI found itself, for the first time in its life, out of debt! Though the fund-raising challenges were still significant, an enormous burden had been lifted. A miraculous wind propelled the URI forward toward the birth of a new millennium and the birth of the URI.

This miraculous wind did not seem to be moving the effort to write a purpose statement any nearer a final version everyone could agreed on. The following excerpts from a letter from Charles Gibbs to the members of the purpose statement *listserv* reflects the turmoil and the range of issues heading into the OD Team meeting in late September:

September 13, 1999

DEAR FRIENDS,

Greetings of love and peace. I have been long
absent from the ongoing online conversation about
the proposed new purpose statement....I have,
though, had the opportunity to talk with a few people
over the phone about the ongoing conversation. So
through that and an after-the-fact reading of weeks of
an email dialogue, I have a sense of the depth and
passion of this conversation. I sense, for the first time
in my work for the URI, the potential for the kind of
rift within our community that we hope to heal in the
world. No peace there unless peace here, I tell myself,
and yet, as with the God-No God issue, people
seemed to be committed to differences in wording
that seemed irreconcilable. Some people insist on the
importance of stating the purpose in a positive way
that reflects what we want to build, not what we want
to eliminate. Others feel the power of a negative – to
end religious violence....

I find myself with feet in two places, and while I
am unclear about how to bring them together, I
believe that how we resolve this conflict is extremely
important to the future of the URI.... The foundational methodology for this dialogue has been Appreciative Inquiry with its focus, not on "problem
solving," but on creating a shared, positive vision of
the future we want to create together, on discovering
the positive resources we share and on exploring how
we can bring those resources into alignment in service
of that vision.

I believe in my bones in the power of positive
visioning and find the passionate conviction that we

must be guided by positive images of the future compelling....On the other side of the issue, I have been
in the company of people for whom the stark reality
of religious violence is a daily threat to their ability to
live a free life, a hopeful life, a positive life....

[Though we are challenged in this effort, it seems
to me that we must] push onward to one expression
of the purpose and hopefully settle on it in a way that
leaves all who are a part of this dialogue heard and
having something of substance and power they feel
they can move forward with energetically. As much as
I would like to see a way through to this happy solution, I don't at this point, but I will continue to pray
and work for it.

Again, thanks to all of you who have shared in this
dialogue. I look forward to hearing from those of you
who care to respond.

Love, Charles

Though this letter did not resolve any of the key issues involved
in the purpose discussion, it reassured many participants that essential
differences of opinion were being honored and that every effort
would be made to find a purpose statement that could hold these differences in creative tension.

The organizational design team met September 27–29 and made
the minor revisions to the preamble and principles called for by the
Global Summit. The organizational concept and structure were finalized. The challenging work to translate this concept and structures
into bylaws was begun in earnest through the pro bono services of
attorney Peter Phleger. The deadline was looming to have a set of
draft bylaws ready. The pace and direction of the work led to a decision that the productive partnership between the URI and Dee Hock
and the Chaordic Alliance had accomplished as much as it could.
Peter Phleger, working with Sally Mahé and Charles Gibbs, now led

the effort to have a workable draft ready to present at the meeting.

On Monday, the first day of its September meeting, the organization design team also produced a revision of the purpose statement: *The purpose of the United Religions Initiative is to end religious violence and create cultures of peace and justice as a sacred trust for future generations.* This draft, which lacked key elements of a statement that had been evolving through an Internet conversation, was circulated immediately on the internet listserv with requests for responses that would be considered on Wednesday, when the organization design team would finalize the draft it was to send to the board and TAG for their approval. The responses that came in over the next two days ranged from "Great, let's move forward" to deep disappointment at both the words and the process. Many believed that the email conversation had been little more than window dressing and wondered if they still had a place in the URI. The conversation continued to be a spirited one and focused more intently on how to present the strong feelings of many on the listserv to the Board and TAG when they met in early November.

THE BOARD OF DIRECTORS MEETS WITH TAG

This vortex of engagement set the stage for the first meeting of the URI board of directors and the TAG from November 8–9, 1999, at the Golden Gate Club in San Francisco's Presidio National Park. For the first time outside a Global Summit, the URI was going to make decisions as a globally representative body. TAG members arrived from India, Pakistan, Korea, the United Kingdom, the Netherlands, Kenya, Mozambique, Argentina, Brazil, and New Zealand and from New York and Virginia, bringing with them items of special significance from their faith tradition. In an effort to save money and build community, most were hosted by board members or staff.

As always seemed the case, the URI forced an ambitious agenda in San Francisco. The extent of ambitiousness wasn't yet visible when the participants placed sacred objects on a table and then convened outdoors for an indigenous ceremony of blessing. Three years earlier, the attendees of the first Global Summit had hiked through the Presidio, finishing with a ceremony in the Interfaith Chapel in the Presidio, which was visible just up the hill. As people gathered for this sacred ceremony it was clear how far the URI had come in those years, how near it was to the moment of birth organizers had dreamed of, and how much work still remained to be done.

Betsy Stang led the ceremony, beginning with a traditional smudging with sage for purification and then invoking the four directions and Mother Earth and Father Sky. In this sacred opening, the participants invited the wisdom of their traditions to guide the deliberations. The participants invited those who cared passionately about the URI but were not a part of this gathering to support them with their spirits and spiritual intentions. Following the ceremony, the group took part in a simple appreciative interview:

1. What has been one high point in your URI experience to date?

2. Imagine it is now June 2001, a year after the birth of the new URI. What is the URI doing in your locale and/or globally? What do you feel best about what the URI has accomplished during its first year? What has your role been?

3. In the transition that has taken place between November 1999 and June 2001, what were the most important values that we attended to in making the transition successful? How did the board and TAG take on its challenging responsibility to provide the first example of a global council that serves the whole of the URI?

The sacred opening and the interviews effected a transformation from two separate groups (board and TAG) into one group. This group clearly held the responsibility for guiding the URI through the transition leading to the charter and birth. This change did not remove the necessity for a significant amount of group formation work. How were people going to carry on discussions? Were people's diverse voices going to be invited and honored? Would people truly listen to each other? How would this group make decisions? This group formation work had to take place in relation to some specific issue. It became immediately clear that this issue was the purpose statement.

In retrospect, the agenda was exquisitely crafted and laughably unrealistic. The planning and facilitation team imagined that, through a combination of large and small group work, group members would finish with the PPP and the rest of the charter and bylaws in time for a midafternoon break. At that point, they would move onto such crucial issues as the 72 Hours Project, the Global Summit and Charter Signing, and the 2000 budget. When the midafternoon break arrived, they were still on the purpose statement. At the end of the day they were still on the purpose statement, but had made great progress. Where the group had come in with one proposed purpose statement, it now had ten!

When the group members broke for lunch the second and last day of the meeting, they were still working on the purpose statement; the end seemed nowhere in sight. The group needed every prayer, every moment of silence, and every appreciative practice of listening to keep moving forward. Many times the participants seemed close to agreement, only to have an alternative point of view transform what seemed to be a growing consensus back into the chaotic vortex. Many times the participants seemed close to moving on to the vast amount of essential work still to be done, only to be drawn back into the chaos of continued purpose discussions.

As group members sat down after lunch, facing their last four hours together, agreement seemed farther away than ever. They even discussed having a charter with multiple purpose statements, or with no purpose statement at all, allowing each CC to write its own statement. And yet, somehow, the center held. They reached a crucial moment when frustration and the specter of the important work they had not touched led one member to demand a binding vote to select one of the two surviving statements.

The ensuing vote was a swift and conclusive endorsement of one of the two versions and the process of refining that version. The vote was a ringing endorsement of the value of diverse voices, of collective deliberation, and of the trust of representatives of the collective to finish the work in a way that honored all who had gone before. At the time, it was obvious the group had achieved a hard-won victory on the purpose statement. Months later it became clear that the group had also created an important model for working as a group. This model would allow a great deal of other work to go forward and would be central in the establishment of working committees when the group reconvened in April 2000. The April meeting was four months after a wildly successful 72 Hours Project and two months before the global charter signing and summit. In the closing few hours of its San Francisco meeting, the group touched on the rest of the major agenda items, including the passing of a resolution to keep the "Initiative" in URI, paving the way for the birth, not of the United Religions, but of the truly global United Religions Initiative.

Within a week, a finished purpose statement was circulated to the board/TAG and the listserve group: "The Purpose of the United Religions Initiative is to promote enduring, daily interfaith cooperation, to end religiously motivated violence, and to create cultures of peace, justice, and healing for the Earth and all living beings." It received unanimous support! Michael Ingham was able to find God in this statement. Jinwol Lee was able, as a Buddhist, to embrace it wholeheartedly. The following email, from Craig Russell of the URI United Kingdom, reflected the general response:

> DEAR FRIENDS,
>
> It is now the early hours of 17th November. I have a very deep joy to be with you.
>
> The messages from Sally and Charles must have been posted at approximately the same time as my last one – the one with the note of impatience. I could not hide that the wait for their messages had been a

very painful one. My fear and speculation were of the worst.

Now, with their news of the new purpose statement, it is a time of jubilation and dance. The feeling of a shared, strong, and united heart is one to be held and celebrated.

It will be a struggle to tear down the edifices of war, oppression, and exploitation and build our new homes together. But the great joint purpose we are forming is one which will have the power to unite people of the greatest diversity and the greatest hopes. We are not only saving ourselves from our worst sides, we are seeking to serve God through the gift of the Earth and all that she contains. No higher purpose, no greater calling, no more challenging demand.

Who will be the people to stand against this purpose, call, and demand?

The people who will stand against this will be ourselves. I feel myself implicated by every word I speak. The change will start here, and it will not stop. Wrestling between our higher and lower selves will give us the insights and strength to prepare for the battles ahead.

I am glad I am with you – to learn from your wisdom and skill the ways of this world and the next.

God be with you.

Craig

With the purpose finalized, the organizational design team's work turned to finalizing the rest of the charter and bylaws. Meanwhile, the URI community around the world gave itself with growing excitement to planning for the approaching millennium and the 72 Hours Project. Throughout the summer and into the fall, Paul Andrews and Sarah Talcott had been broadcasting the invitation to join in this project all over the world. What began as a trickle of responses had grown into a steady stream, as groups around the world expressed their intention to participate.

THE IMPROBABLE PAIRS PROJECT

Paul Andrews conceptualized the Improbable Pairs project as a way to have the 72 Hours featured in the flood of media coverage around the time of the millennium. He imagined a series of brief video clips showing improbable pairs of peacemakers. By early October, he had raised the necessary funds to accomplish the project and was in negotiation with a TV producer to have the spots played several times during TV coverage of the millennium. He had identified two "improbable pairs" who were willing to be filmed. The first pair was an Israeli Jew and a Palestinian Muslim, both of who had lost family members in the violence in the Middle East, but who had come together as part of a bereaved families network working for peace. The other pair was a white South African Air Force officer who had been blinded in a car bomb exploded by the African National Congress and a South African of Indian descent who had planned the attack. In early November, the two pairs were flown to San Francisco, where they were filmed telling their stories at the Interfaith Chapel of the Presidio.

As November drew to an end, work was flying forward on the Improbable Pairs project, on the 72 Hours Project, on the bylaws and designing the charter, on plans for the Charter Signing and Summit, and on the finalization of the budget. Everything came to a brief pause, as most of the staff left San Francisco for Cape Town, South Africa, and the third Parliament of the World's Religions. In addition to most of the URI staff, several members of the board and TAG, as well as other URI supporters from around the world, were among the 7,000 plus who attended this historic celebration of interfaith cooperation in a transforming South Africa. Here a maturing URI could contribute to the global interfaith movement. In addition to staffing a booth to provide information about their work, URI members offered and/or participated in many workshops. Several of these people were members of the Assembly of Religious and Spiritual leaders that met separately for three days. Among the highlights: Bishop Swing preaching from the pulpit that had been used by Desmond Tutu during the height of the struggle against apartheid; stirring speeches by the Dalai Lama and Nelson Mandela, who praised churches for their powerful role in educating the generation of black leaders who were able to overturn apartheid; a ceremony dedicating a peace pole in front of the prison on Robben Island, where Mandela had been imprisoned for 17 years. The Parliament was a wonderful opportunity to share the URI's charter and to invite people into the 72 Hours Project, now less than a month away. The Parliament also provided the overworked URI staff with a refreshing, restoring adventure.

THE 72 HOURS PROJECT

When December 31, 1999, dawned in Adelaide, Australia, where interfaith groups would observe three days of prayer vigils and dedicate two peace poles, most of the rest of the world was still asleep, perhaps dreaming of the 72 hours that lay ahead. But in Pakistan, a band of interfaith pilgrims for peace were moving into the seventh day of a 12-day *Aman Ka Safar* (Journey for Peace). Two buses filled with men, women, and children from many religions and from all over Pakistan had begun in Karachi in southern Pakistan. They were bound for Khyber Pass in northern Pakistan on the border with Afghanistan.

As the sun rose around the world on the last day of the old millennium, interfaith activists in 60 countries also rose with the joy of a commitment to make a gift of peace to the new millennium. Their commitment and joy was magnified by the awareness that each local expression was one node in a vast network of 200 projects that would involve over 1 million people.

Throughout Sri Lanka, the Sarvodaya Shramadana Movement sponsored peace meditation programs, walks, and projects to engage youth in environmental conservation. In Manipur, India, three days of interfaith peace programs culminated in an interfaith peace march on January 2, 2000. More than 1,000 people – Muslims, Sikhs, Jains, Baha'is, Christians, Brahma Kumaris, Hindus, and representatives of traditional religious groups such as Meitei Laininglup and Ragang – shared this tremendous event that included messages of peace from different faiths, as well as interreligious cultural programs. As organizer, Dr. T. D. Singh commented, "This has never happened before. This historic event gave great hope to all."

In Addis Ababa, Ethiopia, more than 300 people from 19 countries gathered at the Organization of African Unity headquarters to dedicate a peace monument. Representatives of Ethiopia's four main religions – Orthodox, Muslim, Catholic, and Protestant – offered messages of hope to welcome the millennium with peace. The 72 Hours was launched on December 30 in Maputo, Mozambique, with a 24-hour peace vigil that featured prayers and songs from Catholics, Protestants, Hindus, Baha'is, Buddhists, Jews, Spiritists, and representatives of the Movement for Peace in Mozambique. On January 1, 2000, they would march through Maputo to the Peace Park to hear a speech by the President of Mozambique, to plant 25 trees, and to dedicate a peace pole. As organizer, Dr. Prafultabai Jaiantilal commented, "There were tears in the eyes of some and a deep feeling of oneness, love, and peace among all present. God be praised."

On the morning of December 31 in Rio de Janeiro, 300 people from 25 religious and spiritual traditions gathered on Corcovado Mountain for a celebration of peace through meditation, prayer, chanting, music, and dance. As organizer Andre Porto commented, "The spirit of togetherness and solidarity was strongly present."

In England, Scotland, Ireland, Malta, Hungary, Slovenia, and Bosnia, the Franciscan Missionaries of Mary organized interfaith prayer vigils for peace. Reporting on these events, Sister Rose Fernando added, "The Franciscan Sisters also engaged in acts of service to the larger community, taking opportunities to speak about peace and reconciliation, reaching out to people who suffered violence in their homes, and taking part in a joint procession."

On December 30 in Imjingak, Korea, 200 people from a variety of traditions gathered for an interreligious service focused on the peaceful reunification of Korea. This began a wide array of formal and informal prayer ceremonies in Korea. Venerable Jinwol Lee explained:

> We, URI Korea, sent letters to all religious denominations to invite them to join our 72 hours peace campaign. Since there would be many denominational ceremonies during the time, we had asked them in the letter to hold peace prayer and meditation in the spirit of our campaign. Even though many people could not attend our own ceremonies, we believe that there were millions of people cooperating in the peace campaign. The project was spread out through AP News and major daily newspapers in Seoul.

The 72 Hours was observed by many events in San Francisco's Bay Area, including an interfaith prayer vigil by inmates on Death Row in the San Quentin Federal Penitentiary and three interfaith walking pilgrimages, one of which began at Downs United Methodist Church in Oakland and ended at the Berkeley Buddhist Monastery, where Bishop Swing spoke:

> Never worry about starting out small.... The idea that Buddhists and Methodists can make peace (and this was not possible a short time ago) – that news is going to inspire Hindus and Sikhs, Muslims and Jews to make the same discovery. Small and large isn't the real measure. The measure is how sincere your heart is. The old century of never looking past your borders is over. Those old walls have come down, and we must now find the people behind those walls. We must build our new world on mutual respect, harmony, and the happiness we feel today.

All over the world, often in the shadow of raucous celebrations, extraordinary, ordinary interfaith peace activists offered living messages of hope for a new millennium. There was no illusion that the world would be instantly transformed over 72 hours, but it was clear that many lives were. The seeds of peace, justice, and healing were planted anew in over a million hearts, and with that planting came a renewed vision and commitment, eloquently expressed by Father James Channan at the end of the peace pilgrimage in Pakistan:

> There are tears in my eyes right now as I am sending you this glorious news that we have arrived back safely in Lahore after successfully completing our *Aman Ka Safar*.... What happened in Khyber Pass was something that never, ever happened before in the history of Pakistan. There were believers of Muslim, Christian, Baha'I, Sikh, Hindu, and Parsi communities. We sang songs of peace, [shared] recitation from different Holy Scriptures and messages of peace from different participants. We prayed for peace in the whole world. Our reaching to Khyber after traveling more than 1,500 miles is not the end of our peace journey, but the BEGINNING.

JOURNEY TO THE CHARTER SIGNING

With the turn of the millennium behind them, the URI staff, with the addition of webmaster Kristin Swenson, turned their attention to preparing for an early February conference call involving the board and TAG. The sole purpose of this call was to give final approval to the charter and bylaws, a tremendous amount of complicated material that had to be reviewed, amended if necessary, and approved in the space of two hours. Brobeck, Phleger and Harrison hosted the call in one of their conference rooms high above San Francisco. The atmosphere was electric, as person after person called in from around the world, until the entire TAG group was present.

The meeting began with prayer and moved immediately into approval of the charter. The preamble and purpose were approved very quickly, but things slowed down when the group reached the principles. Annie Imbens Fransen, a member of the TAG from the Netherlands, had indicated that she would propose a new principle calling for equal participation of women and men in all aspects of the URI. Having worked for two years to develop a broadly accepted group of 19 principles, it seemed likely that this proposal would either be dismissed quickly, leaving a bitter residue, or would lead to a drawn-out discussion that would derail the entire proceeding. The first person to speak after Annie proposed her new principle was Mohinder Singh from New Delhi. He stated how important he thought this principle was, because in India, people would believe they had adequate diversity merely if different religions were represented. They would never stop to think that no women were involved unless the URI principles clearly stated this was important. There was little further discussion. The proposed principle passed unanimously, with a provision that its wording be made consistent with the rest of the principles.

Then a second additional principal was proposed. Since its beginning, the URI had had to counter charges that it sought to make one religion or to blend religions together. This concern had led to the principle that the URI was a bridge-building organization and not a religion. The logical extension of this principal was a proposed principle that stated that the URI encouraged its members to deepen their roots in their own traditions. This principle also passed unanimously. Having accomplished this monumental work, the group moved with deliberate haste through the rest of the charter and the bylaws and the CC and Affiliate application packets, proposing small changes here and there, but giving final approval to the entire package, as the two hours scheduled for the call elapsed. To celebrate, the entire group was led by Masankho Banda, an artist peace activist from Malawi who had joined the staff part-time, in a rousing rendition of a song, "Let Loose the Spirit, Let Loose the Joy." And with that, the charter-writing process came to an end. The work to enroll CCs and Affiliates was begun in earnest as the URI journeyed toward the charter signing and the Global Summit.

The timeline the URI had established required that CC and Affiliate applications be returned to the office in time for the April meeting of the boards. The global staff sent out the application packets, in many cases following them with consultations about unanswered questions and unanticipated issues. This was the first of many times the URI realized the deep wisdom in Dee Hock's insistence to be content with "good enough for now." It was clear that no matter how long the global staff might have taken to refine the application package and no matter how deeply the organizational design team had explored all the possible issues and stumbling blocks in the bylaws (and the organizational design team did explore deeply), it would have been impossible to anticipate all the issues that would come up. "Good enough for now" helped the organization find a mind-set that was open to acknowledging the inevitable imperfections in the fruits of its four-year labors and to be prepared for learning and adaptation that had the potential to surprise, frustrate, and enlighten as the global staff watched the pages fly off the calendar and June draw ever nearer.

The journey to the charter signing and summit grew even more challenging in mid-February when Paul Andrews, the driving force behind the 72 Hours Project, left the URI to play a major leadership role in a new effort to connect technology, business, and philanthropy to serve social good.

CHARLES JOURNEYS TO INDIA

In March, Charles Gibbs traveled to India to connect with potential CCs in Imphal, Manipur state; Mumbai; and Delhi. Manipur, which had hosted an inspiring series of events for the 72 Hours Project, is a high plain nestled inside nine rings of mountains in far eastern India, between Bangladesh and Myanmar. A place of physical beauty and warm, open people, it is plagued by violence from many separatist groups with a stated purpose of severing ties with India. Its geographic location makes drugs a problem. These two issues combine to make Manipuri youth particularly vulnerable.

The aspiring URI CC, which emerged from a group that engaged in the 72 Hours Project, expressed a deep yearning to be an effective force for positive change in this context. The group had planned a large public gathering while the URI's executive director was visiting. To publicize the event, members produced several large banners proclaiming a program about the United Religions Initiative, one of which was hung over the major route from the airport into town. It was an extraordinary testimony to the URI vision that what had been planted in the soul of a sleepless bishop in February 1993 was now planted in the soil and souls in Manipur, India. The wonder continued to unfold as members of the local URI group peppered the executive director with questions, which were prefaced by memorized passages from the charter that clearly inspired and challenged the members. Charles Gibbs later reflected:

> Here I was, nearly 12,000 miles from home, in a part of India between Bangladesh and Myanmar that I hadn't even known existed until I looked it up on a map shortly before the trip, being greeted by members of the Manipur Chapter of the United Religions Initiative! It wasn't that long ago that the URI was an impossible dream shared by a foolish few, and here it was taking root in this remote part of India, where, as Dr. T. D. Singh, who is identified in the program as "His Holiness Bhaktisvarupe Damodara Swami" and referred to informally as "Maharaji," informed me as we were flying in that World War II had ended. I looked at my name and "UNITED RELIGIONS INITIATIVE" both in large letters on the banner and found myself wondering what those idiosyncratic collections of letters signified to this group of 200 or

more people who had shown up on a Sunday afternoon. What had they come out to hear? I found
myself then, and still find myself as I write this,
yearning for the opportunity for those people to
engage in the type of visioning conferences we have
sponsored around the world so I could share with
them in uncovering what the code "UNITED RELI-
GIONS INITIATIVE" pointed to that matched
some deep yearning in themselves.

In addition to its deep commitment to build cultures of peace,
justice, and healing in Manipur, the URI group was eager to take its
place in the global community that was to gather in Pittsburgh. Dr. T.
D. Singh, an internationally recognized leader in the exploration of
the interface between science and religion, as well as one of the spiritual heirs of Swami Prabupadha, founder of the Hare Krishna movement, pledged to bring three of Manipur's famed drummers to
Pittsburgh to perform at the charter-signing ceremony and throughout the week.

The whole URI staff, the production team, and the leadership in
Pittsburgh were simultaneously forming a new partnership and planning the URI's most ambitious global gathering to date. The process
was one of getting acquainted as people worked through a dizzying
array of issues — from those of organizational culture and program
design to practical details so essential to a successful summit. The
group went through cycles of frustration at the challenges of complex
communication and clarity about roles and responsibilities. Group
members also experienced moments of profound epiphany as insights
emerged in unexpected ways from unexpected sources at just the right
moment. With each passing week, the group learned more about
trusting, letting go, holding on and working hard, and of living in the
questions and demanding answers in a timely way.

As so often happened in the URI, initial grand visions tested in
the fires of practicality, priorities, and budget constraints found new

shape. The group had a grand initial vision of holding the charter signing in the middle of one of Pittsburgh's many bridges, followed by a celebratory boat ride on the three rivers that meet in Pittsburgh, ending at a large local park with a festival of faiths and fireworks. Spurred by the insightful counsel of local leadership, headed by Dr. Karen Plavan, and financial pressures, these grand plans were simplified. The group settled on Carnegie Music Hall, a stately, majestic space of great cultural significance in Pittsburgh, and began serious planning for a major production to honor four years of groundbreaking work.

Through all of this, Gurudev Khalsa extended his experience of leading the design and facilitation of URI's summits by skillfully weaving together leadership teams to deal with Sacred Space Coordination, Meeting Room and Break-out Space Preparation, Regional Agenda and Leadership Coordination, Appreciative Inquiry and Storytelling Session, Open-Space Sessions, and Plenary Sharing. Team membership included the URI's global staff, the board and TAG, local leaders from Pittsburgh, and members of the URI's global community. At times, the team's size and diversity made decision making a challenge, but inclusion triumphed over a more narrowly construed desire for efficiency. The group moved forward, forming a new and deeper community each step of the way, making mistakes; forgiving each other; experiencing moments of great insight, great humility, great frustration, and great joy. These people were an imperfect human community committed to high service.

At its March meeting, the URI's board voted to replace its existing bylaws with the bylaws for the new global URI, to become effective upon the signing of the charter and the acceptance of the founding members on June 26. The board also voted to expand and add the TAG as new members. The merging of these two groups, which had happened in fact at the November meeting, now became law. This group would become the Interim Global Council when the charter was signed, and the former board would be officially designated as the Transition Advisory Council, with the special role of providing guidance and continuity during the early years of the new global URI. Also, through March and April, CC and Affiliate applications flowed in and were collated to be presented to the newly constituted board in a systematic way at its April meeting.

The April meeting provided an opportunity to hear, firsthand, stories of the 72 Hours Project from around the world. Also, the group created a committee structure to help it carry out its work. Without question, the highlight of the meeting was the review and approval of applications by potential CCs and Affiliates. The process began with prayerful silence and a request for wisdom and guidance as the board undertook this deep responsibility. For the next two hours, each board member in turn read the name, purpose, decision-making mechanism, and membership of a potential CC and proposed the approval of its application. Following whatever discussion was required, the group voted. Every CC applying for membership was approved. Following each vote for approval, the entire board and staff recited a prayer: "May the members of the (name) CC fulfill their aspirations and live in peace." A similar process was followed for the Affiliate applications. By the end of the process, the board had approved 48 CCs and 1 MCC, which comprised 5 more CCs and over 50 Affiliates, whose membership would become official with the signing of the charter. In those two hours, the seeds of vision and invitation that had launched the movement to create the URI took organizational form. Though the charter signing was still two months away, a new chapter in the URI's life had begun.

Those two months passed with a speed that was at times frightening, considering all the work still to be done on both the production and the program of the charter signing/summit. Each day revealed how much work had been done and how much work remained.

THE MOMENT ARRIVES

URI CHARTER SIGNING
PITTSBURGH, PENNSYLVANIA
JUNE 25–30, 2000

Suddenly it was late June and people boarded flights in Manipur and Calcutta and Delhi and Mumbai and Lahore and Seoul and Denpasar and Manila and London and Nairobi and Kampala and Johannesburg and Addis Ababa and Brussels and Buenos Aires and Quito and Caracas and Rio de Janeiro and Sao Paulo and Trinidad and Christ Church and Osaka and Salt Lake City and Denver and Vancouver and Mexico City and Guatemala City and New York City and San Francisco and Los Angeles and Kuala Lumpur and Cairo and Tel Aviv and Eindhoven and Washington, D.C. and on and on, and flew toward Pittsburgh. Bishops and priests and sheikhs and rabbis and gurus and roshis and shamans and staff carriers and on and on came to Pittsburgh. Teachers and artists and peace activists and journalists and scholars and environmental activists and organizational consultants and students and volunteers and staff and on and on came to Pittsburgh. Women and men and young and old and black and white and red and brown and yellow and short and tall and round and thin and on and on came to Pittsburgh. Old friends and soon-to-be new friends, people who had been on the URI journey from the first moment, and people who were brand new to URI came to Pittsburgh. Pittsburgh, the city of bridges, opened her arms and received everyone.

The San Francisco production team and volunteers were greeted by their counterparts in Pittsburgh. Then the program staff and the diverse planning teams arrived for a day of final planning before the summit began. Many, including members from Pittsburgh, were new to the URI, often meeting face-to-face for the first time. Over the preceding months, they had experienced the blessing (ease of communication) and the curse (a deluge of messages) of email communication. Now came the blessing of being together on the eve of a history-making event. While the program people planned and the production team set up spaces and prepared to receive people journeying from all over the world, Katie Ackerly (a high school senior, daughter of URI staffer Sally Mahé, and a gifted graphic artist) created story-boards telling the story of URI work around the world and information panels that would orient the work for the week. The panels explained the Global Support Network and the path from the charter signing through the selection of the first Global Council to the first Global Assembly scheduled for June 2001. The story-boards offered insights and raised questions and invited people to form strategy sessions around common interests. All of this graphically-rendered information aimed to create a meeting space that was visually alive, informative, enabling, and interactive and that reflected back to the delegates the work they were doing.

The Interim Global Council (IGC) met on early Sunday, the gathering day, to go over its roles and responsibilities during the week, focusing primarily on the IGC's pivotal role in the charter-signing ceremony and on its role as participant/listeners at the regional meetings.

The participants gathered, over 200 strong, on Sunday, June 25, 2000, five years to the day after the interfaith service at Grace Cathedral, on the campus of Carnegie Mellon University. A formal opening began outside with an indigenous ceremony invoking the four directions and asking blessing on the gathering, asking that the group gather in a good way and work together for peace and harmony.

Then the group followed Masankho Banda and the drummers from Manipur into an auditorium for a brief program of welcome before walking down the hill to the Cathedral of Learning at the University of Pittsburgh. There, as everyone shared a multicultural buffet, members of different religious communities in Pittsburgh gave offerings from their diverse cultures — song, dance, music, drama, words — to the delegates.

The next morning, June 26, 2000, 55 years to the day after the signing of the United Nations Charter, the summit formally convened in a large upper room at Carnegie Mellon. The room was filled with Katie Ackerly's vivid graphics, photos, and quotations representing the URI past, present, and future. The air was filled with excitement and people began to anticipate the extraordinary event. Following a general welcome, a sacred opening, and an overview of the week, the balance of the morning was filled with stories of the URI in action in different regions of the world and with appreciative interviews, using the following questions:

1. A STORY OF "BIRTH" FROM YOUR LIFE EXPERIENCES. All of us have had the experience of being present or witnessing the birth of someone or something—the birth of a child or a precious idea, a miracle moment, etc. The experience of new life, of a birth, is often overwhelming, filled with joy, inspiration, fear, awe, or hope.

   A. If you had to name one experience—the birth of a child or a precious idea, a historic moment, a personal shift, etc.—that stands out as a most profound experience of birth in your life so far, what would it be? What happened? Your feelings?

   B. Each of our religious or spiritual traditions has beliefs, practices, or rituals at special times—as when a child is born. Can you share with me something about your religion, community, or spiritual practice from the perspective of its special rituals, ceremonies, prayers, or practices at times of birth or creation? An example?

C. Now describe *your story* as it relates to the
birthing of the URI. . . . What calls you to
this work?
- Ways you have helped make this birthing
possible? Locally? Globally?
- What is the most memorable, powerful,
or significant experience you have had in
your life journey toward interfaith cooperation, peace building, and change?

2. IMAGINE URI GROWING UP—BECOMING STRONG,
HEALTHY, ALIVE, AND CAPABLE OF LIVING ITS
PURPOSE AND BUILDING A BETTER WORLD. The
year is 2010; it is now exactly ten years from the
year of URI's charter signing. From the perspective of URI's great and unknown potential, visualize the kind of URI you would most like to see
in your part of the world and globally—as it
"grows up" beyond its infancy.

Thinking both locally and globally, can you
describe what you see in your imagination? What
does URI look like in your region? Globally? For
example, what do you see in terms of people,
important projects/priorities, ways of being,
connections, and impacts?

3. ONE ANCIENT METAPHOR FOR URI USED
REPEATEDLY IN THE DREAM AND ORGANIZATION
DESIGN PHASES WAS OF INDRA'S NET, which is
about the cosmic web of interrelatedness extend-
ing infinitely in all directions of the universe.
Every intersection of the intertwining web is set

with a glistening jewel, in which all parts of the whole are reflected. Imagine an organization where the reflections making up each CC are an endless amplification of strengths mirroring onto one another, sparkling and glistening. It is an image that is coming alive right now.

A. Thinking very concretely now and from the perspective of your region, what are the three most important things we can do this year to support, encourage, and collaborate in each other's development as CCs?

B. If there were a knowledge-sharing e-network connecting all parts of the URI–a treasury and storehouse of knowledge, training programs, religious wisdom, best practices (e.g. funding proposals that have worked), and empowering stories–what kinds of knowledge would be helpful to you, your region, and your work as CCs?

C. As you think about the year ahead, what is the smallest thing we could do that would have the largest impact on nurturing CCs and their development?

The group ended the morning early to allow for lunch and for people to change into their ceremonial dress in time to follow the drummers down the hill to the Carnegie Music Hall. Everyone waited in the spacious foyer where the reception would be held as the production crew worked frantically inside the hall to iron out last minute technical glitches. The drummers and young Hindu women bearing flowers then led 300 people in religious and cultural dress from 39 spiritual traditions from 44 countries into the music hall. A ceremony five years in the making began.

A shofar, a gong, a conch shell — sacred summonses from three traditions. The participants entered sacred time, sacred space, engaged in a sacred task.

The stage was spare — just flowers. The URI star, created four years before by Walter Gray, projected on a large screen. The charter lay on a large rectangular wooden table, waiting to be signed. The candle, guarded so carefully, had disappeared at the last minute, so the only fire that was burning was the one in people's hearts.

As people speaking in different languages intoned "Welcome to the birth of the United Religions Initiative," Charles Gibbs and Zeenat Shaukat Ali, cohosts of the event, walked onto the stage. They welcomed everyone, honoring the interfaith work that had come before the URI and sounded a theme that would carry through the week: As momentous as signing the charter was, its significance would ultimately depend on the URI's success in making the charter's vision and values a living reality around the world. Success would not be measured by words on the page but by people's actions to promote enduring, daily interfaith cooperation; to end religiously motivated violence; and to create cultures of peace, justice, and healing for the Earth and all living beings.

Mrs. Gedong Oka, revered Gandhian and member of Indonesia's Parliament, led a brief meditation. At the end, she led those assembled in singing a simple song, "Pray for the Peace of Humanity."

Following the meditation, Masankho Banda presented a moving story of interfaith cooperation for peace, which led into a video about the URI. The spoken text was the preamble to the charter:

> We, people of diverse religions, spiritual expres-
> sions, and indigenous traditions, hereby establish the
> United Religions Initiative to promote enduring, daily
> interfaith cooperation, to end religiously motivated
> violence, and to create cultures of peace, justice, and
> healing for the Earth and all living beings.

The images on the screen presented vibrant images of the URI
global, grassroots, interfaith community engaged in dialogue, prayer,
meditation, and action.

Following the video, Bishop Swing spoke about the URI, from
inception to this moment. When he finished his remarks, the bishop
invited Dr. Karen Plavan, representing the Pittsburgh community,
onto the stage and thanked her on behalf of the global URI. Dr. Plavan then introduced Etta Cox, a local jazz singer, who electrified the
crowd with a powerful rendition of a song she had written especially
for the occasion, "Keep Your Hope Alive." This song led into a second video, this one displaying images of the 72 Hours Project from
around the world, as voices spoke words of wisdom and hope from
the world's faith traditions.

As the video ended, Sri Ravi Peruman, of the URI board, and
Ms. Anastasia White, from Johannesburg, South Africa, and the
Interfaith Youth Core, took the stage to moderate a series of greetings
by conference call from URI members around the world, including
those gathered at the UN, at the Camoldolese monastery in Big Sur,
California, and at the Wilgespruit Fellowship Centre in Roodepoort,
South Africa. Sadly, technology failed at that moment. Those gathered never heard the greetings, but they did find out later that the people prepared to offer greetings had enjoyed a mini-summit among
themselves as they spoke with each other for over 30 minutes while
waiting to participate in the ceremony.

The URI's board of directors was then invited to the stage. After
a moment of silence ensued, the invitation to offer silent blessings
from each person's tradition followed. Out of the silence, the purpose

was read by Charles C. K. Franz, a young boy from Pittsburgh, and then by everyone else, in unison. One by one, the members of the board read the 21 principles. The moment to sign the charter had arrived.

Bishop Swing and the board chair, Ms. Rita Semel, stepped to the table together, and together they signed. The bishop leaned over and kissed this document so long in the making, this document filled with equal and extraordinary amounts of hope and challenge. As the rest of the board added their signatures, signature sheets that would be added to the charter book circulated through the audience and the names of the people who had signed over the Internet scrolled down the screen. Masankho Banda led the assembly in singing.

When everyone had finished signing, the board, now officially the Interim Global Council, convened a special meeting to formally accept into membership the previously ratified CCs and Affiliates. As the names of the CCs from around the world were read, their members in attendance stood, figurative points of light illuminating a troubled world. When the charter had been signed, the Interim Global Council inaugurated, and founding CCs and Affiliates accepted, the cohosts proclaimed, "The United Religions Initiative is born! The United Religions Initiative is born! The United Religions Initiative is born!" Computer-generated fireworks exploded on the screen, and the participants erupted in cheers.

Representatives of the Interfaith Youth Core then came onto the stage with a group message of hope and vision. As they finished, the drummers returned to the stage and led a procession from the hall into the foyer, where delegates and those who had come only for the ceremony celebrated the birth of this new hope for the world. They knew that four days of hard work — the prelude to lifetimes of hard work — lay ahead; but in that moment, the ecstatic focus was on what had been accomplished. On June 26, 2000, in the City of Bridges, the sun had shone on a new day for the URI and humanity.

The URI's commitment to action was made even more real in the days following the signing ceremony, as delegates went to work creating a vision and plans for a growing URI presence around the world. During long working days punctuated by periods of prayer and meditation as well as song and dance, the participants met in regional groups to build networks of support for URI development in particular parts of the world. Delegates from Israel and Egypt discussed interreligious peacebuilding possibilities in that part of the world. Delegates from India and Pakistan explored how they might develop a credible interfaith effort to support peace between those two countries. Delegates from Asia and the Pacific discussed the possibility of building on the 72 Hours Project with a project generating 72 days of interfaith pilgrimages for peace around the world.

Latin American delegates planned a major conference of indigenous peoples in Quito, Ecuador, in October to help heal the relationship between indigenous peoples and people of mainstream religion whose ancestors sought to destroy the indigenous culture. European delegates planned a European charter signing at the UNESCO headquarters in Paris in November as a major step forward for the URI in Europe and as a sign of the partnership URI enjoyed with the UNESCO Cultures of Peace initiative. Delegates from Africa discussed peacebuilding efforts in Ethiopia, community education in Uganda, and the possibility of an innovative AIDS prevention program in Sub-Saharan Africa. People from North America discussed a first-ever North American Conference and the positive role North America could take in helping to generate financial resources for URI development around the world. Buddhists from Sri Lanka and a Christian from New Zealand discussed a cooperative interfaith effort to deal with land mines in Sri Lanka.

THE OPEN-SPACE CONCEPT

In addition to time dedicated to regional meetings, there were periods of "open space," where people crossed continental and regional boundaries to work together on a wide variety of issues, including the rights of women and children, the environment, interfaith cooperation through the arts, active peacebuilding, creating CCs, the art of sacred listening, and a vision of a global network to support the future development of the URI around the world. The following piece, prepared for summit participants by Dr. Diana Whitney, characterized the spirit, form, and content of this work.

Welcome to Open Space

Open Space is a simple process for self-organizing among large groups of people who are working together on very complex projects; for example, creating global interfaith cooperation. It is a process used by businesses and communities around the world.

We will be in Open Space for one and a half days — all day Tuesday and Wednesday morning. Tuesday is devoted to sessions that will be convened by participants. We have four time blocks within which sessions will be scheduled. Time blocks range from 1.5–2.0 hours. Wednesday morning we will gather again as a whole community in home groups and plenary to discuss what we learned on Tuesday and to consider implications for the Global Council, which will meet on Thursday afternoon.

Participating in Open Space is Very Easy

1. Anyone can convene a session.
2. You can go to any session you choose. We suggest going to those that sing to your heart. No one is required to go to any session. In Open Space, we say, "Whoever comes are the right people."
3. The "Law of Two Feet" is the only law of Open Space. It says, "If you are not enjoying yourself or contributing in a way that matters to you, use your two feet, leave, and go someplace else." In

Open Space, it is okay to leave one session and go
to another. It is also okay to sit around and wait
for something interesting to happen.

4. In Open Space, there are Bumble Bees and Butterflies. Bumble Bees go from flower to flower cross-
pollinating. In Open Space, Bumble Bees go from
session to session sharing good ideas. Butterflies
are beautiful and attract attention. In Open Space,
Butterflies sit around, attract attention and start
spontaneous dialogues and activities.

The Focus of Our Open Space is
"The URI: Nurturing Our Growth"

Convening an Open-Space Session

You may convene a session on any subject you
choose. We ask only that the session be of interest to
you and be related to the United Religions' preamble,
purpose and principles.

Open-Space sessions are offered as your gift to
the community.

You may convene a session to share ideas, information, or practices; to collect input on a topic
important to you; to plan a project; to build relationships; to educate and learn; and/or to share an activity or experience.

Open-Space sessions may be conversational or
experiential.

Conveners must show up and facilitate their session.

To convene a session, simply write your name and
the name of your session on a large piece of paper.

Please print clearly. We will hang your paper on the wall for all to see.

When session announcements are made, join the line and make a 15-second announcement about your session. Tell us the title and give a brief description of what will happen during the session.

During or after your session, please record the following information:

1. Title of the session.
2. Names of the convener(s) and, if appropriate/feasible, others who participated.
3. Key ideas, outstanding questions, and decisions taken during the session.

Have Fun!

As the regional gatherings generated visions and plans for the URI in action in various parts of the world, the open-space sessions manifested the URI's global connectedness. Together they created the beginnings of an ambitious local-regional-global agenda for the URI into the future.

Midway through the summit, the doors were opened for members of the larger Pittsburgh community to experience this extraordinary global community and to share its vision. The evening opened with an electrifying performance by the drummers from Manipur and was sanctified by blessings from different traditions from different parts of the world. Bishop Swing raised the vision of returning to Pittsburgh in 2050 to celebrate the 50th anniversary of the charter signing and challenged all who were present to work so they might celebrate how far they had come together in realizing the URI's purpose. Three young women from Pittsburgh shared their aspirations for interfaith engagement with a clarity and depth of expression that bore witness to the dynamic presence of young people in the interfaith movement.

Swami Agnivesh, a leader of the Arya Samaj movement, chair of the United Nation's Trust Fund on Contemporary Forms of Slavery, and member of a URI CC in New Delhi, India, spoke passionately of the work the URI must do to help abolish all forms of slavery and bonded labor and to be a voice for a just economic system around the world. Sister Laetitia Borg, a Franciscan nun and leader of the URI effort in Ethiopia, painted a vivid picture of URI work for peace in the war between Ethiopia and Eritrea. She called for the URI to be an active force for peace all over the world, preparing for the day when wars would not be the rule but the rare exception and when active peacebuilding pervaded every corner of the globe and every area of human endeavor.

On Thursday afternoon, the IGC gathered in the midst of the rest of the participants for its first official meeting following the charter signing. The charter said this about the global council:

> The purpose of the global council is to support the membership in making real the vision and values of the Preamble, Purpose, and Principles. The global council's central spirit is not one of control, but rather one of service informed by deep listening to the hopes and aspirations of the whole URI community. The global council will inspire and support the URI worldwide community in cooperative global action. It is envisioned that their deliberations will be tempered with tenderness for one another and for the Earth community. It is envisioned that their actions will reflect a yearning to help people of the URI fulfill their aspirations to be a positive force for peace, justice, and healing in the world.

In the spirit of the charter, the IGC meeting was devoted to its members offering their observations about the hopes and aspirations of the whole URI community as they had heard them during the course of the summit, by being listener/participants in both the regional meetings and the open-space sessions.

On Friday morning, the summit ended as it had begun – in a circle outdoors around a sacred center. Summit participants had been asked to bring a stone that had particular significance to them to the summit. In the closing ceremony, people were asked to arrange themselves in groups of three or four to share the significance of the stone they had brought and to share their hopes for the future, going forward from the summit. The stones were placed in the sacred center, forming a mosaic of rootedness in the depths of the diverse traditions, in the aspirations for a better future, and in the individual and collective commitments to make that future a reality. People from different traditions offered their prayers and spiritual intentions for the future. People then took a stone from the center to take home. Some took the stone they had brought with them, now filled with the energy of this global gathering. Others took a stone offered by a sister or brother from another faith from another part of the world. Two of the stones were offered to the URI global office. One was a chip from the Berlin Wall, offered in the hope that the URI might continue the belief of a new future for humanity that was exemplified in the fall of the Berlin Wall. The other stone was a 500-year-old brick from the Golden Temple in Amritsar, India, the sacred center of the Sikh world, offered with the prayer that the ethos of interfaith cooperation that is built into Sikhism might grow and flourish in the URI.

As the summit ended, people returned home inspired by the lived experience of a global, interfaith community dedicated to peace building. They returned carrying visions, hopes, and plans to put them into action. A Sikh leader from Washington, D.C., expressed a commitment to create a Cooperation Circle of Parliamentarians, aiming to forge bonds of interfaith cooperation among elected officials in governments all over the world. A URI leader from Brazil returned home and helped organize an interfaith ceremony for peace that attracted 25,000 participants as part of a national movement for peace in Brazil. And people around the world began to explore a plan for 72 days of peace pilgrimages around the world.

With the charter signing in Pittsburgh, the global URI was born. In the days that followed, the infant URI began its first movements out into the world. Through the inspiration, commitment, and sacrifice of people around the world, the months and years ahead would see this infant mature into an effective, transformative global organization engaged in enduring, daily cooperation for peace all over the world.

CHAPTER 6

Everyone knew it would take many years to see whether this URI garden would grow into its potential. But even at this early stage, the potential was inspiring and the fruit that was growing was changing local communities, and through them, the world.

Living into the Ideals of the URI

The weeks and months following the birth of the URI were like those following any birth — filled with astonishment that the birth had actually happened and with exhaustion and facing a rising tide of new questions about what lay ahead. The URI found itself in a place similar to where it had been in 1996. Then, it had a compelling vision, but more questions than answers, about how to draft a charter and create an organization that would honor diverse voices and embrace people from diverse faith traditions from all over the world. Now the vision had received inspiring expression in a compelling charter, but the movement into the URI's future was surrounded more by questions than answers.

The journey to the charter had been so consuming that little time had been devoted to life after the charter was signed. The original journey had started down a path in the dark. Now the walk in the dark continued. The URI had become a community of people who trusted each other, who were learning how to walk in the dark together... and who were learning how to live with questions that shaped the next steps. After Pittsburgh, no one really knew how he or she would succeed in creating the kind of global organization called for in the charter. The organization that had been envisioned was magnificent, and nothing like it had existed before! The PPP and organizational design were visionary and evolutionary, but they had not been field-tested.

The infant URI found itself dealing with a jumble of questions. How would the global URI help CCs thrive? What kind of organizational structures and coordination were needed to continue to support and sustain the URI and nurture the flourishing of CCs in the years ahead? What kind of practical support was needed to develop the URI in different regions? How would global staff and regional staff develop and work together? How would the URI take advantage of the existing spiritual wisdom, expertise in organizational development, and advances in technology? How would the URI community build and sustain an organization that could give rise to unlimited numbers of local interfaith groups that were locally rooted and at the same time be able to act effectively as a collective global force for good? How would the URI deepen its identity as a global spiritual community of integrity in service to the sacred? How would the URI create the new learning it would need?

Where would the journey lead now? How would this newly established community of friends live into the PPP and its new identity as a locally effective global organization? How would members sustain the friendships and the possibilities for positive change they had experienced together? Would membership in the URI continue to make a difference in people's lives? Would people's identity as new URI CC members catalyze a spiritual transformation in themselves, in their communities, and in the world? What forces, actions, and behaviors would inhibit and constrain the natural emergence and growth of this organization? How would the values implicit in the URI PPP come alive and truly guide the CC's and the URI's global community?

With the charter signed, the URI had established a new level of knowing and created a vast new unknown to inhabit. In large measure, that unknown would become known through action. Given the nature of the URI, much of that action would be lived out in local settings around the world as fledgling CCs moved past the euphoria of the birth into the work of enduring daily interfaith cooperation. As the URI sought to realize its form and purpose, it would also be carried out with ever-increasing effectiveness on national, regional, and global levels. For years to come, Insh'Allah (God-willing), the URI would be a living experiment, from Buenos Aires to Islamabad, from Jerusalem to Harare, from Seoul to San Francisco.

THE GLOBAL URI

ADDIS ABABA, ETHIOPIA

In Addis Ababa, Ethiopia, the local CC deepened its efforts to be a consistent force for interfaith peace building during the war between Ethiopia and Eritrea. As a testimony to the CC's work of enduring, daily interfaith cooperation, a plaque with the following text hung on the wall of its office:

> On the Occasion of the first National Conference on
> "Building a Culture of Peace – Character, Family
> and Public Service"
> The United Nations Association of Ethiopia,
> Family Federation
> for World Peace and United Nations
> Volunteers Program
> Hereby awarded this
> **Certificate of Merit**
> to
> **United Religions Initiative**
> In recognition of its outstanding Contribution in
> Pioneering in Ethiopia for the first time interfaith
> dialogue among diverse religious groups to build
> a Culture of Peace and create harmony.
> This Certificate of Merit is given
> on this 22nd, December 2000.

The brave work in Ethiopia was one of many small fruits growing around the world from tiny seeds of hope planted in the ground
of shared visions of a future — a future where hatred is transformed
by the healing power of sacrificial love; where violence is transformed
into peace; where children are not taught distrust, enmity, and violence, but mutual respect, cooperation, and peace. Everyone knew it
would take many years to see whether this URI garden would grow
into its potential. But even at this early stage, the potential was inspiring and the fruit that was growing was changing local communities
and, through them, the world.

QUITO, ECUADOR
SEPTEMBER 2000

While the CC in Addis was hard at work locally, with dreams of
being an agent of growth sub-regionally, one could also have traveled
west across Africa, the Atlantic Ocean, and most of South America to
the beauty and thin air of Quito, Ecuador, 9,000' above sea level.
There the URI was convening a regional conference for indigenous
peoples. In September 2000, following Luis Dolan's vision and inspiration, the URI sponsored a conference attended by 60 indigenous
people from 10 pueblos: Nahual (Nicaragua); Miskito (Nicaragua),
Kuna (Panama), Mapuche (Chile), Maya (Guatemala and Mexico),
Shuar (Ecuador), Kolla (Argentina), Quichua (Ecuador), Aymara
(Bolivia), and Inca (Peru). Over the space of three days, the participants shared their ancient "cosmovisions." Their stories revealed a
view of the cosmos that exhibited no distinction between religion and
culture, between the sacred and the secular. The participants also
made it clear what a devastating toll the European conquest had taken
on their traditions. A Nahual man from Nicaragua gave the following
explanation:

> Colonization, primarily by other religions, has
> been a damaging factor for the Nahual. We have lost
> our land, lost our language. We have a fractured cul-

ture that we are struggling to reclaim. We honor the
Earth and are conscious about wise resource use, but
so much has been lost — culture, history, education.
Our sad reality is that we have lost our cosmovision
and our practice of spirituality. We are seeking out
Nahuals from other countries and other sisters and
brothers — the Mayans, for instance — to try to re-
create our cosmovision. Religion is a force that
divides us. For instance, my mother is Roman
Catholic and my brother is Protestant, and they
have a very hard time being together because of
their religious differences.

By the end of the three days, a strong sense of solidarity existed
among these diverse peoples, who delighted in the common ground
they had discovered while celebrating their diversity and uniqueness.
They left with a strong commitment to support each other in their
efforts to reclaim their sacred traditions and to explore dialogue with
the colonizing religions (primarily different branches of Christianity),
recognizing that some who attended this conference were fed by both
their indigenous cosmovision and Christianity. The path to healing
and wholeness was not fully clear. Still, this group took a courageous
and historic step down that path. Not surprisingly, the question of
resources to continue the work presented a major challenge. But, the
URI believed this CC was making an important pioneering effort and
pledged its support to continue what had developed in Quito.

Sadly, the Quito conference was the final URI effort for Luis
Dolan, interfaith pioneer and URI developer in Latin America, who
died from a massive heart attack less than two weeks later as he was
sitting down for lunch with friends, having just celebrated Mass. The
depth of loss was immediately clear as URI participants from around
the world flooded the San Francisco office with remembrances of this
fearless, tireless, and visionary interfaith pioneer. The URI created a
special page on its web site for these tributes. When the IGC gathered

in San Francisco in November, members returned to the interfaith chapel that had hosted the midweek service during the first Global Summit in 1996 and held an interfaith memorial service celebrating Luis' life and renewing their commitment to the work they shared. At the end of the meeting, Maria Eugenia Crespo de Mafia and André Porto, IGC members from Argentina and Brazil, respectively, returned home as interim cocoordinators to continue the work Luis had initiated.

Even as it grieved the loss of a beloved leader, colleague, and friend, the IGC grappled with a vast array of organizational issues. These issues were raised as the abstract constructs of the charter collided with the practical realities of developing a global organization with limitless vision, but limited human and financial resources. As is true for most births, after the ecstasy comes the laundry. The IGC trustees needed time to understand their roles, to develop effective working relationships with staff, and to converse about how best to serve their regions and the URI as a whole. The IGC had only recently created working committees that needed to be developed to effectively address the practical issues of managing the URI. Ideals and values that had found expression in the words of the charter now were applied to the varied and demanding work that presented itself to the trustees: strategic planning, communications, budget decisions, membership issues, regional development and support for CCs, and response to world events. The agenda would have been staggering for a group that met on a weekly basis. The IGC was to meet face-to-face twice a year and by conference call twice a year with committees meeting in between.

THE WORK BEGINS

Recent world events, including an earthquake in India and renewed violence in the Middle East, occupied much formal and informal discussion. IGC members wanted to see the URI be able to live into the fullness of its charter, but again and again, they had to recognize that the URI was an infant organization. Members saw great potential in engaging the community of CCs to address a particular situation, but wrestled with who could speak and/or act on behalf of the whole of the URI, and with whose permission. The group empowered Maria Eugenia to act for the IGC in working with Rosalia Guiterrez on behalf of indigenous children suffering from forced religious education in Argentina, Annie Imbens to represent the IGC at a European conference on the rights of women and children, and Bill Swing to further develop a vision for what the URI might uniquely offer the world as a positive force for peace among religions in the 21st Century.

One urgent organizational issue was the bylaw stipulation that the IGC and the staff engage the global community of CCs in the election of trustees for the first global council, the first global meeting of members, and the first global assembly by June 2001! What had seemed sensible to the organizational design team and the board when the charter was being drafted now seemed impossible. Leading up to the IGC meeting, the group realized that it would be insanity to try to fulfill these original goals in the time allotted in the bylaws. For the first of many times, the IGC and staff took refuge in Principle 19: We are committed to organizational learning and adaptation.

To provide some breathing room for the whole organization, the IGC called for the first bylaw amendment, asking CCs to vote to extend the IGC term of office for an additional year and to postpone the global assembly and the first meeting of members until June 2002. At its April meeting, the IGC culminated a site selection process that took several months by choosing Rio de Janeiro as the host site for the first global assembly. In addition, the IGC also decided to allocate some of the funds that would have supported the global assembly to produce five regional assemblies to help broaden and deepen participation in the URI around the world. Manifesting the trust that had been created in the URI community and organization-wide support for establishing the URI more firmly around the world, the CC network embraced the plan for regional assemblies and voted unanimously for the proposed bylaw change.

A GLOBAL SUPPORT NETWORK

Early in the chartering process, people realized there would need to be a supportive global/regional/local infrastructure if the URI was to flourish around the world. The closer the URI came to finishing the charter, the more real became the questions about how it would sustain the development of the global URI and support the growth and development of CCs all over the world. What would be needed to make the CCs thrive? What kind of infrastructure and coordinating support was vital to encourage the growth in effectiveness and numbers of CCs and Affiliates? How would this global support network infrastructure build on past and current best practices and fit into the evolving URI organizational design?

A draft proposal for a Global Support Network (GSN), with guiding questions for reflection, had been developed by staff and a few URI supporters through a two-day visioning session and follow-up work. The proposal was mailed to the IGC members for review at their April 2000 meeting and to all delegates prior to the Global Summit in June 2000. A chart describing the essential points of the proposal was posted on a wall at the summit. Inquiry worksheets were prepared for all of the delegates, and Charles Gibbs led a workshop for anyone who wanted to discuss the GSN proposal in greater depth.

The proposal imagined a GSN that worked at the behest of the global council to help it fulfill its responsibilities to support existing CCs, to develop new CCs, and to manifest the global connectedness and presence of the whole URI. Like the URI itself, the GSN would be locally rooted and globally connected. It would rely on a professional staff that embodied the PPP and reflected the global diversity of the URI. A substantial effort would be required to engage the expertise and commitment of a wide array of individuals and organizations - volunteer and paid - to provide the capacity to help the URI grow into the full effectiveness of its potential. The resultant organization would be substantial, effective, streamlined, and sustainable. The GSN would serve and lead, and be responsive and proactive. It would be an effective global manifestation of enduring daily interfaith cooperation for the good of all. Finally, it would model mutual learning and global parity of resource allocation. There were five components of the GSN:

- Regional and Global Staffing, which envisioned a robust staffing presence in seven geographic and one multiregional region
- Communications, which envisioned the development of a global communications and a knowledge-sharing infrastructure
- Partners in Leadership, which envisioned a systematic approach to leadership and skill building
- Peace building, which envisioned developing proactive and reactive capacities in this crucial area
- Philanthropy and Finance, which envisioned a global program of resource development and financial accountability

A map of the world, (with the Southern Hemisphere at the top) had been prepared as a backdrop for the Global Summit in Pittsburgh. A circle symbol signifying every founding CC had been placed on the map. Organizers imagined that at some point in the week, artifacts symbolizing the GSN (little cardboard huts that indicated a regional staffing presence, golden string that indicated communication connectivity between CCs and the global council, wrapped presents that indicated in-kind gifts and dollar gifts for Philanthropy and Finance, peace symbols to indicate Peace-building projects) would be ceremoniously placed on the map to provide a view of the GSN vision and to light the direction toward the future.

Reevaluating the Process

The GSN proposal presented a matured vision of the URI organizational future. For the global staff, the GSN plan was a vital and necessary map, a guidepost toward building a clear structure to guide staffing and build necessary support to nurture the global network. However, focused steps toward the further development and implementation of the GSN were delayed by the lukewarm reception it received from the IGC and delegates at the Global Summit in Pittsburgh and by the challenge of raising adequate funds to implement it fully. When the GSN plan was first presented to the IGC and at the Global Summit in June 2000, it met a neutral-to-questioning response. While the tasks and areas of development seemed self-evident and very much wanted and needed, a response among trustees was that perhaps too many decisions had come too fast and that the trustees had not had sufficient opportunity to participate in the visioning and planning.

At the Global Summit, CCs focused on regional issues and little attention was given to the new GSN proposal. The new CCs needed this time to talk about local issues — how to raise money, how to accomplish their programs, and how to connect with other CCs located in the same country or region. In June of 2000, the URI community was not yet ready to tackle the proposal for GSN, one that demanded a long-range and holistic view of the URI global network.

An indicator of this mismatch was that no time opened up during the Global Summit to celebrate the coming of the GSN by placing the GSN artifacts on the map as a visible reminder of good things ahead. This gap between the development and presentation of a new vision and plan by a small group and the larger community's receptivity to it was reminiscent of the dynamic that had been played out for two years between the organization design team and the larger community over the charter. Once again the URI staff learned that it was much easier for a small group to develop a plan than for the larger community to believe it has had adequate input into and ownership of the plan. This dynamic was especially challenging in the URI, with its emphasis on every voice counting. Judging from the reception of the GSN proposal, the URI needed to observe the flow of people's energy and interests and watch for the natural timing of new ideas or proposals to take root and develop. In this case, the GSN plan was ready but the community at large was not ready to embrace it. The seed was planted, but it would take myriad conversations during the next several years for the URI community to grow together into this grand scheme and to share in its development and implementation.

As the URI learned this lesson, they found themselves confronted simultaneously by a major challenge and a potential weakness of the URI's organizational structure and culture: Did the URI have the capacity to plan efficiently and to implement expeditiously? As the organization grew, would every major initiative require the same extended and painstaking process as had the creation of the charter? Or would the URI find increasingly appropriate ways to empower small groups to work on behalf of the whole without creating the appearance of disenfranchising the whole? The answers to these questions rested in a deeper, living exploration of two, seemingly contradictory principles:

> PRINCIPLE 13: We have the authority to make decisions at the most local level that includes all the relevant and affected parties.

> PRINCIPLE 15: Our deliberations and decisions shall be made at every level by bodies and methods that fairly represent the diversity of affected interests and are not dominated by any.

The URI would be living with these questions for a long time as part of an ongoing effort to balance the URI's inclusive ideals with the sometimes urgent practical demands of sustaining and guiding a global organization.

FURTHER STEPS IN REGIONAL COORDINATION

The 2000 Global Summit ended without an endorsement of the GSN proposal. The five areas of operation developed in the proposal were presented. However, the overarching structure that would allow for focused fund-raising and the systematic development of this much-needed infrastructure was neither approved nor rejected. It was simply tabled in favor of other, more urgent issues in the understandable struggle for precious time on the agenda. Though not formally adopted, the GSN vision would help shape future deliberations of the IGC's strategic planning committee and would provide guidance for the global staff as it set about its work to support the growth of the URI. Lacking a ringing endorsement from the larger URI community and lacking sufficient funding to take major steps in implementing its vision, the implementation of the GSN proposal moved forward opportunistically and in piecemeal fashion, rather than strategically and as a whole. But move forward it did, with the staff trusting that some deeper wisdom was at work and that the larger good was being served.

The first steps in creating a network of global support had happened spontaneously and organically, as obvious needs called forth people and opportunities. To take up the incredible challenge and opportunity to develop the URI in Africa, Godwin Hlatshwayo was employed part-time as the coordinator for Africa. To share the vision and develop URI potential in Latin America, Father Luis Dolan had served part-time as a Latin American coordinator. As previously mentioned, after Luis' death in the fall of 2000, Charles Gibbs asked Maria Crespo and Andre Porto, two IGC members, to take up where Luis left off and serve as interim regional staff in Latin America. Josef Boehle, a doctoral candidate studying in the United Kingdom and an early contributor to the charter's preamble, worked for three years as part-time European coordinator. He supported the work of the European Executive Committee (EEC), which had emerged from the 1997 regional conference in Oxford as a volunteer coordinating group. The EEC, which became a CC, included two members of the IGC: Annie Imbens Fransen, a scholar and Christian feminist, and Deepak Naik, a Hindu and Director of Minorities of Europe. Its chair was Patrick Hanjoul, a Catholic priest, who helped direct a large organization, Bond Zonder Naam (Movement Without a Name).

When Josef's dissertation demands prevented him from continuing and funding grew scarce, the role of coordinating URI Europe fell entirely to the EEC. Along the way, the EEC had incorporated as an international charity in Brussels and worked to raise funds to develop the URI in Europe.

At this time, no funding was allotted in the URI budget for regional coordinators in the Pacific, North America, or multiregional region. In the summer of 2001, the URI learned that three IGC trustees from Asia — Father James Channan from Pakistan, Dr. Mohinder Singh from India, and Venerable Jinwol Lee from Korea — had been spending personal funds for URI development efforts in their countries. Thus, a monthly stipend was established to cover their expenses. In addition to these contributors, CC leaders in every region initiated their own coordinating activities and consistently contributed the gift of service and often covered costs for communication and events, all of which was essential to the growth and development of the URI.

In North America, several CC leaders volunteered to coordinate and support other CCs in their areas. In September of 2001, Mary Page Sims organized a quarterly meeting for the URI CCs in the Carolinas and Tennessee. She reported the following:

> The URI of the Carolinas and Tennessee is one year old — a birthday cake was present. We want community as each of us moves in the direction of the URI vision, and we want practical tools, such as Appreciative Inquiry and conflict resolution skills. Recent events included:
>
> In Asheville, a successful AI session and storytelling, planned as a multigenerational event, was a smash success. Next, an interfaith teen retreat is planned. In Black Mountain, the CC is focused on environmental issues and has conducted energy audits in homes and churches. In Hendersonville County, the

CC organized a World Banquet, which dramatized the unequal way food and resources are distributed and consumed in the world.

Some were concerned that not more people knew about the URI, and discussion followed about how to reach folks... Some topics for further discussion came up – How do we develop leadership? How do we deal with religious intolerance?

We see ourselves as pioneers, and sometimes it's lonely because there is a lot of mistrust of the URI in our area.

BUILDING THE URI WEB SITE

Generous volunteer service had helped to build the first URI website, publish the first URI newsletters, and establish and moderate the first email service. Steve Fitzgerald, a Ph.D. candidate in Organizational Development and convener of the City of Angels CC, volunteered to help develop a listserv (an email service) as a means to connect the URI global network. The first experiment was a general list, which proved an invaluable tool in the final development of the purpose statement; more specific lists followed which enabled the work of geographically diverse planning teams for the 2000 Global Summit. Following the charter signing, the general listserv grew to include almost everyone who wanted to connect – CC members, Affiliate members, partnering organizations, and URI friends. As more and more information flowed through this listserv, it seemed natural and necessary to spin off another listserv that would specifically serve the CC network.

The start-up of the CC listserv was a tottering, often frustrating, yet essential, first step. When asked to join this listserv, most people were wary – still being novices with Internet communication. People felt elated and overwhelmed with handling a soaring rise of emails. The URI learned that emails were effective, but many CCs, especially in Africa, did not have computers or had inefficient and costly Internet hookups.

The listserv inaugurated a clear path of relying on computer technology for global communication and knowledge sharing. The challenge to the URI in learning new systems was matched by the thrill of knowing it had entered a new era, when communication would empower the URI membership worldwide. It was another opportunity to walk in the dark. The good news was that members kept walking hand in hand. Here is a sample of how the URI introduced this leap of technology to the CC network:

> DEAR CC CONTACT PERSONS,
>
> We put our heads together to come up with guidelines for use of the CC listserv. We want to thank all of the contact people who have taken on the task of receiving URI emails and figuring out what to do with them. Thank you for your pioneering work!
>
> We are excited by amazing technology that lets us send notes of joy and sympathy and daily news to people in all parts of the world. At the same time, we are trying to figure out effective ways to stay unburdened by too much email.
>
> The purpose of the CC listserv is to:
> 1. Share best practices and highlights in the life of the URI Circles.
> 2. Ask questions and make requests for different kinds of support.
> 3. Pass along essential information relating to the work of the Interim Global Council.
> 4. Offer news about local projects and programs and offer ideas for new programs, resources, fund-raising ideas, and peace-building efforts.
>
> The CC listserv provides a way for CCs to communicate with each other. Each CC can decide to what degree and in what manner its CC will

participate in the listserv. There is usually one contact
person for each CC who handles listserv information,
but there can be more than one. Soon a website will
function for all of the CCs, which will bring us new
solutions and new challenges too!

With thanks,
Steve Fitzgerald and Sally Mahé

Overseeing much of the volunteer work, Kristin Swenson provided visionary and practical leadership in helping the URI take advantage of the sometimes challenging gifts of the world of technology.
She oversaw the redesign of the URI's website to make it more compelling, informative, and inclusive of news from the URI around the
world. Recognizing the need for an increasingly sophisticated communications capacity for the IGC, she worked with Sarah Talcott and
interfaith cyberactivist and URI supporter Bruce Schuman to create a
private website. This site had email capacity and discussion and document centers to support the work of the IGC and its committees.
This site was adapted to create a similar private site to enable the
cooperative efforts of CCs. As with the writing of the charter and the
development of the GSN, this essential, but challenging work with
technology demanded the dedicated effort of a small group. This
cadre took the lead in developing capacity and devoted great attention
to empowering the larger community to be able to make good use of
the capacity that was created. Having an IGC website was of little
value if the individual members of the IGC were unable or unwilling
to use it.

As this communications work was developing, the staff also
attended to publishing periodic newsletters, generating the first annual report in 2000 and making a valiant but small effort at public relations that would generate broader publicity for the URI. This effort
built on Bishop Swing's work to promote the URI. Over the years, he
had traveled extensively, sharing the URI story in China, Japan, Eng-

land, Canada, Italy, Romania, Belgium, France, Pakistan, Korea, India, and the United States, through speeches and on radio and television. He had addressed the Anglican Church's Lambeth Conference, the Episcopal Church's House of Bishops, the community of St. Egidio in Rome, the U.S. House of Representatives and the European Union.

Given this history, it was fitting that among the fruits of the URI's public relations work following the signing of the charter were timely articles in *Fast Company* magazine and *The New York Times*, focusing on Bishop Swing and his leadership of the URI.

Often the U.S.-based global staff found itself learning from URI leaders in other parts of the world, who were doing extraordinary work getting local URI efforts publicized. When, in March 2001, Bishop Swing and Charles Gibbs traveled to Pakistan, James Channan and his partners in Pakistan had arranged various press conferences and an appearance on a nationally televised talk show.

As with most areas of the URI's development, communications saw great growth; yet always more seemingly essential work was waiting to be done.

FOSTERING LEADERSHIP

From the beginning, URI values and AI methodology called for increasing numbers of people to become leaders and to share leadership. With guidance from David Cooperrider and graduate students from SIGMA, responsibility to design and implement URI conferences and global summit gatherings had been steadily handed over to URI staff and to IGC trustees and to CC leaders.

URI summits and conferences required many talents, including conference administration, space design, volunteer coordination, program design and facilitation, and coordination of sacred practices and ceremonies. Months before every gathering there was plenty of work to do, including appropriately inclusive decision making. Under the guiding hand of Gurudev Khalsa, facilitation teams were created and leaders from every region were invited to help plan the global summits. They pioneered the art of email correspondence in managing good conversation, committee planning and group decision making. At the summits, leadership was shared so that men and women, people from different faith backgrounds and different continents, and people of different ages shared responsibility and the spotlight. Since its inception, the URI community had naturally come to expect, trust and enjoy the fruits of diverse and shared leadership.

In 1996, the spirit and practice of AI's open approach to sharing leadership transformed the role of volunteers, who thought they might only be "gofers," to that of active participants and leaders. Volunteers who came to Stanford to assist delegates with airport pickups, hospitality, and snack bar service soon began their own CC and eventually found themselves offering their presence and leadership at a URI gathering on the other side of the ocean (Bali).

URI and AI created a safe space, a space where people from diverse cultures and countries and talents and trades were seen, valued, invited, and encouraged to offer best leadership practices as authentic cocreators of the vision with the URI staff, the interim global council and the SIGMA advisers. The URI learned that salary was not the currency that mattered most. People offered the best of themselves because they shared a purpose they believed in and because they felt appreciated, needed, and in community with people who were kindred spirits. As far as the GSN vision of a formal program of leadership development, there was neither the funding nor the staff time to pursue this particular vision in a broad and focused way.

Formal leadership development seemed to flourish most naturally in the field of peace building.

The 72 Hours Project had raised up the vision of peace building as a core mission and a collective action for the URI. Building on the successes of 72 Hours, it was clear the URI needed to proactively support CCs that wanted to expand and deepen their skills in peace building. At one point, a Peace-Building Institute had been envisioned to provide training in a wide range of skills, such as dialogue, meditation, intercultural sensitivity, exploration of religious/spiritual practices, and development of the practices of reconciliation and healing. 72 Hours had also brought back stories of highly successful partnerships with like-minded organizations and groups. The URI needed to find a way to stay attentive to creating these kinds of partnerships and in finding resources that would enrich the peace-building skills of its members.

PEACE-BUILDING INITIATIVES

In addition, 72 Hours had proven that a collective global action was possible and highly desirable. In the future, there needed to be a way to inspire and lead other global efforts like 72 Hours that would call forth the URI community in a unified and collective global action. Cynthia Sampson, coeditor of *Religion, the Missing Dimension of Statecraft* and soon-to-be founder of Peace Discovery Initiatives, had enthusiastically offered her service and expertise to the URI community and was waiting in the wings for a way to help. Barbara Hartford, a multitalented staff member, was eager to leave administrative duties and unleash her passion to contribute to URI peace-building efforts. A first step in this effort was to send Barbara and Kristine Kisembo, a member of a CC in Uganda, to a peace-building course at Eastern Mennonite University. This experience raised the possibility of more extensive training for a larger number of URI activists who could then become a resource for training and support within the CC community. As with so many parts of the URI, a need for adequate financial support was compelling vision.

Another key development in peace building came as Bishop Swing's desire to find URI's unique contribution to peace among religions evolved into the "Vision for Peace among Religions in the Twenty-First Century" project. This project envisioned building on what had been learned in the URI chartering process to create a global inquiry, involving millions of people and many partner organizations, to raise up a new vision and strategies for peace among religions. Grounded in the belief that the 21st Century must witness an end to killing in the name of the divine, a new level of accountability for global good, and new life-giving cooperative relationships among people and organizations of different faiths, the project sought to engage people from all areas of human endeavor to identify the resources for peace in their faith traditions and vocations. The URI had come to believe that dialogue was a form of action that could lead to more action. Thus, the organizers imagined that this global inquiry would create new relationships, spawn myriad diverse peace-building projects around the world, and produce a widely-owned document that synthesized the findings of this three-year effort to establish a new standard for relationships among different faiths. Seed funding allowed for the first phase of this project to begin in the winter of 2002, launching pilot inquiries in each region as preparation for sharing the project with the entire URI community at the first global assembly in Rio de Janeiro in August 2002.

Meeting the Financial Challenge

From the beginning, Bishop Swing had accepted major fund-raising responsibilities for the URI without compensation. He often said that a key to interfaith work was money, because without it, one would be unable to do the work. Seeing fund-raising as a sacred calling, he gave himself tirelessly and successfully to this effort. The URI was blessed by some "early believers" who had the financial capacity to make major multiyear contributions. They sustained the organization in the early years, helped it climb out of deep debt, and launched it into the post-charter-signing world with an adequate financial base to ensure survival, as the URI sought to grow into a truly global organization.

Along the way, the bishop's efforts were supported by a range of volunteers, including Jim Lord. Lord's pioneering work in applying AI to the field of philanthropy offered a vision of how the URI might create a program of global philanthropy that was consistent with its organizational values. Bill Rankin was the first staff person in the global office with responsibility for raising money. His efforts to extend the bishop's work helped the URI climb out of debt and, thus, to fund the charter signing and summit. When, after two years, Bill left to found the Global Aids Interfaith Alliance Cooperation Circle, the URI began a protracted search that led to the hiring of Jennifer Kirk as Head of Philanthropy and global fund-raising. She brought considerable expertise in global philanthropy from her work with the Asia Foundation and a passionate commitment to developing a program of global philanthropy for the URI that would be consistent with its deepest values.

While Bill Swing worked tirelessly as URI's first and primary fund-raiser, Mary Swing, his wife, worked equally tirelessly as his support and the URI's first financial manager. With grace and competence, Mary created and maintained a system of financial reporting and accountability for this evolving organization. She made sure the staff was paid and their benefits maintained, that financial reports were produced on a monthly basis, and that money was moved around the world — all in a way that would satisfy the requirements of the Internal Revenue Service's annual audit. Inevitably, the financial demands of a rapidly growing global organization demanded that the URI hire a full-time financial manager to oversee the URI's increasingly complex financial affairs and begin to envision and implement systems to be consistent with Principle 18: *We maintain the highest standards of integrity and ethical conduct, prudent use of resources, and fair and accurate disclosure of information.* Siv Winberg became the URI's first financial manager; after much foundational work, she was followed by Ray Signer.

DREAMS TO REALITY

Thus, the global support network evolved. There were so many decisions to make and so much to learn about how to share with others. In the months following the birth, the learning curve only seemed to get steeper. The URI was learning day-by-day what it meant to operate in a decentralized organization, where decisions were to be made by all relevant and affected parties.

Moving forward together was proving awkward, the tendency was for mistakes and a time of constant learning. Questions were far more prevalent than answers. Sometimes people felt left out of decisions that affected them. Sometimes people felt overwhelmed by conversation and email intrusions asking them to respond to something. For instance, soon after the Pittsburgh summit, a questionnaire was sent to CCs that asked them to share information about their best practices, needs, and resources as a first step toward understanding how CCs could benefit from a global support network. The inquiry was not followed up, producing only a handful of responses. It was an imperfect and unpolished dance into the future. The primary partners in the dance were the global staff, regional coordinators, interim global council trustees, and CC leaders. Planning and decision making was a dance where all of the relevant and affected parties were in the position of sometimes leading and sometimes following. As always, world events provided the drumbeat. Divergent interests and constraints provided the music. The dancers continually stepped on each other's feet, but no one hurt for too long. And most importantly, the dance continued.

During the IGC teleconference meeting in September 2000, Hamed Ehsani, trustee from Kenya, raised the issue in his distinctively respectful manner that perhaps the funds slated to produce the first global assembly, then scheduled for June 2001 at Stanford University, might be redirected to the regional gatherings. He suggested that such a change would allow for more participation in the regions and would help strengthen the existing CCs and inspire new ones. Hamed believed this would be a good investment of money, a timely way to further decentralize the URI and to build up the regions. There was a brief silence, but no time in a packed agenda for further discussion of Hamed's important and provocative suggestion. But in the weeks that followed, staff, advisers, IGC members, and CC members in every region explored the possibility. Building on this conversation, in November 2000, the IGC decided to replace the Global Assembly of June 2001 with five regional assemblies. The IGC also agreed that the budget be distributed to different URI regions to host the assemblies, hopefully accomplishing some leadership development along the way.

Originally slated to be spent for the Global Assembly, $300,000 was to be distributed equally, providing $60,000 for each assembly: Asia and the Pacific, Africa, Europe and the Middle East, Latin America, and North America. Representatives of CCs from the multiregional region were invited to join the assembly in the region where they lived. In each region, IGC members explored workable dates and locations for assemblies and stepped forward as key organizers and leaders in the planning committees. Along the way, the budget and operations committee of the IGC amended its earlier budget decision, partly in response to lower income expectations and partly in response to the desire to create global/regional funding partnerships. The committee proposed a structure that provided $50,000 from the global budget for each regional assembly and asked that the planning team in each region take responsibility for raising the additional $10,000 in cash or in-kind service.

In December 2000, Charles Gibbs wrote to the URI community and summed up the changes taking place.

When the URI charter was signed at the global gathering in Pittsburgh, this past June, we celebrated the completion of a four-year process of shared creation. At the same, time we were clear that the measure of the charter would not be its creation, but the process of making it come alive through prayer and meditation, dialogue, and cooperative action – a globally connected community every day. Each day we live into that challenge and over the past six months, we have seen a flowering of activity in response. A few examples: We have seen a CC in Brazil sponsor an interfaith service attended by 10,000 people as part of a major effort to say no to violence and to build cultures of peace. We have seen a CC in Spain host a charter-signing gathering that attracted 600 people. We have seen a CC in Ethiopia enter a partnership agreement with the World Faiths Development Dialogue. We have seen an MCC in Israel renew its commitment to use dialogue and conversation among people of different faiths as an effective method to build lasting peace in that turbulent part of the world. These stories, among many others that could be told, say that there is a great deal to celebrate.

We have also heard of the challenges many CCs are facing. We've heard CCs challenged to find the resources — human and financial — to help bring their plans to reality. We have heard the call for guidance and support from the larger URI community. Clearly, we have a lot of growing and strengthening to do. And we have so much to learn from each other as we grow into an increasingly effective global community.

Also, it is in awareness of the tremendous resources that the Circles represent and the needs that face us all that the IGC decided to replace the Global Assembly in 2001 with regional assemblies. Having more assemblies, more locally, will allow more participation by and greater strengthening of the URI Circles around the world. These regional assemblies will enable us to come together to share our visions, our plans, our questions, and our resources.

We are in the earliest stages of planning these assemblies but will get you information about locations and dates as that becomes available. In return, you might send us ideas, questions, and concerns that can help us shape the planning of these assemblies.

Finally, as this year unfolds, we intend to begin extending URI staff presence into all seven regions of the world. We aren't sure exactly how this will happen, but initial exploration is under way. Please share the thoughts you might have about this. We will keep you informed as the exploration proceeds. Again, thanks

to each of you for being part of the URI and for
sharing this exciting and challenging birth. May each
of you feel the blessing of your work, because it is a
blessing to the world.

Love, Charles

THE REGIONS FLOWER

By January 2001, six months after the charter signing, a bold new
direction was set and the regions began to spin into motion. Each
region was distinct. Planning and leadership evolved differently. IGC
members rose to the challenge and became primary conveners of the
planning teams and invited others in the regions to join them. The
global staff in San Francisco held general financial oversight for the
regional assemblies and helped the planning teams enliven the spirit
of the URI and honor its expression in the charter. Sally Mahé and
Gurudev Khalsa took up the task of serving as global coordinators for
all five assemblies. Questions arose about how to ensure appropriate
global presence, fiscal accountability, continuity, use of best practices,
and inspiring connection from one assembly to the next.

Each planning team was given questions to guide their planning,
including these: How might the centrality of the charter, its creation
story, and its core values be enlivened in each assembly? How might
regional assemblies include stories from the URI around the world?
The global staff fell short of the initial intention to have in-depth
conversations with each planning team along the way to help guide
their conference choices. With the planning teams eager to provide
exemplary assemblies, the process unfolded differently in each region.
Common to each region were local CCs, living models of global connection and regional/local contextualization. In the interests of
regional leadership development, it was best for global staff to follow
the lead of the regional assembly planning teams rather than get in
their way with well-meaning shoulds and oughts. So the global staff
offered proactive support in different ways and then watched each

process unfold, intervening only when invited by the regional team or compelled by urgent circumstances. The result was not a perfect process, but invigorated regional leadership, exciting assemblies, a great deal of organizational learning, and the foundation for vital regional/local/global partnerships that would serve the URI's development for years to come.

Instead of following a known path toward another global gathering, the URI community had chosen to change course and commit substantial funds to producing five assemblies on five continents. The decision could have been seen as too risky, a preposterously ambitious and out-of-control undertaking; instead, the decision produced an electric excitement. The decision was the right response to a shared recognition that it was time to give the regions room to thrive. It unleashed energy, resourcefulness, and enthusiasm in regional and local leaders and allowed everyone involved to rejoice together in discovering ways to practice the principles the participants valued. At this juncture, the lesson for the URI community was to notice and allow for change. The IGC and global staff quickly redirected their work to align with the needs of regional assemblies and increased regional leadership. The URI was thrilled to be going in this new direction, and it was, as usual, a walk in the dark, with questions looming at every turn. How would the URI community develop five regional assemblies in such a way as to deepen the roots of the URI vision globally? How would the regional assemblies generate more Circles and help existing CCs create important partnerships? How would the assemblies meet the needs of the CCs, be fiscally accountable, and raise up new leaders?

NORTH AMERICA ASSEMBLY
CIRCLES IN MOTION, GIFTS TO SHARE, SALT LAKE CITY, UTAH, MAY 27–30, 2001

When people from North America met together at the Global Summit in Pittsburgh, they were intent on advancing a plan for a coordinating structure to help support CCs and develop the URI in

North America. Buoyed by the enthusiasm engendered by these conversations for more active URI development in North America, a swell of committed volunteer leaders from the United States and Canada quickly formed an *ad hoc* planning team and began planning a URI U.S. summit, *Circles in Motion, Gifts to Share*, which was to be the first step toward a broader engagement of all of North America. Planning for this summit was well under way when the IGC made its decision to replace the global assembly with regional assemblies. After consultation, the planning team agreed to expand their vision of *Circles in Motion, Gifts to Share* in order to have it function as one of the regional assemblies, including all of North America.

In spite of the change, the team held to a previous decision to raise its own money to fund the assembly and not to rely on the URI global budget for support. The team eagerly assumed full responsibility for all aspects of the assembly. The Utah Interfaith Council, a Circle led by Dave Randle, a former minister with the United Church of Christ (UCC) and a community organizer in Utah, was able to secure the University of Utah, Salt Lake City, as the site. Volunteers stepped forward to manage a growing database and to develop an open-door invitation process. For the first time for URI gatherings, no restriction was placed on the number of invited guests. Planning team members helped arrange economical flights and distributed a number of travel scholarships. They managed registration, offered extensive interviews with CCs prior to the assembly, organized host support in Salt Lake City, and planned an ambitious five-day program. The assembly date was set for May 31–June 4, 2001.

Paul Chaffee, a UCC minister and director of the Interfaith Chapel at the Presidio, San Francisco, and URI trustee, teamed with Steve Fitzgerald, a member of the Church of Religious Science and leader of a URI Circle in Los Angeles, as coconveners of the facilitation team. The team quickly grew from 10 volunteers to nearly 30.

The planning group depended almost entirely on the Internet, which cut some folks out. Nevertheless, over two dozen braved cyberspace and made a number of phone calls to do the planning. This group contributed over $38,000, or over a third of the cost of the event. Beyond this, most of the cost was covered by registration fees. It was a perfect example of Principle 17 at work and happened because the first donor's enthusiasm and up-front giving sparked everyone else. People cared enough about the event that they gave hundreds of hours, and those who could afford it gave considerable sums of money. The Utah site team and the planning team worked to keep everything frugal without sacrificing the quality of the event. We were also blessed by special circumstances – being named an Olympic cultural event, thereby receiving low-cost accommodations. As it was, over half of those attending received some sort of financial aid. The result was a phenomenal level of diversity, including 25 young people.

We depended on the gifts and expertise of our own people, and it almost always meant things went better and cost less than if we had brought in outsiders. Perhaps the best decision was to make one very large space serve for the business of the summit and for worship and celebration, which, under Jack Lundin's leadership, was sensitively woven into the daily flow of events. Another critical decision was to make the event open to everyone committed to interfaith cooperation. This open-door policy made the whole space welcoming to everyone.

The one person we hired, a URI seasoned facilitator, Penny Williamson, played a crucial role in creating a five-day process that really worked. We could not

have done it without her and her colleague, Diana
Whitney, who donated hundreds of professional
hours. The leadership core kept enlarging the number
of people who were invited to join the leadership
team. People were invited and given the freedom to
tackle an issue and then were kept in a communications loop as plans went forward. As a result, many,
many leaders surfaced and made contributions to this
event. – Paul Chaffee, Assembly Organizer

THE ASSEMBLY

One hundred sixty people attended the gathering in Salt Lake
City. A five-day program began with extensive AI interviews. The
delegates produced and enjoyed a shared history of interfaith
advances, a picture book of dreams for the Twenty-First century, a
diverse selection of workshops, an explosion of open-space sessions,
and a host of newly formed task groups committed to the future
growth of the URI in North America. The work was interspersed
with in-depth prayer and meditation offerings from a broad array of
faith backgrounds. One evening was set aside for a banquet, a time
for everyone to sing together and celebrate each other's talents. URI
veterans and newcomers alike stepped into the spotlight of leadership. Twelve young people from the Buddhist Youth Fellowship drove
caravan-style from Berkeley, California, and met other young adults
from across North America. At night in the dorms, folk guitar, harmonica jazz, Buddhist chant, storytelling, digital video, eating, laughing, hanging out, card playing, and meditating all tumbled together
in the fourth floor dorm lounge. And something more that these
late-night extracurricular parties was offered – a spirit of welcome.
There was no age discrimination here. The older, but still young at
heart, delegates were warmly welcomed by the youth into this special
space each evening.

A cadre of these same young adults happily accepted an invitation from the planning team to organize a public entertainment

evening so local people from Salt Lake City could participate in and learn about the conference. The program, brilliantly anchored by Masankho Banda and Johanna Hardy and performed almost entirely by young adults, presented a richness of talent, wisdom, and actualized visions of the URI in action. The skits, songs, poetry, video clips, and diversity of talent offered illuminated a way of being that invited people to offer their gifts freely to one another in service of the URI. This allowed people to exult in friendship, improvisation, and mutual respect no matter what their background. It called forth an abundance of leaders of all ages, perspectives, and talents!

What could the URI learn from the planning processes that created this kind of ease and trust among people? How could the URI deepen its understanding of its vision and purpose that drew these people together? How could the URI re-create the organizational methodology that released this kind of generosity of spirit?

EVENTS OF 9/11

Before the next regional assembly took place in Nairobi, Kenya, a terrorist attack on the World Trade Towers in New York and the Pentagon in Washington, D.C. rocked the world. Once again the URI was challenged to respond to tragic, menacing world events. Within hours, the email network was busy as CC members around the world expressed their horror at the attack, their solidarity with their sisters and brothers in the United States, and their determination to redouble their commitment to end religiously motivated violence. A special page was set up on the URI website to share these messages with the world. One such message came from the Philippines.

> DEAR FELLOW WORKERS IN THE LIGHT,
> In the wake of the tragedy in New York and Washington D.C., we, the members of the Peacemakers' Circle of the Philippines, wish to express to the people of the United States our deepest sympathy. We pray that in the midst of this darkness, the light of

divine wisdom and love will prevail and shine forth from our hearts. Let us remain steadfast in our faith. Let us not allow the darkness of fear, anger, and hatred to overcome us. Let us continue to pray and to journey in peace together as one Earth community.

Many lives have been lost in this tragedy. The scale and magnitude of the destruction is awesome and horrifying. The process of meting justice and of healing will have to begin anew when the smoke disperses and the rubble is cleared. But the night will be long and the darkness will settle for a while. Yet hope must not be lost. We, peoples of diverse religions, spiritual expressions, and indigenous traditions all over the world must continue to believe in our shared vision and work together to MAKE PEACE OUR EVERY STEP.

Perhaps, one day, this tragedy will be remembered as the end of the old era of conflict and violence and the beginning of a new era of peace building in our midst, especially in the arena of international relations. Our global movement of peoples of diverse religions and beliefs must now rise from the rubble and bring to the fore the highest values and teachings of our faith in dialogue and initiatives that promote peace and healing of the Earth and all beings.

We pray for all the people suffering from this tragedy in the United States and all over the world. We pray that divine justice, peace, and healing may prevail all over the Earth.

Yours sincerely,
Marites Guingona-Africa
for The Peacemakers' Circle Foundation, Manila, Philippines (Founding Cooperation Circle of the United Religions Initiative)

A prescheduled IGC conference call on September 12 took on a somber new significance. The first 45 minutes of the scheduled two-hour call was given over to trustees and staff sharing their shock and resolve. All agreed they must continue, even redouble their efforts. And all agreed the IGC had to issue some sort of statement on behalf of the URI. Moving swiftly, the IGC had a statement ready within two days:

> We, members of the United Religions Initiative's Interim Global Council, express our deep sorrow and grief at the acts of terrorism against the United States and all humanity on Tuesday, September 11, 2001. As people of diverse religions, spiritual expressions, and indigenous traditions throughout the world, we unite in mourning for those who lost their lives, and we offer our prayers for their families and loved ones and for all of humanity.
>
> In an instant, an explosion of hatred and fear darkened the skies over the United States and around the world. The forces of hatred and violence are suddenly so visible. People call for killing in response to this killing, for acts of war in response to this act of war.
>
> In our shock, grief, and fear and in response to the rising tide of hatred and violence, we give thanks for our existing interreligious relationships dedicated to peace, justice, and healing. We – Buddhists, Bahai's, Christians, Hindus, indigenous peoples, Jews, Muslims, Sikhs, Taoists, and many other faiths – declare our intention to grieve together and to support all others who grieve.
>
> We pledge together to offer the gift of prayer and meditation for peace; for justice, not revenge; for healing, not further violence. We state our commitment to build new relationships of peace, justice, and healing

until no one is left out. We pledge together to give our
lives to the challenging daily work of peace building
so humanity might claim out of this tragedy a new
day of compassion, healing, and light.

In the weeks immediately following September 11, URI CCs around the world hosted interfaith services of remembrance. Bishop Swing was hosted at the UN Center in New York by the URI UN CC, where he spoke powerfully about 9/11 being a call to people of all faiths to work to bridge the chasm of hatred and violence that resulted in 9/11 and other acts of interreligious violence around the world. Charles Gibbs and Barbara Hartford joined Cynthia Sampson, David Cooperrider and about 70 other people for the "Positive Approaches to Peace Building Conference," of which the URI was a coconvener, in Washington, D.C., at the end of September. People seemed newly convinced of the essential importance of the URI's work and of the need to do something, now.

As the bombing of Afghanistan began, the dialogue within the URI community heated up. There was no one who did not condemn the terror of September 11, but there were many around the world concerned about the bombing of Afghanistan. They believed that many other acts of terror taking place around the world also needed global attention. This was the global context within which the regional assembly for Africa occurred.

Africa Regional Assembly
Nairobi, Kenya, October 8–11, 2001
Our Quest For Peace – A Sacred Dialogue for Life

In Africa, Godwin Hlatshwayo launched a written campaign to seek proposals from different countries to host the assembly. In the end, Hamed Ehsani's offer to host the Africa Assembly at the Village Market Square in Nairobi, Kenya, was accepted. Godwin generated a flurry of conference organizational material to CCs throughout Africa and attempted to organize planning teams that would communicate via email to plan the conference. However, planning and preparation work by email was somewhat ineffective in Africa because most of the CC leaders did not have adequate access to the Internet. Nonetheless, spearheaded by Godwin, Hamed, and fellow IGC member Joyce N'goma and using a combination of phone calls, emails, and visits, eight separate organizing teams were created and over 15 CC leaders participated and shouldered various responsibilities in preparing for the assembly. These teams came together a few days before the assembly to complete their plans and preparations. In a two-day whirl of focused organizing, an Africa assembly program materialized, providing time for community building, including Appreciative Interviews, subregional planning and priority setting, reflection on the global situation, and exploration of Africa's unique offering for peace.

The following communiqué provides an overview of the work of the assembly.

We, the 128 representatives from 29 URI Cooperation Circles in Africa, met in Nairobi, Kenya, for three days for the first-ever URI Africa Regional Assembly. We represent Burundi, Ethiopia, Democratic Republic of Congo (DRC), Kenya, Malawi, Mozambique, Rwanda, Uganda, Zambia, and Zimbabwe. Also present are special observers from the URI in Latin America, North America, and the URI hub. Our theme is *"Our Quest for Peace and Development — Sacred Dialogue for Life."*

We are guided by the following objectives:
- To experience URI as a foretaste of a diverse and inclusive peaceful community of the future
- To facilitate leadership development through collective participation by all people at the assembly

- To search for and develop peace-building initiatives for URI communities across Africa
- To develop a URI African development strategy for the coming three years

Driven by our overall compelling theme for peace and development, we participated on appreciative inquiry interview conversations and we shared personal stories of URI presence in Africa. Workshops were held on the introduction of the URI, formation of URI CCs, experiences of women and youth in armed conflict, organization for outreach, peace building practices, religious dialogue, resource networking, situation in areas of armed conflicts, the issue of HIV/AIDS in terms of the opportunity and hazard to peace building, and interfaith dialogue. All these sessions and workshops helped us in sharing experiences. We identified issues for us, as URI, to address in Africa.

Motivated and united in the common purpose of the URI "to promote enduring daily interfaith cooperation; to end religiously motivated violence; and to create cultures of peace, justice, and healing for the earth and all living beings," we set out to chart a way for creating a conducive African environment for peace and development.

We realize the following areas as being of critical concern and requiring urgent address from Africa to achieve peace and development.
- Communications
- Financial support for URI Africa
- URI social involvement in global agenda
- Peace-building initiatives
- URI partnerships and networks

Taking into cognizance areas of our activities as identified and reflected upon, we the members here present outline the following areas of action and adopt them as a strategic plan of action for our beloved continent.

- Work toward peace building through development of various initiatives
- Address the issue of HIV/AIDS
- Conduct reconciliatory workshops/meetings
- Enhance the communication within and outside URI in the continent
- Mobilize funds for the objectives of URI in the continent

Committed to the URI preamble and principles and as ambassadors of peace, we the Africa Assembly feel equally concerned with the conflicts in other regions and especially with the war involving the United States and Afghanistan. We offer solidarity and prayers of peace to those who are dehumanized and who lost their lives, their relatives, their property, and their peace. We also offer ourselves to be used as instruments of peace in mediation between the two countries.

Signed
Nairobi, Kenya
12 October 2001

MUSLIM RESPONSE TO 9/11

In addition to the previous communiqué from the entire assembly, the Muslim community issued a separate statement, which received broad assent from the whole assembly:

Statement from the Muslim Community

In the Name of God most Gracious, most Merciful.

We, members of the Muslim community gathered here, feel greatly honored to be part of URI in its quest for world peace. The word Islam comes from an Arabic root world Salam which means peace. Therefore, ideally, Islam should be at the forefront of the promotion of peace in the world.

Of recent, Islam has been portrayed as a religion of terrorists, murderers, and intolerant people. We totally object to this and reaffirm that Islam stands for peace. It does not teach violence, nor does it encourage violence toward members of other faiths. The Holy Quran and the sayings of prophet Muhammad are a clear testimony to this.

It is also true that many people have used the name of Islam to cause violence for their selfish ends. Such acts of violence need to be condemned and disowned by all peace-loving people the world over. We must remember that terrorists and extremists are found in all religions and political systems. We should, therefore, not blame the evils of a few misguided individuals on their religions.

We, the Muslims gathered here, condemn in the strongest terms the terrorist activities of September 11, 2001, on New York and Washington and support all efforts by the world community to bring the culprits to justice, whatever religion they belong to.

We are, however, appealing for caution in hunting down the perpetrators of terrorism. We must exercise restraint in the process so we do not ourselves turn into terrorists by killing and imprisoning innocent people all in the name of hunting down the perpetrators of terrorism.

We are concerned about the war unfolding in Afghanistan right now, where innocent civilians are being killed. That country has endured decades of destruction, and the current war does not help Afghans in any way we can understand.

These innocent lives being lost in Afghanistan now are as precious as those that were lost in America, and the world community should not just be quiet while America and its allies continue to bomb innocent and defenseless civilians in Afghanistan. If this is left to continue, we do not see how this cycle of violence and death will end. We believe military power will not end terrorism, but dialogue can. As people of faith, we should call for peace.

We recommend that for lasting peace, the world community needs to address all the injustices in the world, be they in Sudan, Palestine, Kashmir, etc. We also recommend that the United Nations, rather than individual countries, take the lead in the current global fight against terrorism. The world is for all of us, and it requires collective efforts and contributions from across the world.

We end with inspirational words of Hans Kung:

"There will be no peace among nations until there is peace among religions and there will be no peace among religions until there is dialogue among them."

Let us remember this is the call and vocation of URI.

May peace prevail on earth.

The Muslim statement was received as a timely and significant addition to the Africa Assembly report and both reports were quickly broadcast by Internet.

In the midst of a world in turmoil, the assembly found moments of laughter and joy. Dave Randle, who had journeyed from Salt Lake City to represent URI North America at this gathering, offered the following reflection:

> All the experiences helped build community in their own right, but none of them came close to Hamed's ingenious strategy for community building at the Village Market Mall. The second night of the conference, before we departed for dinner, we were divided into teams of seven people and taken to a bowling alley, where we were instructed to bowl for peace points.
>
> From the look of things, I may have been the only one to have ever bowled before. People dropping balls, being afraid to roll the ball because it might break or hurt the floor, not understanding why they didn't get a second ball if they got a strike, etc., made the event an incredible time of fun and laughter that really brought the community together. I thought bowling for this group was the craziest thing that could have been done, but it turned out to be one of the most effective community-building exercises I have ever experienced. I think more than anything, it is the spirit of the African people who seem to be able to find ways to celebrate life in all of its phases that even allows bowling to be a community builder. It was certainly a time of bringing energy and hope to many people of many faiths. It was also a time to learn many ways to create sacred dialogue.

RESPONDING TO TRAGEDY IN PAKISTAN

Two short weeks after the end of the Africa assembly, the URI community was rocked once again by an incident of religiously motivated violence in Bahawalpur, Pakistan. IGC member Father James Channan, who had recently relocated to Multan, was informed of a massacre in a Catholic church. He traveled quickly to the scene and sent the following message to the URI community:

DEAR BROTHERS AND SISTERS,

I am very grateful to all members of the URI who have expressed their shock over the massacre of 15 innocent Christians and one innocent Muslim police guard in Pakistan on Sunday, 28th of October, at 9 a.m. I do appreciate your prayers and words of sympathy very much. It has comforted me and comforted our poor Christian minority community of Pakistan.

It is hard to believe that such a horrific act of terrorism has taken place in the country and the wrath of some fanatic fundamentalists has been manifested in such a cruel way.

The government of Pakistan, right from top to bottom, feels ashamed of this incident. They are taking some measures to catch the culprits. As usual some government officials are blaming "foreign hand" in this event. It is only a scapegoat. These people are killed by the people who are around us and who do not want us to live in peace and promote peace and harmony.

The incident could have been much worse had the Holy Mass started shortly after 9 a.m. At the time, more than 300 Catholics used to gather for Sunday celebration. Thank God the time was changed and the worst has not happened.

I condemn this act of terrorism in the strongest word. It is a crime against humanity. It is crime against the solidarity of our country. We do favor the policies of our government in their commitment in fighting against terrorism and terrorist organizations.

This tragic incident has further strengthened our vision promoting and preaching peace. Every person in Pakistan who has a heart of human flesh is mourning and expressing deep shock and solidarity with poor, harmless, peace-loving Christians of Pakistan. Our newspapers are full of condolence messages from all over the country. They include thousands of Muslim religious, political, and social leaders and human rights activists and government officials at all levels.

Bahawalpur is at the distance of a two-hour drive from Multan. St. Dominic's Church is our Dominican church (as you may know, I am a Dominican priest and belong to the Dominican religious order). We have two Dominican priests there, one Pakistani and the other American. There are also four Dominican nuns there. We are running one high school and one middle school. This is all for the welfare and good of the people, with discrimination toward none. St Dominic's Church was built in 1962.

Please keep us in your prayers. We need them very much at this time of broken hearts and souls.

With wounded and broken heart, I am,
James Channan

A week later James would have the opportunity to share his story on a San Francisco Sunday morning radio show, God Talk, hosted by former IGC member Ravi Peruman.

ASIA AND THE PACIFIC REGIONAL ASSEMBLY
BALI, INDONESIA, DECEMBER 13–15, 2001
PILGRIMS OF PEACE

Unlike Africa, there had never been a paid coordinator to help develop the URI in Asia and the Pacific. The IGC members from these regions had simply done what they could to help coordinate the existing CCs in their regions and to encourage the formation of new Circles and interfaith initiatives.

When it came time to plan for the assembly, the IGC members again volunteered their service. They shared information by email about possible venues. Dr. T. D. Singh, also known as His Holiness Bhaktisvarupe Damodara Swami, a leader of ISHKON and a convener of a URI Circle in Manipur, India, inquired about visa requirements and the political environment in places such as Bangkok and Singapore. T. D. Singh spoke with an old friend, Mrs. Ibu Gedong Oka, who had participated in the URI Global Summits at Stanford and in Pittsburgh, and led a URI CC in Bali, Indonesia. Mrs. Oka was a member of the Parliament of Indonesia and a highly regarded Gandhi scholar. T. D. Singh and Mrs. Oka endorsed Bali as the best spot for the assembly, and the IGC members and Charles Gibbs agreed. It was decided that Bali would be the place and December 13–15, 2001, would be the date. The place and date were decided, but it was unclear what local hosting capacity was possible in Bali. Mrs. Oka was busy with government work that often called her away to Jakarta. T. D. Singh was the spiritual leader of two ashrams in Bali, but the URI was virtually unheard of there; it was unknown whether people would be willing and able to take on hosting team responsibilities for a major interfaith gathering.

To fill out the assembly planning team and add gender balance, Marites Africa, a CC leader from Manila, Philippines, and Sally Mahé, from the URI global staff, San Francisco, joined. The new team – comprised of Mohinder Singh, a Sikh scholar of Punjab studies from Delhi; George Armstrong, an Anglican priest from New Zealand; the Venerable Jinwol Lee, a Buddhist monk from Korea;

Marites Africa, a Catholic woman from Manila; and Sally Mahé, a Christian URI staff member – converged in Denpasar, Bali, in late July. While everyone had high hopes that the facilities and organizational infrastructure in Bali would be adequate, when the team first gathered in the hot, humid morning air in the lobby of the Radisson Hotel, just about everything was uncertain. It was unknown whether T. D. Singh, just recuperating from surgery in India, had been able to locate local people in Bali to help. It was unknown whether Mrs. Oka and her young assistant, Agus Indra, would be able to return from Jakarta to Denpasar to participate in the planning meetings.

Marites Africa, who seemed a good choice to serve as overall coordinator for the assembly, was unknown to most of the team. It was unknown how the team – composed of people from diverse perspectives – would work together. The possibility of support from diverse religious groups in Bali was unknown. It was unknown how over 100 people from different faith traditions and from the vast regions of Asia and the Pacific, plus local people from Indonesia, could productively come together.

The planning team, all of whom were unfamiliar with Bali, began a true adventure into undiscovered territory. Team members started to search out suitable venues for the assembly, to learn about the unique gifts Bali offered, to share breathtaking heat, to try numerous fresh fruit drinks and unusual food, and to envision and plan for a gathering of people that would extend and deepen the possibility for interfaith work in all parts of Asia and the Pacific.

About an hour passed that first morning without any sign that local people would actually come to help. Then, as if by divine appointment, three people appeared who introduced themselves as devotees of Dr. T. D. Singh and said they were happy to offer their assistance full-time for the next three days. Professionally, Sundara Das was a travel agent; his wife, Prema Manjari, a dentist; and their friend, Guna, a successful businessperson. Soon everyone piled into a van and set off hotel-hopping, hoping to find a site that was not too expensive and too full of tourists and one that offered an authentic experience of Bali in a serene and inspiring setting.

Planning ideas started to flow in the van rides as planning team members began to share their visions and hopes for the assembly. Back at the Radisson, they gathered in a meeting room several hours each day and mapped the evolution of ideas on flip charts and George Armstrong's laptop computer. Marites accepted the role of coordinator and led discussions about the theme, goals, and possible activities. At the end of three days, the team found the Bali Intan Cottages, a hotel that offered simple accommodations at a good price. Team members had a theme, "Pilgrims of Peace," and they developed a promising outline for a three-day program. Marites integrated everything the team had experienced and the plans the team had designed during the three-day trip and wrote an invitation letter that gave prospective delegates a view of what to expect.

> The program will include a variety of dialogue and lecture, activities, rituals and ceremonies, and a peace walk that will be woven together like intricate patterns of batik (hand-painted cloth). Images of light and bamboo torches, of a profusion of colors painted on intricate wood carvings, and of Lord Ganesh welcoming in the weary pilgrim against the music of the kukul from the bamboo gamelan that punctuates the sound of the roaring ocean will serve as the setting for this assembly of Pilgrims.

The invitations were mailed just before September 11, 2001. For several weeks, it was unclear whether the assembly should go forward or be canceled. In mid-November, about four weeks before the opening day, the planning team made a final decision to go forward. They were assured Bali was safe and believed it was more timely and important than ever to be a visible force for peace among religions!

Ninety-four people attended the assembly: three from the Philippines, one from Australia, thirty-two from various parts of India, twenty-nine from Bali and five from other parts in Indonesia, three from New Zealand, nine from Pakistan, one from Nepal, three from Korea, one representing Vietnam, one from Latin America, and three from North America.

After keynote speeches by former president of Indonesia Waheed and Swami Agnivesh, a URI Circle member and human rights activist in India, the delegates participated in appreciative interviews and afterward gathered in groups of six to answer this question: As Pilgrims of Peace, what statement do you want to make to the world?

These statements give evidence of the diversity of voices of people who engaged with one another to renew their fervor for peace:

> Besides chanting and praying, we must feel love in seeing and hearing the plants, the animals, the earth, the air, the weather, the sea, the atmosphere, the sun, the moon always smiling — all of them beings of peace.

> We accept Swami Agnivesh's idea that we have to unite in concrete actions which will lead us to more united actions. We must not control others, but allow ourselves to be controlled by God. God's kingdom must become a reality one day.

> God creates the universe in plurality. The rainbow has many colors, and there are people of many ethnic groups. So why can't we look at religions also in terms of plurality, as the will of God, so that we can look at one another in peace.

> Washing away blood with more blood by war cleans nothing. Blood is washed away by the water of forgiveness.

We want to join all of the URI CCs and all other peace initiatives the world over to organize a global interfaith march for peace with justice.

———————————

Peace is not a distant goal to be attained in the future, but humankind's spiritual birthright, squandered in the pursuit of power. As people of diverse faiths united in the pursuit of peace, we denounce the hijacking of religion and the disowning of spirituality in the pursuit of war and violence.

———————————

Because the URI is an organization that is free from politics and power struggles and reliable to all the peoples of the world, it is the right time to initiate actions to change the mentality to help people become ajathasathas, meaning "people who have no enemy."

———————————

All religions advocate peace, love, and compassion. The URI needs to carry this message to people of all traditions.

———————————

Recognition and celebration of any differences can be achieved by inner conversion, by becoming agents of change ourselves.

These statements were reviewed and incorporated into a Statement of Commitment written by a dedicated group of delegates and signed by all the delegates.

The assembly finale was a *Padayatra*, or sacred pilgrimage walk. Over 1,000 people joined the delegates for a two-kilometer pilgrimage through the streets of Denpasar from the Gandhi ashram to the Parliament building, where everyone participated in a closing ceremony that honored the cultural and religious arts of Bali. It was the rainy season, but no one worried it would rain on any of the assembly activities. Why not? Because the Bali host team hired "professional rain stoppers" to keep the rain away. Not one drop fell the entire three days of the assembly. The rain started once again 24 hours after the last delegates departed for home, taking with them inspiration and a renewed and deepened commitment to be and to lead the change they wished to see in the world.

LATIN AMERICA AND THE CARIBBEAN REGIONAL ASSEMBLY SEARCHING OUR IDENTITY – BUILDING BRIDGES, OAXTAPEC, MEXICO, JANUARY 23–26, 2002

After several attempts to settle on a location, the planning team agreed on Oaxtapec, Mexico. The local host team came from two important interfaith organizations in Mexico City, Instituto Luz Sobre Luz, led by Sufi Sheik Amina and her staff, and the Mexico Interfaith Council, led by Jonathon Rose and his staff, who were able to draw in several religious leaders and government officials. André Porto, one of the primary organizers, wrote:

> It wasn't easy to pull this together. It took one year to prepare for the assembly. Many dedicated people were involved in defining the place, the theme, and the goals and in planning the program and networking to increase attendance. The contribution of everyone was a special gift since we all had to deal with a big emptiness after the passage of Father Luis Dolan.

On January 23, a diverse group of 80 people – men and women, young and old – from many different religions, spiritual expressions, and indigenous traditions throughout Latin America gathered to celebrate the development of the URI in their part of the world and to develop an agenda for future development. As had become the norm with URI gatherings, each day was grounded in shared experiences of the sacred.

Every morning before the sessions we had prayers
and celebrations from different traditions. These practices were optional and announced publicly. Sikhs
offered their spiritual practices; Catholics attended the
Mass; Muslims did their suplicas; members of the
Orixa Cult performed their ritual; Jews did their
prayers; there was an ecumenical celebration of the
Eucharist; an Aztec indigenous ceremony was offered
in the sulfur water lake near the hotel. It was remarkable that most of the participants fed themselves in
their own tradition's practice but also respectfully
attended other's prayers to learn about their rituals.
The "Oratorio," a special room designated for worship would have a Mass, Muslim suplicas, and Jewish
Prayers one after the other in the same morning and
attended by the same people.

— André Porto, Assembly Organizer

In true URI/AI partnership fashion, the assembly began with
appreciative interviews in pairs, moving into groups of eight where
people spoke about their spiritual identity and their motivation for
being involved in peace building and interfaith activities. The AI
process was led by Antonio Valenca from Recife, Brazil, an expert in
Appreciative Inquiry methodology. Much of the program was organized into workshops based on the Action Agenda items in the URI
charter. The Action Agenda, which had been so prominent in the
URI charter development and that would provide the organizing
framework for the Global Assembly in Rio in August 2002, was used
for the first time since the birth of the URI to provide the broad
themes for the assembly's workshops:
  • Sharing the Wisdom and Cultures of Faith Traditions
  • Nurturing Cultures of Healing and Peace

- Human Rights and Responsibilities
- Ecological Imperatives
- Sustainable Just Economics
- Supporting the Overall URI

Led by URI leaders from different parts of Latin America, these workshops provided an opportunity for participants to share their experiences and to deepen their vision and skills in a particular action area. Beyond that, people in each area formed a working group for future development, including input for planning the global assembly.

Once again, a URI gathering was enriched by the presence of indigenous people – and challenged by the enduring legacy of colonialism and continuing predatory practices, particularly by certain Christian groups, which threatened the cultural survival of tribal peoples. Rosalia Guiterrez had arranged for the eight indigenous people from six different countries to meet for a day before the conference began to find common ground for themselves before the larger group gathered. By the end of the assembly, they had decided to form a CC to help them stay in touch with each other and to continue to explore a mutually beneficial partnership between the URI and native peoples in Latin America and around the world.

After a full day of work, the evenings were dedicated to a celebration of the diverse cultures and spirit of Latin America. The evenings were a time for singing, for dancing, for storytelling, and for sharing food and the riches of different cultures. A highlight was an evening hosted by Jonathan Rose and his wife at their home.

> The greatest Mexican cultural experience took place at Jonathan and Margarita's house, half an hour away from Oaxtapec, in the mystic and charming town of Tepoztlan. Our generous hosts, dedicated URI members from Jewish and Catholic origins, provided the group with a unique taste of Catholic and Mexican culture and fine food in a party called Posa-

da. The guests were invited to break the hanging piña-
ta filled with sweets and to challenge the spinning fireworks bull carried by the gracious Alejandrino
Quispe, an indigenous man from Peru. Every detail
and the soul of the night were carefully prepared. People gathered naturally in three different areas and celebrated in their own way. One group, blessed with
great guitar players and full of singers, offered a
stream of the greatest Latin songs. It was exciting to
hear an Anglican priest from Mexico singing
Sephardic songs with a Rabbi. Another group sang
traditional indigenous songs, while others danced near
the swimming pool.... There was a lot of improvisation and creativity. The language of music was important to provide different levels of communication.

— André Porto, Assembly Organizer

Once again, in the simple but profound act of sharing and celebrating distinct expressions of a common humanity, the URI was
being what it sought to become.

André Porto summed up the impact of the assembly in these
words:

In January 2002, a Muslim Sheik from Buenos
Aires experienced for the first time the spiritual Jewish
ceremony of Shabat. Afterward, he shared with the
whole group of participants at the URI Latin American Regional Assembly in Mexico his hope for peace
and his desire to attend many other Shabats. It wasn't
only a beautiful statement. Mr. Mohsen Ali went back
home full of ideas and inspiration to promote interfaith understanding. Good news such as this usually is
rare to find in the mainstream media. However, stories

like this have been blooming out of all URI regional assemblies. In Oaxtapec, Mexico, from the 23rd through 26th of January 2002, 80 people exercised interfaith dialog aiming to understand one another and design a common agenda for action through workshops. When these 80 people went back to their communities, they were all carrying good news. They represent something extremely needed in the world these days — people who are breaking through the cycle of ignorance, hatred, violence, and revenge; people who can listen and forgive one another; people able to share the sacred and who wish to cooperate to serve the planet.

EUROPE AND THE MIDDLE EAST
FACING VIOLENCE AS A WAY TO PEACE, BERLIN, GERMANY, APRIL 6–10, 2002

IGC trustees Annie Imbens Fransen and Deepak Naik worked with members of the URI European Executive Committee; with the host team in Berlin; and with Yehuda Stolov, an IGC member from the Middle East to design and manage the assembly for Europe and the Middle East. As with the other regional assemblies, the leadership was provided by people who had other "day jobs" and who were given modest, if any, financial remuneration for their effort to organize this interfaith gathering. Early on, the planning team was inspired to create a conference that would use Berlin, a city once divided, as a symbol of a country and a people who were able to reunite after a painful history of separation. The overall theme focused on how to use an environment of violence and hatred as a vehicle for reconciliation and peace — not to avoid a history of hatred, but to face hatred, working toward a way to peace and justice.

Forty-two delegates from 16 countries and 13 faith traditions met one another and talked about their experiences in facing religiously motivated violence and discrimination. Participants came from Germany, England, the Netherlands, Belgium, Spain, Croatia, Israel, Jordan, and Egypt. In the center of the hotel meeting room was a simple table adorned with candles and flowers. Each delegate added an object he or she brought from home and was invited to share a story about it. An inquiry (organized so conversations took place in triads) was entitled "Knowing Your Neighbor" and, a few of the questions were as follows:

> Are there aspects, structures, or texts in your faith traditions that can be used to motivate violence and injustice towards others because of race, color, sex, religion, national or social origin, property, birth, or status?

> What kind of violence has been done or is still happening in the name of your faith tradition and against which group of people? What is needed to prevent this violence motivated by people of your faith tradition? What can you contribute to prevent this violence?

> What aspects of your faith tradition motivate and inspire you to end religiously motivated violence and create cultures of peace, justice, and healing for the Earth and all living beings?

Another special exercise invited everyone to learn about each other's faith traditions. On large pieces of paper, people were asked to write down what they thought they knew about another faith tradition or what they had heard from listening to the media. A member of each representative faith tradition stood up and illuminated which impressions were valid and which were not. Conversations seeded the beginning of friendships.

Anne Roth, a visiting delegate from the United States, remarked:

"The personal stories I heard will stay with me. I spoke with a woman from Jerusalem whose son was badly wounded by a suicide bomber and for whom coming to Germany was very hard, but who said she was going home feeling empowered. I spoke with a man who had been jailed several times for his active role within the Islamic community teaching modern interpretations of the Qur'an. This man had fled his home for his life and had not seen his children in 20 years. In spite of their wounds, these were the kinds of high souls that I want to celebrate, honor, and encourage."

The crisis in the Middle East prevented several delegates from attending, but participants did come from Egypt, Jordan, and Israel. Dr. Mohamed Masaad from Egypt commented that, "All participants from all sides came to Berlin not only to speak up from their hearts, but to listen to others and understand the Other as well. For some participants, it was the first time in their life to see a Jew, let alone an Israeli."

After originally rejecting the idea of separate meetings, the delegates from the Middle East changed their minds and decided to meet in special sessions that included only people from the Middle East. An extraordinary fishbowl dialogue/debate took place in this setting. Dr. Mohamed Masaad described this event:

> The participants from the Middle East decided to face their fears directly and courageously. "The root of hatred is fear," they said." What is the point of meeting together if we do not speak up from our hearts and face our fears?" they asked. Soon there were two subgroups, one for Arabs one for Jews, writing down all that they knew about the other side. When the two long lists were finished, each group chose a spokesperson from the other side. An Arab spokesperson was chosen to speak for a Jew. A Jewish spokesperson had to present for the Arabs. By doing this, the painful subject was put into a humorous yet

challenging light. Before starting this "debate," the two representatives exchanged their hats, and that made everyone laugh and relax. At the end of this heated session, each group enthusiastically cheered its representative and emphasized its satisfaction with his performance. Naturally, the debate did not end in the winning or losing of one side or the other. Nor did any side abandon its narrative. At the end, everyone knew that there was another narrative, another story, that *did* exist that they must know.

Workshops were offered by assembly delegates, and representatives from CCs were given an opportunity to share their experiences, frustrations, and successes. One afternoon the entire group walked to Wiedendammer Bridge to hold a special ceremony to honor the Day of Remembrance for the Holocaust. Delegates brought candles from their conference altar and floated tulips down the river in commemoration of those who had lost their lives and those who had been instrumental in helping to save the lives of their neighbors.

In planning next steps, a flurry of ideas rose up for new CCs and new initiatives. A new Global Youth CC was born on the spot, a new CC in Berlin was organized, an interfaith peace-building event in Bosnia at the Mostar Bridge was imagined, and a second CC in Finland and a new one in Latvia was talked about, as well as several CCs that could take off in Jerusalem and Egypt. Plans emerged for a special conference in the fall for the Middle East, and many participants promised to go home and write articles about their experiences here. Mohamed Masaad remarked that the participants spent their last night together in a friendly environment, taking photos and wandering in neighborhoods near the hotel. As the group of Europeans, Jews, and Arabs found their way back to the hotel, laughing and talking with one another, it looked as though Berlin had witnessed the removal of another wall.

SUMMARY

The URI had traveled an enormous distance from the spring of 1997, when it held three conferences within a month, to the spring of 2001, when it launched five regional assemblies around the world. In many ways, the organization still moved in invincible ignorance, continually living in the questions. CCs were still learning what it meant to be a CC. The IGC was developing an ever-deeper appreciation of its unique role and responsibilities and struggling with how to live into those roles as a diverse, dispersed global community working with limited human and financial resources. The global staff was evolving from an almost ad hoc group that could fit into one room, where everyone knew what everyone else was doing, into a professional staff with clearly understood areas of responsibility, authority, and expertise. This learning was accompanied by open channels of communication while people were modeling the URI's nonhierarchical values in their work – working to discern where and how to lead, where and how to serve, and where and how to step aside so others could lead and serve.

The URI was continually grappling with the practical realities and profound questions of how to put an adequate values-based financial foundation under the organization. How could the URI empower work around the world without creating the unhealthy cultures of scarcity and dependency that had characterized so much international work? How could the organization develop a global program of philanthropy that was sensitive to differing cultural realities and that honored the generosity and giving potential of people all over the world, yet was not blind to the dramatically different economic conditions in different regions of the world?

Yes, the URI still lived in the questions and often those questions were deeper and more complex than they had been in the early years. And yet the URI had learned a great deal as well. The organization knew for certain that the partnership between URI and AI had created an organizing methodology that had welcomed, honored, and inspired people from diverse backgrounds all over the world. It had invited them into a safe space where they could discover new friends, dare to dream together about a better world for all life, and offer what was most precious to them from their traditions to make that dream a reality through the ongoing cocreation of the URI. The URI/AI partnership continued to hold great promise for the growth of this effort to promote enduring daily interfaith cooperation; to end religiously motivated violence; and to create cultures of peace, justice, and healing for the Earth and all living beings.

Original URI logo, symbols representing fourteen faith traditions
and an open circle representing all religions not represented here
and those still to come.

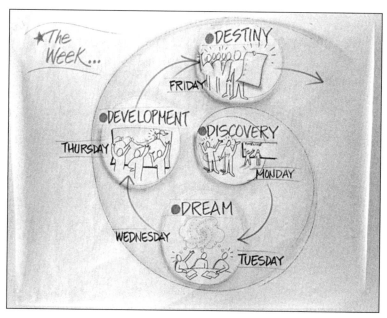

4D-Cycle of Appreciative Inquiry
URI Global Summit 1997
Artist: Diana Arsenian

First Regional Summit, 1997
Brahma Kumaris Global Retreat Center, Oxford, UK

Charles Gibbs explaining URI Transition
Global Summit 1999
Stanford University, CA

Sally Mahé and David Cooperrider explaining Cooperation Circles
Global Summit, 1999, Stanford University, CA

Participants engage in "bib" conversations
URI Global Summit, 2000, Pittsburgh, PA

Interfaith Ceremony for Peaceful Reunification of Korea,
URI 72 Hours Project, December 30, 1999
Imjigak Joint Security Area between North and South Korea

Children for Peace, Berkeley Buddhist Monastery
URI 72 Hours Project, January 2, 2000
Berkeley, CA

North America and Multi-Regional Assembly
May 2001, Salt Lake City, Utah, USA

Africa Regional Assembly
October 2001, Nairobi, Kenya

Asia and Pacific Regional Assembly
December 2001, Bali, Indonesia

Latin America and the Caribbean Regional Assembly
January 2002, Oaxtepec, Mexico

Europe and the MIddle East Regional Assembly
April 2002, Berlin, Germany

Participants in A Journey for
Peace from Karachi to Khyber Pass
celebrate their success,
URI 72 Hours Project,
December 1999, Pakistan

URI Interfaith Peace March marks the dawn of the 21st century
in Manipur, India.

"We, the world community, are waging peace. It is difficult, hard work.
It is constant and we must not let up."

Dr. Robert Muller, former Assistant Secretary General of the UN

CHAPTER 7

The URI's dance into the future is about developing an organization that inspires, welcomes, and supports an ever-increasing number of people from diverse religions, spiritual expressions, and indigenous traditions throughout the world as they initiate effective actions to promote enduring daily interfaith cooperation for positive change.... It is about creating an organization whose foundations reach into the depths and are grounded on the bedrock of stillness, where the ultimate may be experienced.

CHAPTER 7
·························

The Future:
A Dance of Movement
and Stillness

A SPIRITUAL ORGANIZATION

There is a need to be silent as all this is happening. But how can people within an organization experience stillness in the din of building the plane as they are flying forward? How, in the URI's intensely demanding pace of change and development, can its members reflect on and be renewed by the fruits of what they are creating together? When people continue to find themselves walking in the dark, where do they find the spiritual resources to continue to trust their next steps? How can people actualize the vision of the URI as more and more people take the initiative to promote enduring daily interfaith cooperation to make peace a reality in all parts of the world? How can the organization support all participants as they deepen their convictions and broaden their effectiveness? How can the URI amplify the impact of local activities so they reverberate on the world stage?

The URI's dance into the future is about developing an organization that inspires, welcomes, and supports an ever-increasing number of people from diverse religions, spiritual expressions, and indigenous traditions throughout the world as they initiate effective actions to promote enduring daily interfaith cooperation for positive change. It

is about creating an organization that listens and responds to its participants. It is about creating an organization whose foundations reach
into the depths and are grounded on the bedrock of stillness, where
the ultimate may be experienced.

The URI is learning that people persevere in making their
dreams come true when they find a balanced rhythm of movement
and stillness in their lives. In the fast track of modernity, it is very hard
to make room for stillness. The URI office in San Francisco reserves
one room for meditation. Chants and serene music emanate from the
room three times a day and beckon the staff to take a break and be
still. However, in the demands and pace of work, they rarely stop to
listen in silence to the music or to take off their shoes and enter the
quiet space. The silence is present and waits for them always. The
meditation room is a physical reminder of the grounding of the URI
in a sacred place that holds those – of an empty center.

Recently a CC leader from Manipur, India, offered this insight at
the Asia and Pacific Regional Assembly: "The URI is a global body
that is free from politics and power mongers. It is a spiritual organization and is the hope of citizens of the world." So far, the development
of the URI as a global organization has elicited trust primarily
because people experience a consistency between word and deed. The
future asks the participants to sustain the URI as a trustworthy light.
Nirmala Deshpande, a member of a URI CC in Delhi, India, and a
Gandhian philosopher and teacher, called upon the URI to be an
organization that offered the world a new spiritual paradigm that
replaced the love of power with the power of love.

The stillness in the meditation room invites people to know stillness inside themselves. Regardless of tradition, this stillness can connect them with the Source of vision, strength, and conviction, with
the Source of integrity and service. In this stillness, they can let go of
ego defenses and fears and can recommit to the power of love. In this
stillness, people can connect in an invisible way with the careholders
of the URI vision all over the world.

THE URI AT TWO YEARS OLD

Almost two years after the birth of the URI in Pittsburgh, the URI has grown to over 180 CCs spread across five continents. The URI global support network exists to help people in CCs connect globally, increase their skills, deepen their local effectiveness, and inspire a global effort toward peace among religions.

Sadly, each day brings in emails telling of new outbreaks of violence, of large numbers of children at risk for HIV/AIDS, of environmental devastation, and of ongoing suffering that is ravaging countries where URI CCs are working. Thankfully, each day also brings in 10 to 20 email messages from URI CCs around the world talking about their work for a better world. Though the flood of bad news can sometimes overwhelm the good, URI members are sustained in their work, knowing there are more contributions to cultures of peace, justice, and healing than there would be without the URI and its allies in so many other organizations dedicated to positive change around the world.

ILLUSTRATION IN INDIA

Following the outbreak of violence and bloodshed between Muslims and Hindus in Gujarat, India, in March 2002, URI CCs in various cities in India used their networks to mount a response. Mohinder Singh communicated their efforts to the URI global community:

> We in India need your sincere prayers at a time when there are again serious communal tensions in Gujarat resulting in more than 400 deaths of our brothers and sisters and loss of private and state properties.
>
> Last evening Dr. Nirmala Deshpande took the initiative of organizing a prayer meeting in Rajghat – the memorial of Mahatma Gandhi yesterday. She invited the various CCs from Delhi – Swami

Agnivesh; Reverend Valson Thampu; Maulana
Obedullah Azmi, prominent Muslim leader and member of the Indian Parliament; Sayeda Saiden, a prominent Muslim woman activist; intellectuals from various
universities in the capital; and a large number of college and school students. In the evening, a candlelight
vigil was arranged during a strategy session as to how
to deal with the aftermath of Godhra (Gujarat)
tragedy. Before the strategy session, a press statement
was issued condemning revenge killings and an appeal
was made to the NDA Govt. in the centre to ensure
safety and security of the minorities by deploying
Army wherever required. An appeal was also made to
people of India to resist all divisive propaganda, maintain communal harmony, and unite in protecting the
unity and integrity of our secular democracy.

After the prayer meeting in Rajghat, we had a
strategy session, and it was decided that we should
request prominent religious leaders from different
communities to visit areas in their respective cities
which are prone to communal tensions as a measure
of goodwill building and inspiring confidence
amongst the minorities. We appeal to the URI CCs in
various parts of India to become active in keeping
with the preamble of the URI charter and act as
bridges of friendship and restore peace and communal harmony in their respective areas.

I am sending a copy of this email to various CCs
in India to ask them to play their role as peacemakers
during these terrible days.

With best wishes and prayers for peace in the world,

Sincerely,
Mohinder Singh

In forming a new CC in Zambia, Bwalya Peters said she was motivated to initiate a URI Circle because she "loves her country and wants to see Zambia all one — people living in harmony. With the current AIDS crisis and history of tribalism, there is much instability and division in the country." Bwalya believes there must be a better way for the people of her country. She sees people of different religions working together as the best chance of making a positive difference. Her Circle is currently working with street kids, bringing them together, offering them food and information about AIDS, and connecting them with mentors and educational opportunities.

Rosalia Gutierrez, a leader of the Kolla people of Argentina and leader of the indigenous people of an Argentina CC, responds to the URI Global Council Trustee Selection process. The process, designed to be in accord with California state statutory requirements for board elections for a nonprofit membership organization, is not an indigenous people's way of making these kinds of decisions. Rosalia speaks up:

> Our circle feels that we need a little more time to discuss the nomination process... because we have a different way of thinking, a different way of seeing the world. Many of us live in a time and a space that is circular — in which time does not have a beginning or an end, where our values are taken from the Earth in order to live in harmony with our environment, where we are far from thinking in rapid terms. Respecting the diversity, the different thought processes of the different CCs, we want you to accept our way of thinking — not to judge if it is better or worse, but only to recognize a different thought process, which we would like to share. In our way of thinking, the notion of duality is complementary and not polarized. This perhaps could serve URI as a tool for better understanding religions and cultures.

Indigenous peoples have suffered great genocide and massacres because of foreign religions imposing systems that did not support our way of thinking. The dominant systems have created models of domination, and those models have resulted in further arguments about power and constant conflicts that cause people to kill each other in order to impose their own will. Many of us are leaving behind those models in our community. As a result, we do not elect representatives by vote. No one is directly elected. All of us know what function we serve in the space and time that we live in. We are recovering different ways to honor these functions. We have taken the values of our ancestors from our Mother Earth, and this form that we know well is for us a returning to the forms that we have carried from the beginning.

In conclusion, our circle is suggesting that you be willing to understand our way of thinking. We are seeing this different process for nomination as a reality. Please tell us you understand. We suggest or propose that we would like to participate in the global council without having to take part in a system that does not agree with our way of thinking. It would be good to have further conversation with you all to come to a better understanding. We need you to communicate with us, with the mediation / translation help of Yoland Trevino. We are grateful for the possibility that you have given us to be a powerful part of URI. We want to express to you our thinking, which has been silent for much time — or perhaps hidden, as some indigenous say. For us, it is the first time that you have given us this opportunity to express ourselves from our vision. It is for that reason that we respect being part of this family.

ONGOING PROJECTS

On the same day Rosalia sent her eloquent reaction to corporate voting procedures in the United States, Erik Schwartz, from the URI Washington D.C. CC, called to talk about a strategic partnership between the URI, other interfaith organizations, and Habitat for Humanity. He said the Washington D.C. CC was taking the lead with Habitat in developing *Interfaith Habitat*, a program that would expand the effective Habitat work to include an interfaith dimension.

Erik enthusiastically described the plans:

> The project will be coordinated worldwide by Habitat for Humanity International in partnership with the URI and other religious organizations. The home building will be organized by Habitat and URI CCs along with other congregations and interfaith groups. Persons of all faiths will come together to build, beginning the day in prayer or meditation, eating lunch communally, and learning more about each other as they build a house for someone in need.

About the same time, nine members of the Bridge CC, dedicated to ongoing cooperation between the URI and the Council for the Parliament of the World's Religions, met on a spring afternoon in Berkeley, California. The group included a Wiccan priestess, a Jewish couple, a retired dean of a Lutheran seminary, a Lutheran pastor (taking time away from her sermon preparation), a UCC pastor, a bishop of the Church of Divine Man (a Christian church that incorporates psychic training), a student at the Unitarian seminary, and others. They gathered to put final planning in place for a Bay Area-wide gathering of 80 to100 clergy and members of faith congregations interested in finding ways to reach out to people of different faiths. Their project was called *Bringing the Global Ethic Home*. They designed a full-day workshop, incorporating appreciative interviews that engaged people with a historic document, *Towards a Global Ethic*, developed by

Hans Kung and signed by over 300 faith leaders at the Parliament of
the World's Religions in 1993.

The URI's dance into the future includes the *21st Century Vision for
Peace Among Religions,* a global inquiry that builds upon the learning and
successes of the 72 Hours Project. The program, intended to begin
within the URI community but to reach out far beyond it to include
many partner organizations and over a million people, will invite a
worldwide cascade of appreciative conversations that ask people to
unleash the power of their imaginations to see the world's religious
and spiritual communities as leaders for peace in the twenty-first century. IGC member Reverend Heng Sure offers the following reflection on the project:

> In the Vision for Peace Among Religions for the
> 21st, I hear Bishop Swing saying we have to ask deep-
> er questions. Once we are together working for endur-
> ing daily interfaith cooperation, do we still assume it
> is OK to hate and fight each other in the name of the
> Sacred? This is a question we must understand. If we
> simply come together and do not address this ques-
> tion, we will continue to have bloodshed. I see the
> bishop getting deeper to the real cause of the blood-
> shed, the misunderstanding, the antagonism, the
> hatred, and the hostility among religions. Peace Vision
> for the 21st Century is meant to be a contemplation
> and a conversation of the heart. It is a means to shine
> light on what the deeper purpose of the URI really is.
>
> In the Vision for Peace Among Religions for the
> 21st, I hear Bishop Swing asking for an authentic
> flowering as the next step for the URI. He is saying,
> "We have taken a huge step; now let's take a further
> step and go down to the wound and pull the thorn
> out." It's the same challenge, but it's deeper. It is where
> deeper healing needs to be done. Where fundamental

questions need to be addressed:

Why do we, as good-hearted religious people, assume that it is still OK to fight in the name of the Sacred – to fight and stay separate because of our religion? Why do people of different religions allow sibling rivalry to bring us to shed blood?

I carry around with me Bishop Swing's statement about the Vision for Peace Among Religions for the 21st Century. It calls upon people to take it everywhere and get people's responses. Take it to the jails, to the League of Women Voters, to the lunchrooms, to churches, schools, everywhere you can find people who are meeting, and get their response because this has got to be truly global change of heart.

Peace Vision is about the heart. The URI as it exists today is about the body – people taking action and initiative in order to bring positive change in their communities. We have over 150 CCs all doing good things. The Vision for Peace Among Religions for the 21st is offered as a contemplation while we are doing the work.

Wouldn't it be wonderful if while we were active in our programs, we were also contemplating ending the hostility in our hearts? This invisible part in ourselves is still unaddressed. The Peace Vision says, to name what it is that has kept us at each other's throats. Why do we think it is OK to continue hostilities? The Peace Vision is about questions and conversations, not action. It is about changing our eyes and allowing for change of heart by asking questions. The Peace Vision uses the Appreciative Inquiry process to provide a form and methodology for the conversations. People can see into it what they want and add to it, enter it and shape it as it makes sense to them. It is an invitation, an open and unpredictable harvest of fruits.

So, as the URI matures, it is called to get down to the real stuff — to stop the hostilities, hatreds, and violence among people of faith. I applaud that! What a leader to have that kind of guts and courage. He could have relaxed and wrapped himself in the URI and stopped there. But, instead, he is saying, "We have begun and now there is more."

Authors' Perspective

The fourth principle in the URI charter states, "We encourage our members to deepen their roots in their own tradition." Certainly, the authors have found their roots in Christianity deepened by their involvement in the URI. As we near the end of this birth story, we offer a perspective that has arisen from that deepening. The magnificent story of the URI, from the birth of the vision to its dance in movement and stillness into the future, illuminates the words "your kingdom come" from the Our Father, the Lord's Prayer, the prayer Jesus taught his followers. These words beckon us to see a spiritual truth: the greatest achievement in life is not in achieving the kingdom. The greatest achievement happens in the course of the journey we take toward its coming. The journey — who we are in every moment, who we become, and how we choose to take the first step and then the second and third — is the context in which God's peaceable kingdom is found. Our fervent efforts may never result in the fullness of the kingdom we seek, one that offers the extraordinary gift of peace, justice, and healing on Earth. The words "your kingdom come" say the end result is not here yet, and may never be here. But these words say that is okay because what is important is to recognize the fruits of the kingdom along the way.

The Gospel of Thomas says, "The reign of God is spread across the Earth but the people do not see it." Another way of illuminating the story of the URI is to say that the URI's vision is already alive within creation. It is up to people to see it, to cherish it, and to choose it above other things. The glory of the unfolding story of the URI in these first years is the recognition that we are, in fact, being what we want to become. We do not wait for the kingdom or for peace on Earth to happen before the URI is successful. We know the URI is making real its vision when indigenous people from tribes alienated from each other gather around a bonfire and reverently listen to one another and joyfully dance. We know the URI is making real its vision when a grieving priest in Pakistan feels his broken heart begin to heal through the outpouring of support from people of all faiths all over the world. We know the URI is making real its vision when each day around the world, people of different faiths join hands as sisters and brothers and work together for the good of all.

Pete Seeger, the American folk singer, once said: "You know, my involvement in causes and marches may not have made very much of a difference. But I can tell you one thing, that involvement in these issues means you are involved with the good people, the people with the live hearts, the live eyes, and live heads. . . ."

AI is a methodology that draws out the live eyes, live heads, and live hearts in people. It is a perspective and methodology that holds the human spirit in high esteem and creates a safe space for the spirit to soar. It is a process that gives people a way to practice living in a spiritual democracy, where every voice matters and people are invited to rise up, one by one, as valuable members of the whole human family. AI is a methodology that looks to see the beauty, not the ugliness. It supports the human spirit, elicits individual stories, and releases the awesome potential of humanity. AI trusts the capacity of people to do good. Kelvin Sauls, a Methodist minister and member of the IGC, said, "The forces of evil have been arrayed in the world for a long time; it is time we mobilize the forces of good."

URI and AI are a matched set that help people recall their core values. They invite people to discover the best in themselves and others, to share their dreams, to step into leadership, to create, to share good ideas, to develop friendships, to support one another, to take initiative, to draw forth what is already inside.

The greatest gifts in the story of the URI thus far are the moments of recognition when we realized we were being what we wanted to become. A veil was lifted and the separation vanished between the *not yet* and the *here now* — dancing with tribal leaders under the stars in Itatatia, Brazil, celebrating the birth of the URI in Pittsburgh, looking at each other, and saying, "YOU ARE I;" attending a URI staff meeting and taking hold of a Masai "talking stick" to share our vision about the URI. We heard our voices speak, but we also felt the spirit in our souls soar as we spoke about our core values and our passions. We shared with one another what made our hearts feel full and happy.

The story of the birth of the URI is about the birth of a vision and about a bishop who invited the whole world to join him on an inconceivable quest to make that vision real — to encourage religions to stop fighting; to make peace with one another; and to build together a world of peace, justice, and healing. It is the story of AI, an inclusive philosophy and methodology that holds people in high regard and invites them to make a positive difference. It is story about an ambitious organizational design that experiments with organizational structures, allowing people's core values to manifest themselves. The URI story is about committed people finding sources of renewal within themselves (in movement and in stillness, in action and in prayer or meditation) so they are able to offer themselves every day to endless questions and an overwhelming workload. It is a story about the blossoming of friendships — people from different religions, spiritual expressions, and indigenous traditions who are surprised by friendship that transcends differences and that forms a brotherhood and sisterhood dedicated to a shared vision.

The Road Ahead

The future for the URI may be like its first five years — a circuitous and bumpy walk full of unpredictable turning points, a walk in the dark. Questions loom: Will the URI get bogged down in procedures and soon feel like it is an old freighter rather than a light, agile skiff? Will the URI, like the organization that inspired its birth, the United Nations, find itself, in a few years, hobbled by the weight of almost paralyzing decision-making structures? Will the URI be refreshed by the joy of stillness? Will it learn how to live with change? Will it reach for the fresh, magnificent light of new possibilities symbolized in the star logo that guides it way?

We do not know the answers to these questions, but we will move toward them one step at a time. In 1997, the rallying cry was "Impossible, so let's do it!" Today people trust the URI to sustain itself as a locally rooted and globally connected organization with spiritual heart and soul that provides solutions to ancient hostilities and alternatives to traditional hierarchical organizational behavior. The rallying cry still is "Impossible, so let's do it!"

The challenge for everyone in the URI and for all those who are yet to be a part of this vision is to embrace the values that give our souls life and the URI its integrity. We will find our way together into the future as we take heart and leap into this impossible dream together. Pardon us if, at the end of this book, we and all the URI smell of feathers and are sticky with glue. Like you, we are standing on the precipice of hope. Come, let's fly.

> To hope means to take a playful leap
> into the future...
> to dare to spring from firm ground,
> to play trustingly, invest energy, laughter.
> And one good leap encourages another.
> On then with the dance.
>
> Joan Erikson

AFTERWORD

The world today is far different from when Bishop Swing received a call from the United Nations in 1993. Far different from even a year ago at URI's second birthday in June 2002. Our world is fractured. Menace and cynicism abound. Trust and authentic hope are hard to find, and yet the URI story reveals that there is a blossoming of trust and cooperative accomplishment all over the world. This rise of a global community rooted in universal values remains mostly unseen.

In the past year, URI's global community has grown to include 204 Cooperation Circles with over 26,000 members in nearly 50 countries. True to deep roots in Appreciative Inquiry, each prospective Cooperation Circle is given an appreciative interview by a global council trustee or staff. The interview is not an interrogation or an evaluation of new members but creates, through respectful conversation, a bond of mutual understanding built on careful listening and shared values.

These interviews in themselves can be transformative. When URI received its first CC application from the Palestinian Territories, from the Nablus Youth Federation, it fell to Yehuda Stolov, a Global Council Trustee and an Orthodox Jew living in Israel to interview Majed TBelih, a Palestinian Muslim and contact person for the prospective CC. Their contact not only laid the groundwork for the CC's approval, it built a bridge of understanding that will connect this new CC with existing CCs in Israel and throughout the Middle East and the world. Yehuda's comment about an event where members of the Nablus Youth Federation met with members of the Interfaith Encounter Association MCC (Multiple Cooperation Circle) are inspiring: "It looks so natural that we nearly forget how unique this is." A connection of trust in a fractured world. Authentic hope blossoming.

In August 2002, URI held its first global assembly — *Sharing the Sacred, Serving the World* — outside the United States. 320 participants from 37 countries and nearly 60 faith traditions created a global community in Rio de Janeiro, hosted by the Rio Interfaith Network CC, the Sao Paulo CC, and Viva Rio, and webcast around the world by Yahoo.com. In addition, thousands of Brazilians joined with those attending the assembly through a sacred music festival and a sacred village which were open to the public.

As in past global summits, Appreciative Inquiry created the *ground of being* for this gathering that was distinguished by the committed and passionate interaction of people dedicated to interfaith cooperation. This assembly belonged to the participants, who created much of its content as the week unfolded. Participants organized regional cultural celebrations and sacred ceremonies, they spoke earnestly about how their faith traditions supported and blocked their ability to accept religions and cultures different from their own, and they contributed their ideas to create a Spiritual Agenda for Action — visions of actions for the 21st century that would lead to peace. They visited some of Rio's favelas to meet the people and to learn about successful community education projects. Perhaps most importantly, they were nurtured by the sheer joy of being part of a global community engaged in shared learning to empower greater service in the world. In a world torn by war, commitment for peace and friendships across cultures and religions blossomed.

Dame Dr. Prof. Meher Master-Moos, President of the Zoroastrian College in Mumbai, shared these observations about the assembly:

This was the BEST Inter Faith Peace Conference I have ever attended any where in the past 50 years. What made it so special? Not just the URI organizers taking on the great financial burden of bringing all of ustogether from everywhere, as far away as Tajikistan and the Shaman of Siberia — not just giving all of us such lavish hospitality in the Grand Old Gloria Hotel and keeping everybody under one roof, not just the musical evenings, the Spiritual "Exhibition", the sumptuous daily banquets for breakfast, elevenses, lunch, tea and dinner of the best array of foods – but the MOST MEANINGFUL sharings.

What made this conference unique was the close – few persons in a group – round table sharings. Learning the Peace Process from each other's experiences. What's happening in Africa and Afghanistan, with people in Pakistan and Philippines, Israel and Iraq, all over the Globe; the great learning method was No Speeches – only sharing. The different "Tracks" were so interesting, giving a special emphasis to various aspects of the Peace process. This was the only Conference I have ever attended where there was not a single "hot air platform lecture" from pompous speakers.

The Global Assembly created an almost unbelievable new reality – participants experienced themselves as a global community with a glorious diversity of expression and talent united in a commitment to share the sacred and serve the world. You had only to walk into the main conference room and see Jews and Muslims from the Middle East leading the community in prayer, or Hindus, Buddhists, Sikhs, Zoroastrians, Baha'is and Christians from India, Sri Lanka, Pakistan, Korea, Philippines, Viet Nam, New Zealand, and Bali leading a celebration of Asian and Pacific culture, or people from all over the world sharing from the depths of their traditions about the teachings and practices that lead to peace, to see authentic hope blossoming.

Also at the Global Assembly, URI inaugurated its first Global Council (GC). With members from 21 countries, the GC is rapidly becoming a global community of its own, enabled by a commitment to listening to the needs of the whole URI network and to fair and transparent procedures for participatory governance. The GC stayed on two days after the assembly and quickly went to work. Trustees self-selected committees on which to serve, chose committee chairs, considered possible at-large trustees, and developed agendas. The GC decided to meet three times a year by conference call and once a year face-to-face. In addition, GC committees meet regularly by conference call and via the internet.

As always in the URI, friendships and sharing experiences of the sacred remains central. When the Global Council gathered for its first face-to-face meeting after Rio at the Bishop's Ranch, a retreat and conference center in Healdsburg, CA. in May 2003, the meeting opened with a Buddha washing ceremony in honor of the Buddha's birthday and closed four days later with an indigenous ceremony honoring Pachamama, our sacred Mother Earth. Meeting time was framed and enriched by sacred offerings from different traditions, and by a special ceremony to dedicate a peace pole. Through friendship, committed work, and shared experiences of diverse forms of prayer and ceremony, the URI Global Council is forging connections of trust in a fractured world.

The practice of using questions as good pathfinders, remains central to URI's journey. Key questions continue to surface. How does URI grow to have a true global impact? How much money does the organization need to operate well and how will funds be raised? How will the GC and staff balance conflicting needs — the need to support CC initiatives and provide for effective communication among CCs with the need to lead URI's growth by inspiring collective global actions and by offering training in peacebuilding and leadership skills?

QUESTIONS OF BALANCE

URI has been successful in creating a global community of Cooperation Circles united by a Preamble, Purpose and Principles, and free to live into the PPP in ways they determine locally. URI has created a communications infrastructure to help CCs participate in a global community, but the organization has only begun to tap the potential of this infrastructure. Many in the URI yearn for a sense of shared global action such as was experienced during the 72 Hours Project. But the URI community has really just begun to explore how to have a global voice. These are issues of connectedness, but they are also issues of scale and urgency. At the heart of these questions, is how to balance leadership from the whole, represented by the Global Council and staff, with initiatives from individual CCs. A corollary issue is how to balance resources necessary to maintain and build the global network with resources for specific action projects, skill building and collective global actions.

FUNDING AND FINANCING

The question of resource generation is also central. CCs around the world generate the financial and other resources needed to do their work. In 2002, 85 CCs had raised nearly $500,000 to support their work. Volunteers throughout the URI network give hundreds of thousands of hours to fulfill URI's purpose. Yet the overwhelming majority of financial resources to support URI's regional and global development has been raised through the global hub in San Francisco. Clearly, URI must create much greater diversity in funding. Self-sustainability is a goal for every part of the URI – local, regional, global – but with that goal comes the question of how to achieve it in a way that doesn't recreate within URI the economic inequity that exists in the larger world. An important question is how to mirror the growing culture of generosity of service that is a hallmark of the URI community with a culture of financing and giving where each part of the URI is responsible for itself and is able to offer money gifts to other parts in need. Leading the way, some CCs have already discovered other CCs in need and sent them a financial gift.

TELLING THE URI STORY

Key to URI's finding the balance between local and global needs and financial sustainability is the question of how effectively to tell URI's story to the world. Each day within the URI community stories of significant events, exciting projects, mutual support, and effective local actions are generated. These stories are shared through a CC listserv, included in monthly e-updates. They are posted on the URI's global website (www.uri.org), and through regional websites or regional newsletters. Around the world, URI members work to have the stories of their efforts told in the public media and a global newsletter is mailed to a broad based world community twice a year. And yet, URI is still an infant in this area. For busy people, it is taxing to take time to reflect on their activities and write up their stories. Assessing effective technology for a global community with a wide and varied range of capacity is complex and often costly. And yet the need for the URI to be seen is paramount. The accumulation of URI stories is like a shining stained glass window: each local action constitutes one bright piece of colored glass. When these stories are told and reflected back as a whole, they reflect a reality much larger than each piece. URI seeks ways to tell its unfolding stories effectively and broadly so that the collective power and beauty is recognized.

There are no easy answers to the questions URI faces. It remains a key spiritual discipline to allow the questions not to be seen a burdens or problems but as pathfinders, guiding everyone's consideration and input, and opening new, creative and unanticipated ways forward. The answers will only be found by living into the questions, something URI has a great deal of experience doing.

In a fractured world where menace and cynicism abound, we have no choice to but continue living with these questions, seeking the best answers for now. In a world where trust and authentic hope are hard to find, and yet are blossoming everywhere, mostly unseen, URI continues to support this blossoming and make it more visible around the world. URI's commitment to build a truly global community creating cultures of peace, justice and healing is more needed than ever.

July, 2003

Appendices

APPENDIX 1

Discovering the Steps to a United Religions Charter

1. Welcome Letter from Bishop William E. Swing

Welcome!

Welcome to San Francisco; welcome to a week of dreaming, sharing, and growing;

Welcome to a small community of 60 colleagues; and welcome to the challenge of planning the first phase that will lead to the creation of a United Religions.

Of all the abundant surprises and gifts that this initiative has received this past year, none was greater than a telephone call from Cleveland, Ohio. The Social Innovations in Global Management (SIGMA) Program at Case Western Reserve University was intrigued with the prospects of working with us. Since that call, we have worked together, and at this Summit we will have the privilege of their leadership.

The collecting of people for this Summit has not happened in a system-atic way. An accidental meeting in Rome, a lunch in Oxford, a slip of paper with a name and telephone number, an opportune letter from Costa Rica, then all of a sudden, a spectacular array of a wide cross-sec-tion of expertise! A tiny nucleus of folks from the Bay Area has labored to bring all of this together. Special thanks go to Charles Gibbs, master tailor of weaving.

Once upon a time, Robert Traer said at a conspicuous new beginning: "All we need do is love our religious and cultural traditions, our hymns and our chants, our prayers and our precepts, our scriptures and our sutras, our rituals and our lives, and then live so that we all may live." Those are still good words.

Welcome,
William E. Swing

2. AGENDA for WEEK
Discovering the Steps to a United Religions Charter

Sunday, June 23

	Arrival in San Francisco
6:30 pm	Dinner at the Fairmont for hotel guests *(Masons Room)*

Monday, June 24

7:30 - 8 am	Optional group meditation
7:45 – 8:45	Breakfast
8:45 – 9:00	Gathering for morning session
9 am -12:30	**Morning Session** *(including break)*

Discovery (Who is here?):
- Opening prayer / meditation / silence / sharing
- Welcome by Bishop Swing
- Mutual Interviews and group sharing to meet and to discover the collective energy, experiences, and resources we bring to this work

12:30 – 1:30	Lunch
1:30 - 5 pm	**Afternoon Session** *(including break)*

Discovery (The Past):
- Opening prayer / meditation / silence / sharing
- Create and interpret timelines to contextualize the UR initiative
- Create "Mindmap" of trends supporting this initiative now

6:15 pm	Board bus to Bishop Swing's home
6:30 pm	Dinner at Bishop Swing's home
9:15 pm	Bus returns to the Fairmont

Tuesday, June 25

7:25 – 7:55am	Group meditation
7:45 – 8:45	Breakfast
9:00 – 12:30	**Morning Session** *(including break)*

Discovery (The Present)
- opening prayer / meditation / silence / sharing
- Interpret "Mindmap"
- Share personal artifacts
- What do we want to continue / let go of?

12:30 – 1:30	Lunch on *Cathedral Close*

1:30 – 5:00	**Afternoon Session** (including break)
	Dream (of United Religions):
	• Opening prayer / meditation / silence / sharing
	• Work with a vision of a United Religions: What might it be? What might it be like? What might it accomplish?
5:30 pm	Board bus to social gathering for drinks, hors d'oeuvres, view of the Bay Area
8:30 pm	Bus returns to Fairmont

Wednesday, June 26

7:30 – 8:00 am	Optional group meditation
7:45 - 8:45	Breakfast
9:00 -12:30	**Morning Session** (including break)
	Dream (of the UR Initiative)
	• Opening prayer / meditation / silence / sharing
	• Dream of the ideal year to lead to a Charter-writing Conference
12:40 pm	Board bus to Presidio
	Afternoon Renewal:
	• Lunch
	• Opening prayer / meditation / silence / sharing
	• Walking tour through the Presidio National Park, ending with a gathering at the Interfaith Center in the Presidio
5:30 pm	Board bus to Fairmont – Evening free

Thursday, June 27

7:30 – 8:00 am	Optional group meditation
7:45 - 8:45	Breakfast
9:00 - 12:30	**Morning Session** (including break)
	Design (of the next year)
	• Opening prayer / meditation / silence / sharing
	• Visioning the action process for the next year
	• Discovering common ground for action
12:30 – 1:30	Lunch
1:30 – 5:00	**Afternoon Session** (including break)
	Design (continued)
	• Opening prayer / meditation / silence / sharing

	• Organizing and mobilizing action for the next year
6:30 pm	Dinner in the *Garden Room* at the Fairmont, where the UN Charter was signed, June 1945.

Friday, June 28

7:30 – 8:00 am	Optional group meditation
7:45 - 8:45	Breakfast
9:00 - 12:30	**Morning Session** *(including break)*
	Destiny:
	• Opening prayer / meditation / silence / sharing
	• Commitments / next steps
12:00 pm	Lunch and Beginning of the next year

3. Opening Speech by The Rt. Rev. William E. Swing

Greetings! I marvel that I am standing here talking about something that has never happened in the world and almost everyone who has had access to my ears has told me will never happen. I marvel even more that you are seated there in earnest, listening to this. Today indeed is a special moment. Credulity trembles. And delirious hope gasps for a first breath. An entire new life for the world beckons us to step ahead.

I would like to begin by speaking of **A Floating Vision**. A floating vision. As a regular bishop chasing after a regular diocese, my days are spent in a wide range of concerns. Churches, schools, social service ministries, et al. The tiniest part of my attention has been given to interfaith work. Until three years ago when a telephone call came from the United Nations asking for a great interfaith service to be held at Grace Cathedral in celebration of the UN's 50th Anniversary. What hit me so profoundly was not the telephone call from the UN or the prospects of the great worship services. It was a floating vision I had while tossing and turning that night. I was assaulted by the scandal that the nations of the world have spent 50 years together struggling for global good while the religions have never dared to come together in a responsible daily forum to struggle for global good. I arose from that floating vision of religions determined, amateur that I was in interfaith, to press for a United Religions.

The first thing that this vision compelled me to do was to telephone the experts, the veterans who have been serving in the established venues of interfaith work. My invitation to them to meet in New York on June 21, 1993, was graciously accepted by the likes of Marcus Braybrooke,

Bill Vendley, Daniel Gomez-Ibanez, Luis Dolan, Chung Ok Lee, Bawa Jain, Jim Morton, and many others. Looking back I am astonished that they made such time for such a rookie. But they did and they recommended that I go back to San Francisco and plan an Interfaith Youth Conference to be held immediately before the UN50 Celebration. I was encouraged to launch the vision with young leaders who will live the next 50 years.

I will not belabor this history which many of you know. The Interfaith Youth Conference did happen on June 22-24 on the University of San Francisco campus. With 200 young adults, with world-renowned speakers, it was an intense, spiritual, and deeply moving experience. In addition, international interfaith leaders took part. In special separate meetings during the Conference this question was put forward to these interfaith leaders: "Should I continue to present the vision of a United Religions?" By and large the answer was "yes". Following the Youth Conference was the memorable UN50 Celebration at Grace Cathedral where the floating vision was brought before the world of ambassadors, and the informal response was favorable.

Next came the time of **Testing The Vision**. Testing the vision. A small group of people who planned the June 1995 events gathered in July 1995 to take the vision to the next level. This group of local interfaith people called ourselves, "The United Religions Initiative" and we went through the process of becoming an official organization with officers, meeting, brochures, etc. The first test was one of becoming a visible entity.

Next Charles Gibbs and I went to New York in September, 1995 where we made a presentation to the Religious NGOs at the United Nations. In October/November I went to China and presented the vision to the national Head of the Chinese Christian Council, Bishop K.H. Ting, and to the head of the Amity Foundations, Dr. Han Wensau. In addition I gave speeches on the subject in Beifing, Nanjing, Shanghai, Hong Kong, and Taipei.

From February to May I traveled in India, Pakistan, Egypt, Israel, Jordan, Switzerland, Turkey, Germany, Italy, and England testing this vision with conspicuous religious leaders. Their reactions have been written up and you have seen them. At an Interfaith Conference in Oxford this springtime, I had an opportunity to address a few people from South America and Sri Lanka. And next month I leave for Japan and Korea. Suffice it to say that in one year I have given the vision a real road test.

Thus far I have garnered some learning and developed some guesses concering the scope of a United Religions. Here are some samples

1. A United Religions could end up being basically a spiritual resource for peace among religions, healing among nations, and wholeness in the realm of nature.

2. I think in terms of three circles. The smallest circle out from the center has points on the circumference for local interfaith groups in cities, interfaith groups on university campuses, interfaith chaplaincies at institutions, religious communities specializing in interfaith, regional interfaith dialogues and others. The second circle out from the center has international interfaith groups on the circumference. The World Conference of Religion and Peace, the Temple of Understanding, The Council for a Parliament of World Religions, The Peace Council, Thanksgiving Square. The Congress of Religions, The Global Ethic, The International Association for Religious Freedom and others. The third circle out from the center has interfaith work of the great religions-The Roman Catholic dialogue, the Islamic dialogues of the Crown Prince of Jordan, dialogues of Orthodox, Anglicans, Buddhists, Hindus, Jews, and others. Lines of communication run from all points on the circumference through the center and make contact with opposite points on the circumference. I can see the center as having a life of its own, created by all points on the circumference. The center would be The United Religions.

3. Nothing takes the place of one-to-one, face-to-face, interfaith work.

4. The quickest recognition for the creation of a United Religions came from ambassadors and diplomats. Also politicians, economists, scientists (especially ecologists) were most supportive.

5. The most basic issue is whether or not a religion believes that the world holds together in an ultimate unity.

6. A United Religions would not be another international interfaith organization. The kind of distinction between the Red Cross/Crescent on the one hand and the United Nations on the other hand, must be made between international interfaith groups on the one hand and a United Religions on the other hand.

7. A United Religions would be the place where religions could find some wiggle room in the midst of intractable situations.

8. The most powerful teachers of interfaith are the media and one's own religious tradition. Most often neither teaches what is accurate about other religions.

9. A United Religions would hold each faith in context of all faiths for the sake of all life.

10. Interfaith work among the leading religions is a very new phenomenon. The Vatican could point to 30 years while Lambeth Palace pointed to five.

11. Prayer among the religions is a touchy subject. It suggests to some that everyone believes the same thing and has the same Deity. It therefore doesn't respect the uniqueness of each religion.

The testing of the vision's classic problems always arose. Unwieldy bureaucracy, Third World vs. First World, representativity, syncretism, and all of the expected issues came up so consistently that most people had a hard time seeing beyond the obstacles to the vision. And even then, it was hard for them to see specificity in the vision. Beyond that and finally at the bottom was a hard issue of authority and control. Some folks saw beyond the obstacles, caught a glimpse of the vision, but bailed out because they were not about to share authority and control in a global enterprise. They could respond to small interfaith initiatives and could carry on dialogues where they are completely in control. But to sit among equals in order to strive for global good was not an option for them at this point. So I can say one year later that the vision has been tested as well as the bearer of the vision.

Vision Coalition
Wherever I have been, this question always arose, "Who is bringing forth this vision of a United Religions?" I would respond that a few of us who worked on the UN50 Interfaith Worship Service are the only ones behind it. My answer, though true, never brought confidence to the hearer. We are puny in numbers and in clout! Now we embark on a journey to change that.

The first organization to assist with our effort was the SIGMA (Social Innovations in Global Management) group out of Case Western Reserve's School of Management in Cleveland, Ohio. They happened to read about us in an article in the Cleveland Plain Dealer newspaper. Since then they have spent numerous hours readying for this conference, helped us in recruiting, and have been soul-brothers and sisters in this effort. And we are set to plan together for the First Charter-Writing Session of the United Religions to be held in San Francisco, June 16-17, 1997.

This Summit that we commence today is an invitation to the folks here to be the first people in the world to align with the initiative to create the United Religions. We aren't just looking for your name and endorsement of your organization. We want to enlist your imagination to become pioneers on a spiritual quest to serve all of God's creation beginning with religions and ending with religions. Up to now religions have primarily spent themselves on their unique revelations, wisdoms and community with no concern for joining with other religions to provide a global presence for good. The challenge ahead is to grow in understanding a world-wide calling. To attempt to expand the thinking patterns of religions is a daunting task of highest challenge. Nevertheless, having traveled and probed, I do believe that the world of religions is waiting for the challenge.

When we leave here on June 28, at 1:30 p.m., I hope that you will have jumped into the waters at the deep end of this pool and discovered your own buoyancy. I hope that you personally will add your name to the list of sponsors, you will help us identify other promising leaders, and you will go home to talk to your constituency to see if an entire body could back the process to create a United Religions.

It is getting later in the game and being puny will not be tolerable much longer. Vision Coalition is needed. Please understand that this will not be a closed coalition. It is intended to draw individuals, corporations, leading persons, international interfaith groups, local interfaith endeavors, and finally the great religions themselves into the dialogue of what a United Religions should look like. Today is the first day of a long march toward coalition-binding around the vision.

Vision Realized

I am convinced that someday there will be a United Religions. There has to be. There is not going to be a time in the near future when one religion converts, conquers, subjugates all of the other religions to itself. Furthermore, religions are going to have to learn to live together. No longer can one religion use terror, law, threat to excise other religions from its territory. Communication crosses borders and enters homes, so people are now exposed to other religions. The sooner we find a way for religions to share the same geographic space, the sooner life will be enhanced. The sooner we can get religions to come together to serve the common good, the sooner global issues will have a chance for solution. I know that eventually there will be a United Religions because there has to be. Now the question is, sooner or later?

At the first of this century, there was a time when human beings knew in their bones that we should fly. So all kinds of people glued feathers to the arms, climbed to the top of the barn, began flapping, and jumped off. And sure enough, right around there, we learned to fly. I don't mind standing in front of you today smelling of feathers and sticking with glue. I'll tell you right now, I'm jumping.

This Summit comes down to one invitation to you around the creation of a United Religions. "Come, let's fly!"

The Rt. Rev. William E. Swing
Episcopal Bishop of California

4. An Appreciative Inquiry[1]
Discovering the Steps to a United Religions Charter

We live in a time of remarkable change, a time for re-thinking relationships among groups and communities of all kinds. World historic changes like the ending of the system of racial separateness/apartheid in South Africa; the collapse of totalitarian regimes and the bi-polar world; the rapid spread of global communications potential; the birth of millions of grassroots organizations joining in the fight against global challenges of poverty and environmental decline; unprecedented inter-religious cooperation and action (like the Parliament of the World's Religions and 100s of international interfaith gatherings) – all of these signal a very open moment in world history. And yet excitements are quickly tempered: clearly we are still infants when it comes to our capacity for nurturing a global *communitas* congenial to the life of the planet and responsive to the best in our spiritual traditions. It is within this context that the current initiative of discovery is being carried out. The vision: that *there needs to be, in today's complicated and interconnected world, a United Religions, which would, in spiritually appropriate ways, parallel that of a United Nations.*

On the following pages are several questions we would like pairs to reflect on in the form of a mutual interview process. Data, stories, and learnings from these interviews will be drawn upon *periodically throughout the week* as the conference seeks to discover the potentials in the United Religions vision and, more concretely, discover the steps for evolving a successful charter writing process. Please take good notes as you conduct the interviews. One aim is to be able to put together, at the end of the conference, a complete and compelling report of the deliberations. Every voice matters, and like the story about the blind persons and the elephant our collective discoveries will be more richly textured than any single account. At the end of the interview take time to thank your partner and share back with them what was striking, uplifting, challenging, or especially meaningful about what you learned from them.

---

1 For more on the Organization Development background behind Appreciative Inquiry and the Future Search Conference approaches, see Cooperrider D.L. and Svivastava S., Appreciative Inquiry into Organizational Life in Srivastva, S. and Cooperrider, D., *Appreciative Management and Leadership*, Revised Edition (1999), Lakeshore Communications, Euclid, Ohio. For more on Future Search conference see, Weisbord M. *Discovering Common Ground: How Future Search Methods Bring People Together to Achieve Breakthrough Innovation, Empowerment, Shared Vision, and Collaborative Action.* San Francisco: Berrett-Koehler, 1992.

United Religions – **as a permanent gathering center where all religions of the world are united on a daily basis in bringing their spiritual gifts to a common table to enrich, wherever possible, all life on this earth** – is not yet an organizational reality. It is an urge. How to collectively act on this urge, and join with a world waiting for the birth of new light, is the task of this discovery.

To start, I'd like to learn a little bit about who you are, what interests, excites, or draws you to participate in this conference? What was it that compelled or called you to this work?

1. **A "High Point" in your Life.** To get to know you better as it relates to experiences that you have had that might make a difference here during the course of this conference, I would like you to reflect upon your life and life's work. Obviously you have experienced ups and downs, peaks and valleys, etc. For the moment I would like you to reflect on a "high point' – a time when you were involved with something significant or meaningful and felt most alive, proud,
creative, effective, engaged, etc. Share the story of this high point experience. What made it a peak experience? What felt truly special? Are there lessons that might be brought to this work?

2. **Valuing:** There are many different qualities and skills, resources, positive global changes and trends, and historical experiences that can be drawn upon as a United Religions vision is given birth and grows. We would like to engage in a process of valuing those many resources, at several different levels (yourself, your religion or faith community, and global trends).

   A) **Yourself:** Without being too humble, what is it that you value most about yourself as it relates to things you bring to this conference and work of interfaith cooperation? What are your best qualities, skills, approaches, experiences, etc.?

   B) **Your religion or faith community.** Each of our communities of faith have special gifts – traditions, beliefs, practices, values – to bring to the arena of interfaith cooperation and action. As you think about your community of faith, what are some of its most positive qualities or gifts that make it capable of entering into cooperation with others to build something like a United Religions?
      - Are there special texts or passages or quotes that stand out for you?
      - A story or parable?
      - Historical experiences?
      - Capabilities or commitments?
      - Values?

C) **Constructive world trends, changes, or potentials.**
Against the background of many world problems and conflicts
(The *1996 Encyclopedia of World Problems and Human Potential*
lists over 15,000 global problems) there is also a hopeful story
which offers a glimmer of what is possible when we find ways to
promote peace rather than war, cooperation rather than competition and prejudice, and sustainable development rather than
environmental degradation and human oppression. As you
reflect on our conference task, what are the global or local
trends, events or milestones that are most positive or promising
– societal trends or changes that give you the most hope in the
possibility of some day creating a vital and effective United Religions type entity?

3. **Have you ever been part of the successful development of a
global organization, or collaborative alliance of diverse
organizations (inter-religious or other types)?** What was special about that experience or example? What were some of the critical turning points, challenges and responses, that are useful to learn
from?

4. **The emerging story of interfaith relationships.** Against a
bleak and clearly conflicted back-drop is a hopeful story which
offers a glimmer of what is possible when the spiritual impulse
promotes peace rather than war, cooperation rather than competition and prejudice. Though the story is largely untold, a million or so people of faith are reaching across religious and racial
differences to work together. To help us put together a brief
record of the story of important interfaith work, please help us
make a list from your vantage point of some of the maker initiatives, activities, or developments of recent times.

* What is the storyline you see evolving?
* What is happening in the interfaith world that you want to
see *continue to happen*, even as things change in the future?

5. **Visions of a better world, and your image of how a truly
effective United Religions might contribute and serve.**

* Put yourself 30 years into the future, the year is about 2026.
Visualize the kind of world we are being called to realize, a
better world, the kind of world you really want. What is life
like in this vision of a better world?
* Assuming an *effective* United Religions type of entity came to
existence just before the turn of the century; imagine the
variety and types of contributions it might well have made to
the global good. List its special (imagined possibilities)
accomplishments since 1999.

6. **Discovering the steps to building a United Religions "Charter"**

   * Assuming now that the world's religions were ready, that the current interfaith strengths and structures were mobilized, and that together we could build the kind of United Religions the world is calling for–then, **would you want it?** Why? What are your cautions, doubts, or significant concerns?

   * Suppose that one night during the conference, when all were asleep, there was a miracle and everything needed to build a United Religions was put into place. How would you know? What would be different? What would be happening?

   * In the ideal, what kind of process, (the 3-5 key steps) can you envision or recommend for arriving successfully at a United Religions "charter writing" conference in the next 1-2 years?

5. Discovering Our Collective History (The Past)

Purpose
To generate a visual historical perspective of noteworthy events over the last century in global, religious and interfaith affairs.

Guidelines:
On your own, make notes of memorable events that represent to you notable milestones and/or turning points in the history of a) the world; b) your religion or community of faith and c) interfaith efforts.

Use a magic marker to transfer your notes to the appropriate time lines.

GLOBAL EVENTS
What happened? Why important?

1890s – 1920s

_____

_____

_____

1930s – 1950s

_____

_____

_____

1960s – 1970s

_____

_____

_____

1980s – 1990s

_____

_____

_____

6. Events in Your Religion or Community of Faith

What happened? Why important?

1890 – 1920

_____

_____

_____

_____

1930 – 1950

_____

_____

_____

_____

1960 – 1970

_____

_____

_____

_____

1980 – 1990

_____

_____

_____

_____

7. "Open Space" Group Action Planning

Group Task: _____

Purpose:
To decide on short and long term action steps. For each task group, what are the steps you will take as a group to work toward a creation of a United Religions, specifically a Charter writing conference in June, 1997?

Group Members:

_____

_____

_____

Short term actions (next two months):

_____

_____

_____

WHAT   HELP NEEDED FROM   DUE DATE

_____

_____

_____

Long term actions (next year and beyond):

_____

_____

_____

WHAT   HELP NEEDED FROM   DUE DATE

_____

_____

_____

8. Interpreting Our Collective History
Group report-outs will begin at _____ o'clock

Purpose
Identify themes and patterns that have shaped the environment for interfaith initiatives. Establish a context for our future work.

Guidelines:
- Self-manage: Revisit leadership roles for your group.
- Each table interprets our history from a different perspective.
- Discuss the timelines and write your summary on flip charts.
- Prepare a three minute summary report.

Table Assignments:

I. TABLE(S) _____

- Looking at the Global timeline, what story can you tell about recent world history as it relates to this initiative?
- Scan the other timelines. What connections do you see?

II. TABLE(S) _____

- Looking at the Religions timeline, what story can you tell about the recent history of our religions and communities of faith?
- Scan the other timelines. What connections do you see?

III. TABLE(S) _____

- Looking at the Interfaith timeline, what story can you tell about the recent history of interfaith efforts?
- Scan the other timelines. What connections do you see?

Notes:

9. Discovery – Group Mind Map (The Present)

Group Mind Map -– Trends Affecting Us Now

Purpose
To build a shared context of the trends affecting the United Religions Initiative now.

Task
As a total group, create a "mind map" of trends affecting us in this initiative now.

Guidelines:
This is a group brainstorm – no evaluation, no censorship.

The person who names the issue says where it goes on the map.

Give examples to clarify what your trend refers to.

Contradictory trends are OK.

Notes:

Prouds" And "Sorries" Of Our Institutions
Group Report-outs Will Begin At _____ O'clock

Purpose
Assess the PRESENT (current reality) in our institutional relationship to the possible creation of a "united religions" and to other stakeholders. [NOTE: This is an experience in owning up to what is, not blaming or problem-solving. The motto is: "Own it, don't moan it."]

Guidelines:
- For institutional groupings as follows:

  - International interfaith organizations

  - Local interfaith and religious organizations

  - Private sector (profit and nonprofit) organizations

  - Universities

- Self-manage: Decide on leadership roles for your group.

- List what your institution is doing RIGHT NOW that you are PROUD of in your relationship to our conference task.

- List what your institution is doing RIGHT NOW that you are SORRY about in this regard.

- As a group, select you "PROUDEST PROUDS" and "SORRIEST SORRIES."

- Reporters: Prepare a 3-minute report.

Notes:

10. Open Space" Group Action Planning

Group Task: _____

Purpose
To decide on short and long term action steps. For each task group, what are the steps you will take as a group to work toward a creation of a United Religions, specifically a Charter writing conference in June, 1997?

Group Members:

Short term actions (next two months):

WHAT   HELP NEEDED FROM   DUE DATE

Long term actions (next year and beyond):

WHAT   HELP NEEDED FROM   DUE DATE

APPENDIX 2

URI Global Summit
June 21-26, 1998

Living Into the United Religions

1. Explanation of Week's Schedule

Sacred Practices
In order to ground ourselves daily and deeply, these optional morning and midday gatherings will offer a variety of practices under the leadership of various conference members. These might include guided meditations, sharing of sacred texts, movement, music, or contemplative silence. If you would like to be among those offering such a session, please contact Yoland Trevino.

Silence
Recognizing that for many, creation emerges out of silence, and that is a sanctuary, which can revitalize our connection with the sacred, the URI has successfully experimented with several "reminders" of silence. At the Summit, we will have a gong call us to two minutes of silence a few times during the day, and "silence stones" to be held by any participant willing to hold the silence in a group while others carry the dialogue.

Sacred Practices
Each morning and afternoon session of the conference is planned to open with silence and a brief sacred practice by a participant. If you would like to be among them, Yoland Trevino will be coordinating these session openers.

Following Your Calling in the Work of the Conference
We have aimed to create a conference design that offers each participant the opportunity to contribute to the work of the conference in the areas they feel called. During most sessions, you will find several choices among the identified conference tasks and will often have the option to organize a meeting around another topic you propose. During any session you should also feel free to take a break or a walk or a rest, whatever you need to support the full vitality of your presence and contribution.

The Role of "Work Stations" in Organizing Work
Each of the major conference tasks will have a "workstation" located around the perimeter of our conference space. These stations will

feature a visual depiction of the task, a display and handouts of the most current work, and various means of collecting input (an input box, action plans to add your name to, wall drawings, etc.). These stations will function both as a gathering place for input from the various small task groups and as a meeting place for people wishing to talk about and work on that task during a particular conference session. The workstations/talk areas include: 1) Charter Preamble and Purpose; 2) Charter Principles and Organizational Design; 3) Global Religious Cease Fire; 4) Charter Action Agenda (with subheadings for each agenda area);

Talking Circle / Closing

To provide a sacred space for community sharing and reflection the last half hour of our afternoons (5:30pm to 6:00pm on Monday, Tuesday, and Thursday) is reserved as a "Talking Circle", an Open Mike, and will end with an appropriate closing.

2. An Appreciative Inquiry Living into the United Religions via Sacred Conversations

Introduction

As we begin our weeklong journey of charting the future of the United Religions, we hope that at every moment to invoke the presence of the sacred in our conversations. In this first exercise, where pairs will meet to listen to each other's stories and ideas *about* the United Religions and our relationship to it, we will simultaneously be *living into* the United Religions as we relate to one another in a spirit of trust, openness and love.

For some, this process of "appreciative inquiry" will not be new—it seems to have become a standard feature of United Religions conferences around the world. For others, the term may be new, but perhaps not the idea of being in a dialogue with others, where your full curiosity is present and available to discover the best of what your fellow human beings have to offer. In addition, please consider that your own sacred source is present in your conversation, informing and guiding you, each in your own way.

Please ensure that you take turns in this interview, to equally divide the available time between you. If you cannot finish all the questions, it is OK; what is most important is that you have a deep experience of hearing another and of being heard around the kinds of questions that will occupy us throughout the entire week.

We know from past experience, that some extraordinary stories will be told in this setting. If you are able, and so inclined, please record in writing any story that you find especially moving. One of the aims this week is to collect stories of the URI that can carry its essence into all parts of the world. A gathering box and/or a storyboard will be placed near "The URI Story Unfolds" wall graphic, for you to add stories from your interviews and other conversations anytime during the week.

Enjoy yourselves and please return to the tent at the announced time.

Appreciative Interview Guide
These questions are meant to serve as a guide for an interview that will take you through the subject range of the entire conference. Feel free to adapt and supplement them by following your own curiosity in asking questions.

1. **Your Calling to this Work**
   Please tell the story of why you are here. What has called you to this conference and to be involved in the work of the United Religions Initiative? What life experiences have guided you here—tell the story of any particular events or moments that stand out.

2. **The Gifts that You and Your Faith Bring**
   Without being humble, what gifts do you see yourself bringing to this work? What might those who know you say are some of the best qualities, skills, and experiences that you contribute to efforts such as this one? How does your faith, or community, or practice inform and call you to the work of the United Religions?

3. **Living into the United Religions**
   In the past year, what have you done that could be regarded as "living into the United Religions," regardless of whether your actions were taken with this in mind? For some, this may be actions resulting from earlier URI conferences. For many of us, involvement in United Religions Initiative builds upon what we are already doing, linking our work with the purposes of the URI. How have you lived into the URI?

4. **The Draft Charter of the United Religions**
   As you read the draft charter, what most excited you? What in the preamble was most powerful for you? How well did the purpose statement(s) capture your sense of the UR? What was striking to you about the proposed principles? Can you imagine an international organization based on these? And which potential action agendas of the UR are you most interested in and supportive of?

5. **The Global Religious Cease Fire**
   Imagine 72 hours of active peacemaking across the planet (Dec. 31, 1999 – Jan. 2, 2000) when no person is killed in a religious

conflict, when no violence is committed in the name of religion, and when people reach across their religious and spiritual differences in respect and hospitality. What can you imagine happening during those three days? What will be necessary to prepare for this event? What can you see yourself doing to work toward this vision?

6. **Regional Development and a Worldwide Movement**
   Perhaps the most important infrastructure of the future UR is the budding development of regional initiatives all over the world. You will be able to hear about many during this conference—they represent the beginnings of a UR that is decentralized, locally led but globally linked, where the transformative power of our actions draws upon the most sacred practices, the deepest truths and most inspiring wisdom of our various traditions. How do you see this movement spreading in your part of the world? How can the cease fire and the draft charter be used in tandem to inspire people and organizations to participate in cocreating the UR by the year 2000? What do you see yourself doing toward this end?

3. Discovering the Whole of the United Religions Vision

Purpose
To engage in small groups with the whole of the UR Vision, exploring the interrelated themes of this Summit—the draft charter, the cease fire, and regional development. In this way, everyone will have an opportunity to be part of a conversation of the whole, before self-selecting into groups that will gather tomorrow at workstations to further develop each area.

Outcomes
As a product of this work, we ask your group to share some of what's most exciting and most in need of further clarification in the ideas that have been developed to date. **Please fill out the attached worksheet (more are available) with your input** to the groups who will be gathering at the workstations tomorrow.

Topics for Conversation & Input

The Overall Vision

The history of a call for a United Religions organization is lengthy, with many different visionaries proclaiming the need over the last one hundred years. The URI grew out of Bishop Swing's vision, while commemorating the United Nations' 50th anniversary, of an organization that would parallel the UN in spiritually appropriate ways. Since then, the vision has evolved, balancing the desire to involve influential representatives of the historic religions with people of faith from all paths. The UR vision has become more grass-roots oriented, more inclusive of spiritual movements, and sill aims to be inclusive of good leadership from the major religious institutions. With the addition of the drive towards a global religious cease-fire, the UR is simultaneously working towards becoming a movement and a new form of organization.

As you imagine the UR in your own way, what are some of the highlights? Please discuss and record on the worksheets:

What about the overall vision of the UR is most exciting?

What questions, issues, ideas, does this vision raise for you?

Draft Charter

Imagine an organization which is: inclusive, de-centralized, self-sustaining, where decisions are made at local levels, resources are shared, where local actions are connected to form a global presence, where the spiritual wisdom of all faith traditions is revered, and where the deepest values of people are respected and put into action for the good of all. The draft charter intends to create a framework for such an organization. How does it reflect what you imagine?

Input to Work Stations

Input for work stations. Please offer your ideas, questions, issues to the following work station areas. Your ideas will be considered by the task group at that work station.

_____ Overall Vision   _____ Draft Charter
                                                    Preamble & Purpose

_____ Cease Fire   _____ Draft Charter
                                                    Principles & Org. Design

_____ Regional Development   _____ Draft Charter
                                                    Action Agenda

What's most exciting is...   **Questions, issues to**

resolve are...

Overview of Charter Definitions and Work Station Tasks

Please read the following definitions and the tasks designated to each workstation. Choose your work station.

WORKSTATION 1
Preamble and Purpose

Preamble
A statement of the call. What is going on in the world that invites and inspires us to created the UR? Why now?

> **Task:** to share our best thinking and learning from R and D work which will serve as guidance to a writer who will produce a draft preamble.

Purpose
A clear unambiguous statement of intent that draws a community together because they believe it is worthy of pursuit.

> **Task:** to consider R and D work review and revise most current Purpose as a statement worthy of personal and collective pursuit.

WORKSTATION 2
Principles and Organizational Development

Principles
Statements of fundamental beliefs that guide structure, decisions and conduct.

> **Task:** review our current set of principles and apply best thinking form R and D contributions to enhance, improve and modify them.

Organizational Design
A general perception of an organization design that can be trusted to be just, equitable and effective with respect to all discussions, decisions, and actions in pursuit of purpose and in accordance with principles. An image of an organization that enhances cooperation among people and magnifies spirit.

> **Task:** to dream boldly. Building upon R and D conversation and contributions, to generate multiple images of a potential UR organization.

WORKSTATION 3
Agenda for Action

Action Agenda
General areas in which the UR will invite dialogue and cooperative action.

> **Task:** integrate R and D contributions, create a list of inspired action areas in accordance with purpose and principles: give title, definition, and rationale.

Practices
The actions of the members of the community functioning within the organization in pursuit of purpose in accordance with principles.

Workstation 4
The URI Ceasefire (72 hours) Project

The vision of the Ceasefire project is that – for one focused moment around the world (using the millennium opportunity) – people of faith can actually live together the vision of cooperation that the United Religions aims to establish. That lived experience will then create an enormous momentum toward the signing of the United Religions Charter in June 2000.

> **Task:** To develop a plan to move the Ceasefire Project in to action beginning this summer.

4. Instructions for Workstations

WORKSTATION 1
Preamble and Purpose
Instructions

Objective: to imagine a United Religions that answers the call described in the Preamble and fulfills the Purpose we ascribe to it...to know that the Preamble and Purpose we affirm will guide us toward the United Religions we want.

Outcome: input to the Charter Preamble and Purpose that will be incorporated in a revised draft to be affirmed by the Summit.

Tasks:

1. Evoking the Dream: Review the current draft Charter Preamble and Purpose statement, and imagine a United Religions existing in the year 2010 that fulfills these dreams. Do these statements evoke images of the United Religions you believe the world is calling for and that you want to help create? Share with each other some of the most compelling images you see.

2. Charter Preamble: The Preamble is intended to be a statement of the call for a United Religions: what is going on in the world that invites and inspires you to create a UR, and why now? Consider the Preamble in the light of this intention, the history of its development to date, the discussion questions included in the Draft Charter Packet (p.6), and any input contributed to this workstation. In small groups, answer the following three questions, summarizing your responses on flip charts:

What do you like best about the Preamble? What is most compelling, most important to retain in a final version?

What in the Preamble is unclear, questionable, or missing in your view?

Make three suggestions for improving the Preamble that your group agrees upon.

3. Charter Purpose: The Purpose is intended to announce the essence of why the UR exists and what it aims to accomplish. Consider the most recent draft Purpose statement in the light of this intention, the history of its development to date, including the preceding versions, the discussion questions included in the Draft Charter Packet (p.9), and any input contributed to this work station. In small groups, answer the following three questions, summarizing your responses on flip charts.

What concepts, words, or phrases do you feel most strongly about to keep the essence of the Purpose?

What is unclear or missing in the message of the current Purpose statement?

Make three suggestions for improving the Purpose statement that your group agrees upon.

4. Recommendations: Prepare to present the results in a 10 minute presentation.

WORK STATION 2
Principles and Organizational Design
Instructions

Objective: to imagine the United Religions in the future…to envision the principles of organization we truly believe in and want to work toward.

Outcome: input to the Charter Principles that will be incorporated in a revised draft to be affirmed by the Summit.

> **Tasks:** in small groups, discuss the questions in 1-3, and prepare to share your conclusions from 4 with other groups.

As a group review the Draft Charter Principles in terms of their priority importance to the United Religions' future success. Just for now, pick out 3-5 principles that you would really like to work with as a group— the 3-5 principles you feel should be held up as priorities.

Now imagine yourselves 12 years into the future, the year is 2010. Visualize it as if it really exists now.

Now, in 2010, you are tremendously proud and pleased to see how effectively the people of the UR have put these priority *principles into practice*—in the form of good organizational structures, processes, behaviors, effectiveness, etc.

As you look at the United Religions Organization in 2020, what do you see? What is happening that lets us know we are bringing the principles to life in real ways?

Note: some things you may want to consider in your vision of the future: what does the organization look like? Locally? Globally? Members? How many? How are decisions made? Where do resources come from? How is cooperation and synergy achieved? How does the organization learn and grow? What is leadership like? What makes the UR effective in the world? Spend enough time to imagine concretely the United Religions organization you and you group would most like to see and work toward.

Now is the time for improving the Draft Charter Principles. On a flip chart put a line down the middle. On the left hand side, make a list of the five things you like most about the Principles, as they are right now. On the right hand side, identify up to five ways to improve or add to the principles (or recommend the deletion of any).

Prepare to present the highlights and conclusions of your deliberations to the other groups:

- most exciting visions of bringing the principles to life

- what you like most about the principles as they stand

- ways your group recommends improving or adding to the principles

- prepare a 10 minute presentation.

WORKSTATION 3
Charter Action Agenda
Instructions

Charting UR actions and enacting UR Charter
We welcome you to the Action Agenda Workstation where we will develop the future agenda of the United Religions, in the form of both charter language and plans for initiating action now. We are the action people—so we imagine that, in addition to improving the charter's statement about the action agendas, a number of actionable ideas will result from our conversations. Here, you will have the opportunity to join a work group in one of the six areas of the draft charter or a new one you feel drawn to propose.

Objectives:
To chart our best ideas for UR actions into a revised draft of the UR Charter Action Agenda—making it big enough to encompass the most compelling possibilities for UR action.

To begin now living into the UR Charter by sharing actionable ideas that we shape into action plans we enact back home.

Outcome
Input to revise the draft Charter Action Agenda (for affirmation by the Summit) and Plans of Action to "field test" the charter and bring the UR to life over the next year.

Tasks:

1. As a whole group, we will be introduced to the six charter Action Agenda areas, with a brief presentation of the rationale for creating them and projects already proposed to live into them. Then we will invite proposals for any new areas to consider, not covered by the existing six. We will self-select into action agenda groups where each of us feels we can make our best contribution.

2. In the small groups, review and seek to understand (or create, in the case of new areas): the background, rationale and project ideas for your agenda area. Discuss:

   a) What is the most compelling about this action agenda and the projects it suggests? Is it in alignment with the proposed purpose and principles of the UR?

   b) What additional background, rationale, or projects would you propose be added to the charter?

c) What ideas do you have for beginning to enact any of these ideas now in your part of the world? Share you actionable ideas and begin crafting action plans to carry them out over the next year or two. What resources will be needed to carry out these plans?

3. Summarize in writing:

a) Your proposed charter revisions / additions.

b) Your action plans (post them on wallboards).

WORK STATION 4
The URI Global Cease-fire Project
Instructions

Objective:

Our objective at this station is to develop a plan to move the Cease-fire project into action, beginning this summer. We will *share the story* of the Cease-fire as it has developed so far, *dream together* what a Global Cease-fire could be, and *design* an action plan for the Cease-fire

Participants will work on four interrelated tasks:

Task 1 – Creating the Invitation

Create a strategy whereby an invitation will be issued by world religious and spiritual leaders, inviting the world's people of faith to join them in a global cease-fire and peacemaking.

- Create the most inspirational and compelling invitation we can imagine.
- Identify and enroll the people who will issue this invitation.
- Design a media plan and strategy.
- Create the invitation strategy using URI regional groups.

Task 2 – Mobilizing People and Actions

Create a plan for mobilizing people of faith around the world to make peace together on all levels – personally, in local communities, and in the world.

- Discover how sacred traditions make peace.
- Dream of actions the people of the world could do together in that spirit.
- Design projects.
- Make commitments to these projects.
- How can the URI regional groups help create this?

Task 3 – Organizing Cease-fires

Create a plan for what people of faith will actually do to make a difference in places where there is violence ("hot spots").
- Identify hot spots.
- Explore partnerships with other peacemaking efforts.
- Create a hot spot cease-fire plan and commitments.

Task 4 – Holding it together

Create a plan and a strategy to link people and projects together in a global network.
- Spotlight exemplary projects around the world.
- Connect regional and other initiatives together.
- Stage the project – URI providing the infrastructure.

Outcomes:

After this Summit task groups will:

- Create the invitation.
- Mobilize people and actions around the world.
- Support exemplary projects in hot spots.
- Create the appropriate project infrastructure of support.

5. Regional Development Instructions for Entire Assembly

Activity 1: Watering the Regional/Local Roots of the URI

By now, we have heard five regional reports sharing inspiring stories of the work that has been done around the world this past year. We have also spent the last two days delving into the Cease Fire plans and the draft UR Charter—its preamble, purpose and principles, its proposed organizational design, its action agendas. Now, at this midpoint of the conference, is a time to integrate our work into plans that globally root the UR in regions around the world, where it will be lived into action.

Objectives:

To gather as regions and sub-regions to build strategies for living into our purpose and principles, participating in the cease fire and charter circulation, and enacting regional initiatives that build our capacity to act on our agenda.

Outcome:

A brief summary of each region's (or sub-regions) plans for development:

- Draft charter circulation and feedback.
- Cease fire participation.
- Regional/local organizational development and initiatives.

Questions to consider:

1. What are the victories and challenges of our work over this past year?

2. How do we imagine the URI developing regionally over the next two years in:

- the unfolding of a regional structure in alignment with the draft charter
- the proliferation of local initiatives to live into the draft charter
- the circulation of the draft charter, and feedback based on dialogue
- the enactment of plans to support the global religious cease fire

3. What concrete steps/actions/commitments can we agree to now in order to create results in the above areas?

4. How will we follow-up with each other and keep in communication (perhaps within and between regions)?

5. What are the needed resources and where can we seek them out?

Activity 2: Circulation

Objective:
To engage participants in creating a strategy to gather feedback for the draft charter.

Introduction:
Let us envision the UR Charter, now in its gestation period, as the document that holds within it the capability for the awakening of universal peace.

In Africa, a "doula" is a midwife…a person who is fully present during a birth…attending to the needs at hand…listening and engaging with the emergent stages…a holder for the life force which is being born in the moment. URI charter-keepers (i.e., circulators) are those who choose to act as doulas – people who take responsibility as trustees or holders to help in the birth of the UR Charter.

From Webster's dictionary – to circulate means to move in a circle or circuit…through a circuit back to a starting point…as blood in a body.

Imagine:
Can we imagine a draft charter being lived with for one year by many groups of people all over the world to explore its worthiness?

Imagine:

Can we imagine an organization whose purpose and principles are a vital guide to all action, pumping through the system, bringing fresh insights, experiences, and priorities? Might we imagine not only a process of writing a charter but also a global organization where circulation is its way?

Task:

To create a strategy that will invite people from all walks of life, all levels of society, all religions and spiritual communities, individuals and groups, organizations and institutions to live with and reflect upon the draft charter.

To create a system for receiving feedback to the draft charter from people from all over the world.

Emerging Questions

1. Who needs to be invited to experience this draft charter and to respond?

2. How might people engage with the draft charter? In what ways and in what places shall people engage in conversation about the draft charter?

3. How do people connect their learning from group to group, place to place, from the small groups to the whole?

4. How do people sign up at this stage of the process/

5. What can we do to reach the leadership of major institutions?

6. How do we ensure that the circle of voices is inclusive—of indigenous communities and mainstream religious traditions, of spiritual movements and those not formally affiliated with any religion?

APPENDIX 3

The Surprise of Friendship

One of the questions that deserves attention is "what exactly is it that happens in the intimacy of a deep appreciative inquiry interview that creates a momentum for change, often beyond people's expectations, and often very quickly—e.g., in a relational experiencing of one another in less than an hour?"

Obviously there are many answers: people discover common ground, some shared vision, imagine possible joint projects, build bridges of understanding across stereotype, understand one another's values, shift from problem talk to solution talk, and on and on. Dan Young, at GTE for example, believes something physiological happens. He tells the story of his very first AI interview. He is still astounded by the fact that the interview made such an impression. In his memory he can still see the person, can recreate exactly what was talked about, can even remember the feelings generated, etc. In Berger and Luckman's terms it had the qualities of primary socialization (like in a family). What, from your experience, happens?

This week, all day Monday, I had an occasion to work on something that was profound for me in a thousand ways. But the most compelling for present purposes relates to the question "what happens?"

I share the occasion with some hesitancy because of its nascent unfoldment and because of its almost undescribable potential—as you will see, the implications are quite important. But a number of people have asked me to share some of the insights, including the AI interview questions we used, so hopefully it can create more learning. The thoughts are fresh, and half-baked. I hope I'm not presenting too much.

The Occasion
Early in the 1990s on his first trip to Jerusalem His Holiness the Dalai Lama proposed, "If the leadership of the world's religions could simply get to know one another...the world could be a different, a better place."

Reprinted with permission. Cooperrider D. L. (2000). "The Surprise of Friendship at the Carter Center." *The OD Practitioner*, Vol 32, No. 2, pps 46–49. South Orange, NJ.

So on November 9th a one-day meeting among 20 of the world's religious leaders was called in Washington DC. The Dalai Lama, starting at 9 am would open the meeting, explaining his hope and vision. The purpose:

> To create a beginning, a taste, of what ultimately might be made available for the world's religious leaders—a secure, private, small and relatively unstructured forum where leaders can have conversation with one another, know one another in mutually respectful ways, and reflect on the hard issues of the world without binding any institution to another.

The organizers of the event felt the pressure of precious little time, and also knew how easily old patterns of conversation could set in. So they recommended appreciative inquiry as the methodology for guiding the dialogue. I accepted the invitation—with awe as well as feelings of being humbled and challenged beyond my capabilities—to "moderate" the session.

The day was tremendous and powerful beyond words. I will be learning from it for years. Bottom line: the group decided to make major steps forward, and plans were made for two three-day sessions "to get to know one another"—in some cases where groups have not spoken in 400 years. By any measure the day was a success. The forum was launched.

New insights? After His Holiness the Dalai Lama shared his vision we then went into appreciative inquiry interviews, in pairs, across religious tradition and belief, and then the rest of the day engaged in whole group dialogue.

The new insight for me was the "surprise of friendship" that emerged in and through the sincere and deep appreciative interchange—the sharing of stories, the search for understanding life purpose and best qualities, etc. (I will show the AI questions below.) Of important note was that the relational movement one could see was not a coming up with common values, or shared vision, or joint projects and the like, for these, at this stage, would likely not be possible, for example, between people from the Vatican's Roman Catholic group and the Orthodox. But something else more important started. One might call it the positive chemistry of interaction; it was the surprise not only of beginning to know one another, but the surprise of liking one another, the glow of new acquaintance.

It was not the outer structures of common task, or proclamation, or shared vision, or shared outcry over the devastated ecology of life. It was something paradoxically that at once appears more subtle and more powerful, more at the feeling level of the ground of relatedness. Its been said that friendship is not necessarily a union of personalities, or the fusion of differences (almost by definition, with friends we especially cherish and honor and "hold" the differences); indeed friendship is something more, and unexpected attraction, a magnetism of souls.

What happened in and through "the sharing of things precious" was broad realization of the other's good heart. And it happened, I would contend, in conversations that were ordinary, trusting, affectionate, and focused on a search for the positive core of the other's experience. What people described later on was that the touchstone for friendship was evoked, nothing more and nothing less. Articulated was a readiness for friendship. What surfaced as an unmistakable voice—an urge for more connection.

In the end everyone enthusiastically agreed to a three-day next-step session, toward the creation of an enduring forum for dialogue. People clapped. And guess what the suggested name is, for the emerging forum? It is: "The inter-religious forum for friendship among religious leaders."

While I've never seen a book, we might hypothesize it: the key to dialogue and human system change, especially when it is enduring and sustainable, is openness to the surprise of friendship. Likewise then, we might say the central importance of the AI conversation is in its "readiness-creating" contribution to building friendships beyond irreconcilable differences of belief and faith (a great dissertation topic!). We can relate, and have, irreconcilable ontologies, cosmologies, and religions. Indeed, looking back now, it is clear to me I've witnessed this in our recent work with unions. It is also an explanatory factor in the evolution of the International Physicans for Nuclear War, that is, when Dr. Lown and Dr. Chazov of the USSR created their historic partnership. To their surprise, they became "friends". Simply put, it might well be that the people who in actuality serve to keep it all going somehow, someway became friends. We know, similarly, that in lasting marriages people don't try and turn each other into sameness. But they do say things like "my husband or wife is my good friend."

Saint Aelred of Rievaulx, a thirteenth century monk, said, "friendship cannot be based on anything less than the essential goodness of each friend."

Not a bad way for thinking about what happens in Appreciative Inquiry!

So this was my "insight for the day" from Monday. Listed below is the interview protocol that got us going. Many thanks to Diana Whitney, Jim Lord, Dawn Dole, Loy Cooperrider, Charles Gibbs, Suresh Srivastva, people in the GEM certificate program, and the students of Case Western Reserve University for their help.

It is increasingly clear to me that we have only scratched the surface of understanding appreciative inquiry. Maybe we know about five percent...or less. I know I've learned more in the last six months than in the last 15 years. It is exciting. Hope this sparks something for you. I can't wait to know what we will know ten years from now. Maybe, just maybe, I would not have been so nervous beforehand, getting ready for Monday's surprise!

—David L. Cooperrider

Appreciative Inquiry Interview Guide

Overview

MONK: "All these mountains and rivers and the great earth—where do they come from?"

MASTER: "Where does this question of yours come from?"

Early in the 1990s His Holiness the Dalai Lama proposed, "If the leadership of the world's religions could simply get to know one another...the world could be a different, a better place."

Today's meetin might be viewed as a humble start, an exploration, of this idea. The purpose is a simple one:

> To create a beginning, a taste, of what ultimately might be made available for the world's religious leaders—a secure, private, small and relatively unstructured forum where leaders can have conversation with one another, know one another in mutually respectful ways, and reflect on the hard issues of the world without binding any institution to another.

This "workbook" provides a set of questions to spark a dialogue related to the purpose just stated. It explores, for example, hopes that call us here, experiences we bring to this work, our deeper concerns about the world, insights about significant engagement across faiths and religions, and visions of a better world.

The questions are offered as a starting point, a seed, for meaningful conversation.

The flow of the day will be a simple one involving whole group discussion of our agenda with some one-on-one conversation and moments of silence. Even though it is only one day, we do want to create a retreat-like atmosphere of reflection and hospitality.

The opening dialogue sets the stage for a new appreciation of one another, our work in the world, and conditions we feel will make meetings like this a success.

I. OPENING DIALOGUE

Question #1: A story from your life journey...?

One could say a key task in life is to discover and define our life purpose, and then accomplish it to the best of our ability.

- Can you share a story of a moment, or of the period of time, where **clarity about life purpose** emerged for you—for example, a moment where your calling happened, where there was an important awakening or taching, where there was a special experience or event, or where you received some guiding vision?

- Now beyond this story...What do you sense you are supposed to do before your life, this life, is over?

Question #2: Insights from important interfaith encounters— exploring the personal meeting and friendship between people of different religions?

We have all been changed both in outlook and in our lives, because of encounters with people from other spiritual traditions or religions. In your work as a leader you might have had one, two, or perhaps many encounters with people of other traditions that stand out as particularly significant.

- Can you share a story of one experience that stands out in your memory—for example, an encounter outside the normal "safety zone" where you were surprised or humbled, or where there was an experience of healing and hope, or where there was a genuine experience of compassion, joy, love, or friendship?

- Whether it was difficult or easy, what did you come to respect most, not just about that person, but about their particular religion or practice?

Question #3: Qualities that would make meetings like this significant and effective?

You probably already know, based on years of experience, what kinds of things would make this type of meeting between leaders of the world's religions worthwhile, meaningful and successful.

- What qualities of relating would help make it work?

- What qualities or gifts do you and/or your religious tradition bring to this kind of meeting?

- Bottom line: what would make meetings like this worthwhile to you? (Note: This question will be discussed when we come back in the whole group.)

II. INSIGHTS FROM THE PAST

Question #4: World events and trends over the past 100 years?

Taking steps to create an enduring dialogue among leaders of religions does not happen in a vacuum.

- Think about the five most important historical events that have occurred over the past 100 years—global or local events and trends that give YOU a send of urgency, readiness, or calling for our work here. What trends or challenges do you see as most significant? Examples?

III. OUR WORLD TODAY AND THE HARD ISSUES

Question #5: The emerging story of inter-religion relationships?

The *1996 Encyclopedia of World Problems and Human Potential* lists over 15,000 global problems and documents, for example, that half of the armed conflicts in the world in early 1993 were not between nation-states but between groups from different religions. Against the background of many world problems and conflicts there is also a hopeful story which offers a glimmer of what is possible when we find ways to promote peace rather than war, cooperation rather than prejudice, and sustainability rather than environmental degradation and human oppression.

The century since that historic gathering in 1893 in Chicago—the Parliament of World Religions—has seen a vast widening of interfaith dialogue, inter-religious prayer and meditation, pilgrimages, joint action, and study in world religions. Indeed it appears there is a worldwide urge for an enduring, daily cooperation among people of the world's religions to make peace among religions and to serve, in the presence of the sacred, the flourishing of all life. As leaders in these arenas: What are we most proud about? What are we most sorry about?

- Think about the most significant achievements, milestones, developments and infrastructures that have happened locally or globally in your lifetime. What developments are you most proud about?

- Conversely, as you look at events or trends in the world, and the current responses of religious leaders including yourself, what are you most sorry about, or more important, **what should we be doing more of or different?**

IV. LOOKING TO THE FUTURE: VISIONS OF A BETTER WORLD

Question #6: Your vision of a better world, and the special tasks and significance of the world's religions in the new century?

Dag Hammarskold, former UN Secretary General said: "I see no hope for permanent world peace. We have tried and failed miserably. Unless the world has a spiritual rebirth, civilization is doomed. It has been said that the next century will be a spiritual century or it will not be."

Put your thinking about 30 years, a generation or so, into the future. Even though the future is, in so many ways, a mystery, we want to begin to visualize the kind of world you feel we are being called to realize, a better world, the kind of world you really want. What do you see in your vision of a better world?

- Specifically what are **three** changes or developments in your vision? What is happening in the world a generation from now that is positive and different, and how do you know? How would you feel if these three things were realized?

Question #7: Your vision of the relationships between the world's religions and leaders?

The assumption in the invitation to today's meeting is that there needs to be, in today's complicated and interconnected world, an ongoing and sustained conversation among the religious leaders of the world. The simple hypothesis: the world will be a different place, a better place. It is easy to see the value of something like this, is it not?

Let's imaging a scale from 1 to 10—where a rating of ten represents *the ideal kind of relationship among leaders* of the world's religions and spiritual traditions. Leaders of the religions are relating in ways people would be proud to point to—as examples or stories for the world's children.

- What does your "10" look like? The quality of relationships? Kinds of contact and communication?

- Let's assume a significant and growing number of leaders from the world's religions do choose "to get to know one another"—and it begins to succeed. A safe, confidential, ongoing, and non-binding forum is created. How might the world benefit? How might you and your faith community or organization benefit?

V. FUTURE MEETINGS: 1999 AGENDA, HOW OFTEN, AND WHERE

Question #8: Next Steps?

Again, putting yourself in the future, lets suppose that, in fact, a high quality and enduring forum for dialogue has been successfully created—it is a safe and level playing field where leaders and their envoys can come together to talk, in confidence, about the hard issues of the world.

- As you imagine such a forum, and we can design it in any way we wanted, and assuming resources are not a constraint, what are some things that could happen, or should happen, to make it a win-win-win for everyone—for the world, for work in our respective traditions, and for inter-faith relationships?

- Bottom line: What would make it significant, exciting or high priority and meaningful to you?

- What are some possible places for a next meeting?

APPENDIX 4

The United Religions Charter

THE UNITED RELIGIONS INITIATIVE (URI) is a growing global community dedicated to promoting enduring, daily interfaith cooperation, ending religiously motivated violence and creating cultures of peace, justice and healing for the Earth and all living beings.

Working on all continents and across continents, people from different religions, spiritual expressions and indigenous traditions are creating unprecedented levels of enduring global cooperation. Today, at its birth, people's hopes are rising with visions of a better world. It is a world where the values and teachings of the great wisdom traditions guide people's service, where people respect one another's beliefs, and where the resourcefulness and passion of ordinary people working together bring healing and a more hopeful future to the Earth community. The URI, in time, aspires to have the visibility of the United Nations.

Since June 1996 thousands of people have shared their visions and worked together to create the URI. It is a new kind of organization for global good rooted in shared spiritual values. People from many different cultures and perspectives have worked to create an organization that is inclusive, non-hierarchical and de-centralized; one that enhances cooperation, autonomy and individual opportunity. This cocreative work offered by people of many cultures has produced a unique organization composed of self-organizing groups which operate locally and are connected globally.

The URI's Charter has been spoken into being by a myriad of voices from around the world. Its essential spirit, values and vision are expressed in the Preamble, Purpose and Principles. Taken together, they inspire, ground and guide all URI activity. The Charter includes:

Preamble - the call that inspires us to create the URI now and continue to create it everyday;

Purpose - the statement that draws us together in common cause;

Principles - the fundamental beliefs that guide our structure, decisions and content;

Organization Design - the way of organizing that enhances cooperation and magnifies spirit;

Guidelines for Action - an action agenda to inspire and guide the worldwide URI community.

The global URI organization will be born in June 2000. You are warmly invited to participate in the birth and the growth of the URI and become part of this extraordinary force for good in the world. This Charter is your invitation to participate in its on-going creation.

Preamble

We, people of diverse religions, spiritual expressions and indigenous traditions throughout the world, hereby establish the United Religions Initiative to promote enduring, daily interfaith cooperation, to end religiously motivated violence and to create cultures of peace, justice and healing for the Earth and all living beings.

We respect the uniqueness of each tradition, and differences of practice or belief.

We value voices that respect others, and believe that sharing our values and wisdom can lead us to act for the good of all.

We believe that our religious, spiritual lives, rather than dividing us, guide us to build community and respect for one another.

Therefore, as interdependent people rooted in our traditions, we now unite for the benefit of our Earth community.

We unite to build cultures of peace and justice.

We unite to heal and protect the Earth.

We unite to build safe places for conflict resolution, healing and reconciliation.

We unite to support freedom of religion and spiritual expression, and the rights of all individuals and peoples as set forth in international law.

We unite in responsible cooperative action to bring the wisdom and values of our religions, spiritual expressions and indigenous traditions to bear on the economic, environmental, political and social challenges facing our Earth community.

We unite to provide a global opportunity for participation by all people, especially by those whose voices are not often heard.

We unite to celebrate the joy of blessings and the light of wisdom in both movement and stillness.

We unite to use our combined resources only for nonviolent, compassionate action, to awaken to our deepest truths, and to manifest love and justice among all life in our Earth community.

Purpose

The purpose of the United Religions Initiative is to promote enduring, daily interfaith cooperation, to end religiously motivated violence and to create cultures of peace, justice and healing for the Earth and all living beings.

Principles

1. We are a bridge-building organization, not a religion.

2. We respect the sacred wisdom of each religion, spiritual expression and indigenous tradition.

3. We respect the differences among religions, spiritual expressions and indigenous traditions.

4. We encourage our members to deepen their roots in their own tradition.

5. We listen and speak with respect to deepen mutual understanding and trust.

6. We give and receive hospitality.

7. We seek and welcome the gift of diversity and model practices that do not discriminate.

8. We practice equitable participation of women and men in all aspects of the URI.

9. We practice healing and reconciliation to resolve conflict without resorting to violence.

10. We act from sound ecological practices to protect and preserve the Earth for both present and future generations.

11. We seek and offer cooperation with other interfaith efforts.

12. We welcome as members all individuals, organizations and associations who subscribe to the Preamble, Purpose and Principles.

13. We have the authority to make decisions at the most local level that includes all the relevant and affected parties.

14. We have the right to organize in any manner, at any scale, in any area, and around any issue or activity which is relevant to and consistent with the Preamble, Purpose and Principles.

15. Our deliberations and decisions shall be made at every level by bodies and methods that fairly represent the diversity of affected interests and are not dominated by any.

16. We (each part of the URI) shall relinquish only such autonomy and resources as are essential to the pursuit of the Preamble, Purpose and Principles.

17. We have the responsibility to develop financial and other resources to meet the needs of our part, and to share financial and other resources to help meet the needs of other parts.

18. We maintain the highest standards of integrity and ethical conduct, prudent use of resources, and fair and accurate disclosure of information.

19. We are committed to organizational learning and adaptation.

20. We honor the richness and diversity of all languages and the right and responsibility of participants to translate and interpret the Charter, Bylaws and related documents in accordance with the Preamble, Purpose and Principles, and the spirit of the United Religions Initiative.

21. Members of the URI shall not be coerced to participate in any ritual or be proselytized.

Organization Design

The URI is an organization where people act from their deepest values and claim their right and responsibility to do extraordinary things to serve interfaith cooperation on a local and a global level. The URI is made up of groups of people all over the world who take many different kinds of actions to serve a common purpose.

Individuals, associations or organizations seeking membership in the URI shall create a Cooperation Circle (CC) or join an existing Cooperation Circle. Groups are called Cooperation Circles because they are created by people who come together to initiate acts of interfaith cooperation. Every URI Circle determines its own unique purpose, membership, and ways of making decisions that are relevant to and consistent with the Preamble, Purpose and Principles. If a Cooperation Circle chooses to coordinate its efforts with other Cooperation Circles, it may decide to form a Multiple Cooperation Circle (MCC). If two or more Multiple Cooperation Circles wish to coordinate efforts they may form a Multi-Multiple Cooperation Circle (MMCC). See diagram on page 9.

To provide initial stability and interfaith diversity, Cooperation Circles must have at least seven (7) members who are from at least three (3) different religions, spiritual expressions or indigenous traditions.

Rights of Members

Each URI Circle has the right:

- to organize in any manner and around any issue or activity which is relevant to and consistent with the Preamble, Purpose and Principles;

- to determine its own process of governance and decision making that is in accordance with the Preamble, Purpose and Principles;

- to choose to combine with or join any other URI Circles;

- to participate in the selection of Trustees to serve on the Global Council;

- to review and accept, on behalf of the URI, applications for membership from individuals, organizations and associations seeking to join in pursuit of the Purpose.

Responsibilities of Members

Each URI Circle accepts the responsibility:

- to act in accordance with the Preamble, Purpose and Principles;

- to determine its own process of governance and decision making that is in accordance with the Preamble, Purpose and Principles;

- to take actions to encourage and ensure that its own members act in accordance with the Preamble, Purpose and Principles;

- to actively use its best efforts to achieve the Purpose in accordance with the Principles;

- to adhere to the Bylaws and operating procedures as they evolve in the life of the URI;

- to communicate best practices, stories and highlights of activities with other parts of the URI;

- to develop financial resources to meet its own needs;

- to share financial and other resources to help meet the needs of other Circles;

- to pay any dues and/or offer such appropriate contribution as the Global Council may establish;

- to keep accurate and current records of its members, financial transactions and activities;

- to indemnify and hold the Trustees, the United Religions Initiative, its employees and representatives, harmless from any liabilities arising out of or in any way caused by a URI Circle's breach of any provision of the Articles, by-laws or operating procedures.

Application For Membership
Individuals, associations, and organizations may form their own Cooperation Circle and may apply for membership directly to the Global Council or to an existing MCC or MMCC.

Affiliates
Individuals, associations and organizations who value and support the URI Preamble, Purpose and Principles may become Affiliates. Affiliates desire to be informed of and to participate in the work of the URI, but do not desire to have the rights and responsibilities of membership. Affiliates may be asked to pay a fee to participate in URI activities and the communication network. Those who wish to become URI Affiliates may apply to the Global Council or to a URI Circle.

The Global Council
The purpose of the Global Council (GC) is to support the Membership in making real the vision and values of the Preamble, Purpose and Principles. The Global Council's central spirit is not one of control, but rather one of service informed by deep listening to the hopes and aspirations of the whole URI community. The Global Council will inspire and support the URI worldwide community in cooperative global action. It isenvisioned that their deliberations will be tempered with tenderness for one another and for the Earth community. It is envisioned that their actions will reflect a yearning to help people of the URI fulfill their aspirations to be a positive force for peace, justice, and healing in the world.

The Global Council is responsible to develop financial and other resources to meet the needs of the URI. The Global Council will accept eligible applicants for membership to the URI and manage the affairs of the URI.

Global Council Trustees
The term Trustee signifies that trustees carry the trust for the URI world membership. The Trustees of the URI will be exemplars who manifest the vision and values of the Preamble, Purpose and Principles, and who will model leadership and service by their actions. They will have a deep commitment to serve the whole of the URI community.

Composition of The Global Council
- A maximum of twenty four (24) trustees elected by the world membership through elections in eight (8) regions.

- A maximum of twelve (12) trustees selected at-large by the GC to meet the need for greater diversity or a particular expertise.

- A maximum of three (3) trustees designated from among the members of a Transition Advisory Committee composed of members of the current URI Board of Directors. The Transition Advisory Committee will remain in place until June 2005 to meet the need for continuity.

- One (1) Trustee shall be the Founding Trustee to honor the unique role of the URI founder.

- One (1) Trustee shall be the Executive Trustee to ensure that the URI staff is represented.

Selection Process For Trustees

To ensure that there are people from diverse geographic perspectives on the Global Council, 24 seats will be filled through an election process. URI Circles within a geographic region can select up to three (3) trustees from among the eight (8) regions listed below. The regions are: Africa, Asia, Europe, Latin America and the Caribbean, the Middle East, North America, and the Pacific. The eighth (8) region is a non-geographic region for URI Circles that are multiregional in composition.

To ensure optimum diversity and to meet the need for particular expertise at the GC, twelve (12) seats will be filled by appointment by the GC.

Trustees are chosen every two years to serve on the GC.

Models of reflection, meditation and prayer which deepen understanding of the qualities of leadership which embody service and spiritual wisdom are encouraged as part of every governance selection process.

Global Assembly

A Global Assembly of all the Members of the URI is planned to take place every two years at a place designated by the Global Council. The Global Assembly will be a vibrant gathering where people deepen their experience of living into the Preamble, Purpose, and Principles as a global community. The Global Assembly will magnify everyone's capacity to carry forward their dreams and initiatives, address visions of collective actions for service in the world, and give voice to collective hopes and aspirations. The Global Assembly will align strengths and call forth unprecedented cooperation. It will celebrate the totality of the URI and offer opportunities to give and receive hospitality, to share work, and to offer help to each other.

Guidelines For Action

In light of the essentially self-organizing nature of the URI which gives members freedom to choose what they want to do, the following Agenda for Action is offered as guidance for URI activities. Inspired by a Javanese phrase, " Memayu Hayuning Bawano" which means "to work for the safety, happiness and welfare of all life," the URI will serve as a moral voice and a source of action grounded in contemplation in each of the following areas:

Sharing the Wisdom and Cultures of Faith Traditions - actions to promote dialogue and kinship among the diverse religions and spiritual traditions of the world.

Nurturing Cultures of Healing and Peace - actions to develop cultures in which all people can live without fear of violence.

Rights and Responsibilities - actions that uphold human rights.

Ecological Imperatives - actions that uphold the welfare and healing of the entire Earth community.

Sustainable Just Economics - actions to bring a spiritual perspective to the tremendous gap between rich and poor.

Supporting the Overall URI - local, regional and global actions that support all URI activities.

Organization Design - Building the URI Together

MULTIPLE COOPERATION CIRCLES: (MCCs) are groups within the URI formed when three or more Cooperation Circles wish to join together in order to enhance their work and create a more enduring coordinating structure.

MULTI-MULTIPLE COOPERATION CIRCLES (MMCCs) are formed when two or more MCCs wish to join together to enhance their work and create a more permanent enduring structure.

COOPERATION CIRCLES (CCs) are the fundamental unit of the URI. Individuals, associations and organizations who seek membership in the URI shall create Cooperation Circles (or join existing ones) and take on the rights and responsibilities of membership.

AFFILIATES are individuals, associations and organizations who value and support the URI Preamble, Purpose and Principles. Affiliates are welcome to participate in URI communication and activities. They do not desire rights and responsibilities of belonging to a URI Circle.

THE GLOBAL COUNCIL (GC) is composed largely of trustees selected by the URI membership. The GC trustees are examplars of the core values of the URI who listen to the hopes and aspirations of the URI worldwide community and serve the best interests of the whole URI.

For More Information
Please contact the URI with your ideas, your hopes and dreams, and your inquiries so that you and/or your group might consider being part of the URI.

P.O. Box 29242
San Francisco, CA 94129

Phone 1-415-561-2300
FAX 1-415-561-2313

Website: www.united-religions.org
email: charter@united-religions.org

© 2000 United Religions Initiative

INDEX